Human Resource Management in Olympic Sport Organisations

Packianathan Chelladurai • Alberto Madella

Master Exécutif en Management des Organisations Sportives
Executive Masters in Sports Organisation Management

Library of Congress Cataloging-in-Publication Data

Chelladurai, P.
Human resource management in Olympic sport organisations / Packianathan Chelladurai, Alberto Madella.
p. cm.
Includes bibliographical references.
ISBN-13: 978-0-7360-6304-3 (soft cover)
ISBN-10: 0-7360-6304-8 (soft cover)
1. Sports administration. 2. Personnel management. 3. Olympics--Management. I. Madella, Alberto, 1956- II. Title.
GV713.C436 2006
796.06'9--dc22

2006002435

ISBN-10: 0-7360-6304-8
ISBN-13: 978-0-7360-6304-3

Copyright © 2006 by Packianathan Chelladurai and Alberto Madella

All rights reserved. Except for use in a review, the reproduction or utilization of this work in any form or by any electronic, mechanical, or other means, now known or hereafter invented, including xerography, photocopying, and recording, and in any information storage and retrieval system, is forbidden without the written permission of the publisher.

The Web addresses cited in this text were current as of November 30, 2005, unless otherwise noted.

Acquisitions Editor: Myles Schrag; **Managing Editor:** Lee Alexander; **Copyeditor:** Patrick Connolly; **Proofreader:** Julie Marx Goodreau; **Permission Manager:** Dalene Reeder; **Graphic Designer:** Nancy Rasmus; **Graphic Artist:** Denise Lowry; **Art Manager:** Kelly Hendren; **Illustrator:** Denise Lowry; **Photographer (cover):** © CIO, Photo: Wataru ABE; **Printer:** Versa Press

Printed in the United States of America 10 9 8 7 6 5 4 3 2 1

Human Kinetics
Web site: www.HumanKinetics.com

United States: Human Kinetics, P.O. Box 5076, Champaign, IL 61825-5076
800-747-4457
e-mail: humank@hkusa.com

Canada: Human Kinetics, 475 Devonshire Road Unit 100, Windsor, ON N8Y 2L5
800-465-7301 (in Canada only)
e-mail: orders@hkcanada.com

Europe: Human Kinetics, 107 Bradford Road, Stanningley, Leeds LS28 6AT, United Kingdom
+44 (0) 113 255 5665
e-mail: hk@hkeurope.com

Australia: Human Kinetics, 57A Price Avenue, Lower Mitcham, South Australia 5062
08 8277 1555
e-mail: liaw@hkaustralia.com

New Zealand: Human Kinetics, Division of Sports Distributors NZ Ltd., P.O. Box 300 226 Albany, North Shore City, Auckland
0064 9 448 1207
e-mail: info@humankinetics.co.nz

Contents

Foreword

The work that you are about to discover—devoted to human resource management—is the third in the MEMOS collection. The two other volumes deal with strategic and performance management (Chappelet and Bayle 2004) and marketing of Olympic sport organisations (Ferrand and Torrigiani 2005), both available from Human Kinetics. Other works are planned by the MEMOS team, in particular a manual on the management of Olympic sport organisations (Camy and Robinson 2006). The MEMOS programme itself could, in fact, be considered as an exercise in the management of human resources, because managing its participants and teaching staff has been part of the programme since it was created in 1995.

From the outset, the objective defined by MEMOS has been to permit management-level staff working in national or international Olympic organisations to develop the necessary knowledge for providing better management of sport today. The programme thus targets the development of the Olympic movement's human capital in the broad sense. For that reason, it receives considerable support from Olympic Solidarity.

The MEMOS programme is intended for sport leaders in executive positions. It therefore needed to be adapted to the time that such individuals have available. The teaching is centred on three intensive modules that are divided over 1 year and whose topics correspond to the first three works in the MEMOS collection (strategic management, marketing management and human resource management). During the year in which they study the three modules, participants must also complete a personal project on the performance of an Olympic organisation (usually the one in which they work). A member of the MEMOS teaching staff provides coaching for the project; this person plays the role of tutor following each of the three modules (personal sessions with the participant) and throughout the entire year (e-tutoring). Participants draw up a report on their project and defend it before a jury consisting of the tutors before presenting it at the Olympic Museum in front of their fellow students and the participants in the next session of the programme. On successful completion of the programme, the participants obtain an Executive Masters in Sports Organisation Management (for which the French acronym is MEMOS).

The first 9 sessions of the MEMOS programme have produced nearly 200 graduates. Each intake is now given a Roman numeral for easier identification. The 10th intake, MEMOS X, will take place from September 2006 to September 2007. Every alternate year, MEMOS intakes are also provided for French- and Spanish-speaking participants. Although MEMOS began in Europe, graduates come from all continents;

there are now few countries that have not sent at least one participant. Women still remain in the minority but nevertheless constitute around one quarter of the graduates. All the graduates make up a genuine learning community and a network that will take on increasing importance within the Olympic movement.

The members of the teaching staff (which consists of about 20 lecturers and tutors) within the programme also participate in this community. They were originally brought together by Professor Jean Camy of the Claude Bernard University in Lyon, France, who founded the programme in 1995 with the assistance of the International Olympic Committee, the European Olympic Committee and the European Union's Socrates programme. Now an emeritus professor, Jean Camy's leadership remains an essential aspect of the programme. The members of the MEMOS teaching staff are mainly from Europe (with the exception of two from Canada), but they nevertheless form a group whose linguistic and cultural diversity is remarkable: The staff includes members from Belgium, France, Germany, Italy, Portugal, Spain, Switzerland and the United Kingdom.

I am currently in charge of this outstanding team whose membership remains an open one. My role is to put into practice many of the concepts handled in the present volume. The two major issues described are the overall short-term personnel administration function (to ensure that the programme functions efficiently each year) and the longer-term task of human capital development. The aim of the latter is to ensure that the MEMOS teaching staff members all derive professional benefit—individually and together—from the programme and can make an effective contribution to better sport management. This involves directing and motivating colleagues who, as in most nonprofit sport organisations, to a large extent work on an unpaid basis. I would like to take this opportunity to thank them all for their exemplary commitment and the confidence they have placed in me.

The coauthors of this work are a perfect illustration of the diversity of the team and the high quality of the MEMOS teaching staff. Packianathan Chelladurai (affectionately known as "Chella" by other sport management specialists) is of Indian origin but completed his entire academic career in Canada and in the United States, where he is currently teaching at the Ohio State University. He has initiated hundreds of students of many different nationalities into sport management, providing an original vision of intercultural management within sport organisations that is based on an unparalleled mastery of literature on human resource management.

Alberto Madella is a sociologist who has long been interested in human relations within sport organisations. He is a professor at the CONI (Italian National Olympic Committee) School of Sport and as such has trained a great many of the country's leaders within amateur sport. Little by little, he has instilled a managerial culture within Italian sport, notably within the National Athletics Federation. Alberto is also a researcher who is renowned for his scientific contribution to human resource management in sport, particularly via the European Observatoire of Sport Employment (EOSE).

Alberto and Chella form an unparalleled team that unites theoretical knowledge and practical experience. This book is the result of their close collaboration on many of the MEMOS modules that they have led jointly, and also of participants' projects tutored by each of them over the years. My wish is that this stimulating work will contribute to the development of human capital for sport organisations, and that readers will discover why and how this fundamental resource should be better managed within the framework of Olympic values.

Professor Jean-Loup Chappelet
Director of MEMOS

Preface

Two features that dominate the global scene are sport and management. One does not have to go beyond the excitement of the Olympics to get a grasp of the ubiquitous nature of sport. Although management as a profession is not highlighted as much as sports, its significance to the daily lives of the world's population cannot be underrated. From birth to death, every human being is affected by various types of organisations that, in turn, are directed and controlled by management.

We are fortunate that the Olympic movement and the international sport federations such as Fédération Internationale de Football Association (International Football Association, or FIFA), International Association of Athletics Federation (IAAF) and Fédération Internationale de Basketball Association (International Basketball Association, or FIBA) have brought the two realms of sport and management together in its staging of international, regional and national competitions. More important, the Olympic Solidarity's projects and programs to enhance the managerial capacity among the administrators of the Olympic sport organisations are laudable. One such program is Executive Masters in Sports Organisation Management (MEMOS), through which administrators from various countries are trained to promote and govern sport in their own countries more effectively. We are all grateful to Olympic Solidarity for these laudable efforts.

This book is written specifically for the students in the MEMOS programme, which is composed of a week-long intensive training in three different areas: strategic management, sport marketing, and human resource management. The fourth requirement is a project that extends over a year. Given these temporal constraints, we were to restrict ourselves to specific topics from the vast and growing literature in human resource management. We have identified certain topics deemed more germane to the management of the Olympic organisations and have elaborated on them. The choice of these topics is based on our interactions with the students in MEMOS in the last 10 years. Further, it is also based on our various areas of expertise and experience. Professor Alberto Madella has long been associated with the Italian Olympic Committee (CONI) and has been teaching in universities in Italy. He is a sought-after speaker and consultant on the international scene. Packianathan Chelladurai had been a national-level player, referee, and coach in India. At the moment he is teaching sport management at the Ohio State University in the United States. We hope that our varied backgrounds have come together to produce a good book. We are confident that it will be helpful not only for current and future MEMOS students but also for the wider community of the managers of Olympic sport organisations at any level.

We are thankful to the MEMOS participants for their valuable insights and comments on the content and delivery of our classes. We are also thankful to Olympic Solidarity and professors Jean Camy and Jean-Loup Chappelet, who have made all of this possible. Finally, our thanks to director Pere Miró and his associates Carolina Bayón and Joanna Zipser-Graves for their support and guidance in running the MEMOS programme.

Introduction

Management in any organisation is concerned with securing and coordinating various kinds of resources, such as finances, facilities, materials and people (i.e., the human resource). Of all these, the human resource is the most critical, as well as the most problematic. It is the most critical because it is the people who convert the other factors into "real" resources. For instance, a computer in the office becomes a resource only if someone uses it in a competent way. A basketball is turned into a resource only when a person starts dribbling and shooting it effectively. An ice rink is a resource only because the skaters and hockey players use it. From a manager's perspective, all the other kinds of resources become valuable if, and only if, the people in the organisation use them effectively. This perspective is also true of any Olympic sport organisation (OSO). OSOs are "organisations that belong to the Olympic system and to the sport movement: clubs, national and sport federations, international federations, national Olympic committees, organizing committees, and so on" (Chappelet and Bayle 2004, p. ix).

OSOs combine numerous features shared in common with other nonprofit organisations, characteristics that are typical of the sport sector in the broadest sense, and others that derive from the values and the main cultural features that are specific to the Olympic movement. In their analysis of the marketing strategies and operations of these kinds of organisations, Ferrand and Torrigiani (2005) have indicated that the main distinctive inspiration behind an organisation in the Olympic movement is that it does not "simply exchange a service for money . . . but carries out a social transaction within which its action procures benefits for its members" (p. 2). Furthermore, these benefits are not just for the members themselves but have an impact on the society at large. These functions can be achieved only if competent people are available to carry out the tasks and if there is competent coordination of their expertise and efforts. Having competent people and coordinating their efforts are the essence of human resource management (HRM).

Despite the critical importance of human resources (e.g., performance of individual athletes and teams) for the success of these organisations, the recognition of and importance attached to human resources are much lower than one would expect. Certainly, in strategic planning documents and in the public pronouncements of OSO leaders, recognition is frequently paid to the human factor. But this recognition does not necessarily translate into proper institutional arrangements or distinctive and sophisticated human resource management practices, and thus such proclamations remain as lip service. This view is supported by the fact that only a few OSOs (normally the largest ones) have a director of human resources position or a human resource department. Only 30 national Olympic committees can be placed in this category. Even when they exist, these functions are normally assigned to staff positions with low resources, low status and little actual power in their respective organisations. The frequent preference given to external consultants when it is necessary to optimize human resource management is another indication of this way of thinking.

The broad field of HRM encompasses many divergent and problematic activities, which include the following:

- Recruitment and staffing
- Career opportunities
- Control and assessment of people at work
- Working systems
- Division of roles, tasks and functions
- Communication, uses of technologies and knowledge management
- Internal conflict
- Delegation and empowerment
- Reward systems and incentives
- Distribution of power
- Formation of powerful boards
- Fairness
- Motivation, commitment and involvement
- Learning and changing a culture
- Professional versus volunteer dynamic
- Managing diversity and empowering minorities
- Optimal leadership

The problematic and critical nature of HRM for organisations such as OSOs is confirmed by the extreme complexity and diversity of these aspects. Actually, many of these organisations are slowly but definitely realizing this, as is shown by the trend to formalize more practices and procedures in the domain of HRM compared to in the past.

As we have already emphasized, human resources are the most problematic because every person is different from every other person. Unlike footballs or hockey sticks, which can all be manufactured to our specifications, people cannot be expected to have exactly the same orientations, attitudes, talents and skills. More important, every worker in the organisation has his or her own mind. In addition, within all organisations, people work and interact with others, building networks, coalitions and groups, either formally or informally, with their own dynamics and structure of relations. The issue becomes even more problematic when the workers speak their mind. When we consider that the managers (including those who are responsible for managing human resources) also have their own minds and often impose them on others, we can realize the magnitude of the challenges related to human resources within organisations. That is why even before the advent of "scientific" management theories and practices, people have often reflected on how to optimize people's work and enlist their strategic co-operation. Consider, for example, the arguments developed by Plato in his book *The Republic*, by Aristotle in *The Politics* or by Machiavelli in *The Prince*. From their analyses and understanding of people's qualities, these renowned thinkers tried to derive some guidelines for collective action and the construction of cohesiveness and social order. This just shows that HRM is pervasive across time, national cultures and organisational areas. It is impossible to manage marketing strategies or campaigns, or to renew and assess production strategies, without being constantly confronted with the way people are mobilized, coordinated and evaluated. Therefore, effective management of human resources is extremely critical to the overall effectiveness of the organisation; it can be a true competitive advantage.

Approaches to Human Resource Management

The previous discussion explains why human resource management is a popular subject in management education and practice. The approaches to the study and practice of human resource management have been varied in terms of perspectives and paradigms. Two of these approaches and their significant "nuances" are especially relevant for our purposes because they facilitate understanding of the issues associated with HRM and how to address those issues. These two approaches are properly labelled as *personnel administration* (or personnel management) and *human capital development.* We must note that other perspectives exist (some of which are extremely critical of other approaches), but they are not based on empirical research and evidence. Hence they are not dealt with in this text.

The first perspective, personnel administration, with a long history in management practice, focuses essentially on the work contracts and, consequently, deals with issues such as employee–management relations, salaries and productivity. It tries to provide answers on key topics such as the following:

- How to recruit good employees
- How to orient and train personnel
- How to provide the best incentives to enhance productivity
- How to supervise and control employees at work
- How to avoid resistance from employees

For those who take this perspective, the main preoccupation is clearly the preservation and improvement of the efficiency of the organisational system, basically through the control of the manpower and the reduction of the associated costs. Many organisations with a human resource department and an HR director deal essentially with these kinds of problems. In numerous countries, the relations between the company and the workers usually fall within this area of human resource management.

The human capital development perspective, on the contrary, is more focused on the following:

- The advancement of people through the management of their careers and competencies
- The optimization of their co-operation, their creativity and their capacity for useful innovation
- The setup of optimal and convenient working and training systems

This perspective has a long history that includes debates and investigations in the social studies of organisations. The efforts in this regard were intensified after the famous research of Elton Mayo on human relations in the workplace in the 1920s and 1930s. The human relations school perspective has clearly demonstrated (based on an experimental approach) that monetary rewards and material incentives cannot fully explain the behavior of people in their working environment nor the variations in their productivity. Social norms and attitudes shared at the group level are fundamental driving factors for an organisation's members. The most recent discussions concerning "organisational culture" (Hofstede 1991; Parker 2000; Schein 1985; Schein 1991) follow this direction and have sparked significant debates in the context of sport organisations (Doherty and Chelladurai 1999; Slack 1997; Weese 1995; Westerbeek 1999).

Within this perspective, which has a strong psychosociological foundation and a more long-term and strategic orientation, organisations are preferably depicted as **co-operative systems** (Barnard 1938) whose performance can be enhanced through dedicated attention and specific investment in people. Salaries paid to persons are not simply costs to be minimised but can be seen as a potential investment. Hence, "investing in people" is a common slogan used nowadays within this framework.

The concept of co-operation is attractive because of its positive view of people and their organised interaction, but we should also note that co-operative systems can often be altered and disrupted by conflict and tensions related to divergent interests and representations by groups or individuals. This is why a primary focus of this approach is the **"political"** dimension of human resource management. It corresponds to the view that organisations, whatever their size, are always political arenas (Heinemann 2004). Important discussions of this political perspective can be found in the works of Crozier and Friedberg (1977), Clegg and Dunkerley (1980), Pfeffer (1981), Mintzberg (1983) and Morgan (1986), but probably the best formulation can be found in the works of Max Weber, for whom it was possible to understand organisations only if they were viewed in the context of conflicting interest (1922). Many organisational processes, especially decision making, cannot be fully understood if we do not consider how power, negotiation and regulation of conflict influence them, much more than rational and technical processes do (Beaumont 1993; March and Simon 1958). According to this view, organisational structures can be understood better as a product of internal struggles rather than a simple result of the application of technical and rational methodologies used to design them. Emphasizing the power relations is then not just a sociological inclination but an essential perspective that has to be integrated into managing human resources, especially in those cases where the human factor is an essential ingredient of organisational change. For example, attempts to change an Olympic organisation into a more service-oriented organisation, or attempts to introduce empowerment practices to encourage creativity and innovation, are always met with resistance. Another example can be the reluctance of some of the best coaches to share knowledge and experience with younger colleagues; this does not facilitate the creation of a true learning organisation. In addition, the political view allows us to identify nonethical approaches to human resource management, especially when management manipulates people and groups. Managers in OSOs must therefore be well aware of and prepared to deal with these political challenges.

In spite of their very different orientations, the two approaches to HRM that we've summarized are not contradictory but are, in fact, complementary to each other. The personnel administration perspective addresses the issue of stability and productivity of the organisation, while the human development perspective is focused on enhancing the welfare of the employees and increasing their capabilities so that they can more effectively contribute to organisational success. But in either perspective, personal and collective needs, preferences and beliefs; cultural factors; and external employment policies, regulations and legislation that govern the labour market or industrial relationships must be taken into consideration. With these in mind and given their mission, history, operational conditions and values, OSOs should be particularly sensitive to the human capital development approach. Successful sport leaders and coaches are often invited by the most prestigious business schools to speak as champions of human development, and this is an indication that OSOs are indeed more focused on human capital development.

At the same time, OSOs need to effectively harmonize the two perspectives—personnel administration and human capital development—because they are so strongly related. For example, sometimes rational formal procedures cannot be successfully implemented in an OSO because the specific culture or power relations within the OSO might impede their effectiveness. However, since the process of cultural change can be quite long, and managers cannot always wait for it to happen, it may become necessary to start with the formal rules and procedures as a first step in facilitating cultural change.

In the last few years, the human capital development approach has received great attention, and its role in strategic management is being more and more emphasized. Another reason for the increased attention given to human development is the decline of unionization of workers and the decline of collective bargaining in many countries. This has put more emphasis on the individual–organisation relationship, facilitating a kind of individual-centred approach to human resource management. Although the sport sector and its labour market tend to follow the same general pattern, managers of OSOs must also consider the specific national or continental aspects of their operations when making decisions related to the human factor in their respective OSOs.

Structure of the Text

In this text, we will discuss some of the current topics and practices of human resource management usually covered in traditional manuals. These topics include organisational justice, staffing, leadership, performance appraisal, reward systems, empowerment of workers, management of diversity, handling of conflict, and so on. Since these concepts need to be applied to Olympic sport organisations, we begin in chapter 1 with a description of the unique features of an OSO with reference to its human resources. Participants (especially competing athletes), volunteers and professional workers are discussed, including the contributions they make and their specific needs and patterns of relationships.

In chapter 2, the main topics within HRM are presented, with particular attention to the specific problems and challenges faced by OSOs. The philosophy behind this text is to offer some guidelines for finding solutions to problems that are specific to OSOs, instead of covering all HRM topics (such as those that have little or no relevance to an OSO or those for which there is no substantial difference for an OSO compared to other kinds of organisations). Since we are convinced that practices of human resource management can be diversified according to the context, culture and structure of an organisation, we do not want to provide a "cookbook" of HRM recipes that are ready to be applied anywhere. We introduce and discuss specific cases to create awareness of the theme and its complexity in order to facilitate the identification of possible solutions. Because of the specific nature of the problems related to the management of people (e.g., national or regional legislations, power relations or cultural issues), we believe that unique solutions can be found "locally" to suit a specific context of an organisation. In other words, HRM cannot be a fully prescriptive discipline, as some writers have suggested. Rather than offering a definitive set of prescriptions or a description of selected practices, we try to develop an analytical framework rich with relevant implications and guidelines for practical action. This is also justified by the fact that HRM tends to evolve along with social and labour market changes.

Based on the philosophy just described, in chapter 2 we present the idea of organisational justice, followed by a wide spectrum of human resource practices. We believe that the concept of justice or fairness should be the foundation of all practices and decisions in the field of human resource management, including staffing, retention, training, conflict management, empowerment and others. Chapter 3 is dedicated to the analysis of organisational structure and designs, being especially sensitive to the human resource management implications of such aspects. All these areas of interest are dealt with from the perspective that managing people means properly managing their diversity. Managers should not be scared by diversity; they should be accustomed to dealing with it and should recognize possible advantages and opportunities as suggested in chapter 4.

Finally, in chapters 5 and 6, we turn to two major areas of concern for managers. Probably the most classic topic in HRM is leadership. In chapter 5, we present Chelladurai's multidimensional model of leadership as applied to OSOs. The model is a synthesis of existing leadership models in industrial and organisational psychology adapted for application to sport teams and then to sport organisations. Chapter 6 is focused on organisational change. Too often managers think that managing change is a purely rational and technical matter, and thus they tend to ignore the positive or negative contributions that people make to any strategically planned organisational change. The chapter discusses the significant role of human resource management in the management of organisational change.

1

one

Distinctive Features of Olympic Sport Organisations From a Human Resource Management Perspective

The management of human resources poses special problems to Olympic sport organisations (OSOs) because of their specific characteristics and environment, and especially because of their great social significance in most countries. This occurs essentially because sports are constantly under scrutiny by the public, the media, political parties and even governments. Accordingly, organisations that deliver and control sport (and consequently their leaders and management practices) are also in the public eye. Emotions can easily interfere in the way these organisations are led, human resources are managed, and changes are planned, communicated and implemented. Thus, managers of OSOs can become targets of praise or blame, depending on the perceived and relative performances of their organisations. Their practices can be perceived as more or less effective, not because of their impact per se, which can be calculated through sophisticated technical models and methods, but much more for the degree of success of the affiliated athletes and teams in a restricted number of competitions. Olympic medals, for example, are usually considered as the main indicator of effectiveness, not only for the specific management of elite athletes but also for a wider range of related aspects. For instance, these aspects can include the way talented athletes are developed, coaches are trained or facilities are managed. In general, this means that a causal relationship, without a clear scientific status or evidence, is usually established between sport success and management practices and structures.

Apart from this high "emotional pressure", numerous other relevant—and quite peculiar—aspects can be identified that have an impact on the human resource management (HRM) dimension. In OSOs, these include

- a distinctive **organisational culture,** in which **many different subcultures may coexist**—for example, elite athletes, coaches, referees (MacIntosh and Doherty 2005)—and create **constellations of interests;** and
- a **wide diversity of the workforce,** such as the high frequency of hiring a part-time or temporary workforce for the organisation of big events.

Another important, distinctive feature is

- the **difficulty in defining the exact boundary of some of these organisations.** Although the existence of "a relative identifiable boundary" has often been indicated as a necessary requirement for all organisations (Robbins 1990), when trying to demarcate members from nonmembers, the case of an OSO presents some peculiar aspects. For example, national federations are in fact "associations of associations", and their organisational setting, impact and effectiveness cannot be easily demarcated from that of their affiliated clubs. Many coaches (both professional and volunteer) work simultaneously for a club and the federation. If we consider the development of elite athletes, who are clearly a critical human resource for the achievement of organisational success, it is sometimes difficult to distinguish how much of their development depends on their club, on the federation, the national Olympic committee or external actors (e.g., sponsors, agents). Their performance is actually more the result of a network of actors and related actions. Curiously, the same performance measure is sometimes used contemporarily to assess the effectiveness of different, even if interrelated, organisations.

However, the most important aspect of these kinds of organisations, even if not exclusive to them, is probably

- the special nature of the combination of voluntary and professional human resources that characterises OSOs.

These specific features, combined with other aspects that are recognizable in any other organisational context, generate a wide range of problems that have a significant impact on the domain of human resource management.

We have tried to reconstruct a general typology of these problem areas based on the accounts of many Olympic sport managers (describing their experience as well as critical incidents). These accounts include complaints about the lack of competent human resources in their organisations and complaints about inadequate attitudes, self-interest and conflict.

The problems that they usually mention refer to diversified conceptual areas, which are difficult to demarcate precisely:

1. **Governance issues**—Empowerment, role of the board, delegation of responsibility, accountability, transparency, elections, balance of elected versus professional personnel and lack of representation
2. **Personnel administration issues**—Recruitment, job turnover, competencies, job evaluation, education and training, remuneration, reward practices, career management and assessment systems
3. **Involvement and commitment issues**—Lack of motivation, role of nonmonetary gratification, negative impact of traditions and effect of bureaucratization on commitment and loyalty
4. **Conflicts within groups of the OSO**—Communication, absence of recognition and rewards, power issues and lack of rationality in managing OSOs

1.1 Olympic Sport Organisations As Volunteer Organisations

The voluntary character of OSOs is one of their fundamental and constitutive features. Therefore, we will explore the nature of voluntary organisations and the consequences of such a nature for human resource management, compared to other kinds of organisations. What does it mean to be a manager with the responsibility for human resources within this context?

Numerous definitions of **voluntary organisations** can be provided. A volunteer organisation can be defined, for example, as

> " . . . an organized group of persons (1) that is formed in order to further some common interest of its members; (2) in which membership is voluntary in the sense that it is neither mandatory nor acquired through birth; and (3) that exists independently of the state" (Sills 1972, p. 363).

Or, again, a volunteer organisation can be defined as

> " . . . a formally organized named group, most of whose members—whether persons or organisations—are not financially recompensed for their participation" (Knoke 1986, p. 2).

We must note that the above definitions do not preclude these organisations from hiring paid workers in different roles. European data show that about 25% of the total paid sport workers work for voluntary organisations (Camy et al. 2004).

From this perspective, a variety of organisations—ranging from a local sport club to national sport governing bodies and international sport organisations—that promote and govern various sports and the interests of participants in sports would all be considered volunteer organisations. The sport environment is densely populated by voluntary associations, and volunteers can be found at any level of the organisations, whatever their degree of professionalisation or the quantitative ratio of professionals to volunteers. However, since several kinds of volunteer organisations exist, it is useful to classify them and to locate an individual sport organisation in that classification in order to better understand some specific management implications. Palisi and Jacobson (1977) have proposed a useful scheme consisting of the following five classes of voluntary organisations.

- **Instrumental (productive for members)**—Those organisations that are created and maintained for the benefit of their members. For instance, the players' associations and referees' or coaches' unions exist to protect and promote the welfare of their respective members.
- **Instrumental (productive for others)**—The volunteer organisations that exist to produce goods or services for the benefit of a whole community or one of the deprived segments of it (e.g., ethnic minorities, disabled persons). The focus of these organisations is on changing or improving something or somebody outside the membership without reference to any benefits for the members of the organisation themselves. Olympic sport governing bodies regulate and govern their activities and those of member units for the benefit of participants in the sport. In addition, they also promote the sport within the respective communities. Numerous organisations involved in "Sport for All" belong to this group.
- **Expressive (pleasure in performance)**—Those organisations that are formed for the purpose of providing facilities for the use of their members as well as organising and conducting sports practices and competitions for their members' enjoyment. The members express themselves by engaging in the activities and derive pleasure in such participation.
- **Expressive (sociability)**—Those volunteer organisations that present a forum for their members to satisfy their sociability needs. The organisation arranges activities where members assemble and satisfy their social needs. Some of the sport clubs may fulfill this function.
- **Expressive (ideological)**—Voluntary associations formed to promote a sacred belief through standardised ritual actions. In America, Athletes in Action is a voluntary group that attempts to promote Christianity through sport. In other countries, such as Italy, some not-for-profit sport organisations have had strong ties with political or religious associations. These sport organisations endorse the main principles of those political or religious associations and promote those values through their sport practices and events.

Most sport organisations fall under the categories of instrumental (productive for members) and instrumental (productive for others). Sport governing bodies are created to be instrumental in promoting and regulating a sport for the benefit of all the participants in the sport. Thus, the participants at large are the *raison d'etre* of the sport governing bodies. However, the possibility of providing support to all the participants is strengthened if the formal membership and the legitimation that stems from that are strong enough. This explains why all these organisations inevitably fight to increase their membership or at least to keep it stable. Going back to the previous list, in the majority of cases, organisations can combine many of the different orientations listed. In spite of this, OSOs usually refrain from pursuing official expressives and ideological functions since the Olympic Charter does not allow any discrimination within the family of its organisations.

1.2 Stakeholders of Olympic Sport Organisations

Even if dedicated mostly to serving their members, OSOs are operating in a more complex environment, and their actions are extremely relevant for a larger public rather than simply their members. The public of an OSO can be thought of as consisting of several stakeholder groups (see figure 1.1).

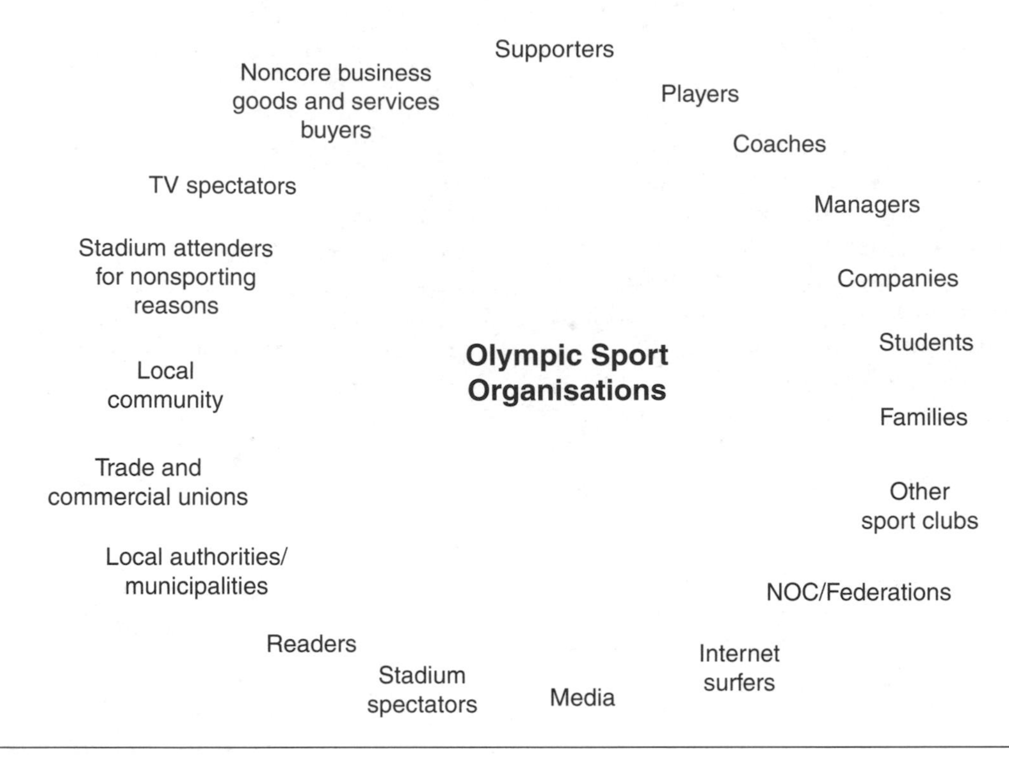

Figure 1.1 Typical stakeholders of OSOs.

Stakeholders can be defined as " . . . persons or groups that have or claim ownership, rights, or interests in a corporation and its activities, past, present, or future" (Clarkson 1995, p. 106). In sport management literature and practice, an effective relationship between the organisations and their stakeholders is normally considered as a key ingredient of high-quality organisational performance as well as a fundamental driver of their strategies. In the already mentioned work by Ferrand and Torrigiani (2005), they put the relation with the stakeholders at the centre of an organisation's marketing practices, differentiated into "internal marketing", "corporate marketing", "fund-raising services" and "social cause marketing" (p. 2).

The importance of the stakeholders is not a unique feature of OSOs, but it certainly applies to all of them. All these stakeholder groups and individuals are affected by the actions carried out and the decisions made at the organisational level. Besides obvious stakeholders—such as athletes, coaches and referees—the stakeholder groups of an OSO could include the media, government agencies, educational institutions, organised supporters (i.e., fan clubs), the private sector, and so on. In addition, other OSOs would constitute another significant stakeholder group of an OSO, because they share the same markets, participant pool, sponsorship and donor sources, spectators, and so on. By the same token, those organisations that have jurisdiction over an OSO, such as the national Olympic committees and the international or continental sport federations, are another significant stakeholder group. The same problems can be identified concerning the relations between international and continental organisations.

The stakeholders must first be identified and then their needs, expectations and involvements must be properly analyzed in order to match the organisational goals and objectives and therefore facilitate success (Di Maggio and Powell 1983; Freeman 1984; Scott 1995). At the same time, organisational performance cannot be evaluated based only on the stakeholders' perceptions (Chappelet and Bayle 2004; Esposito and Madella 2003; Hoye and Cuskelly 2003; Papadimitriou 1999; Wolfe, Hoeber and Babiak 2002).[1]

Of course, the fact that all the stakeholders can be potentially relevant and, consequently, should be identified and recognized does not

1. For an accurate theoretical foundation of this perspective, see Berger and Luckmann (1967).

mean that they are all at the same level. This has often been recognized in the scientific literature, and even more in management practice, through the well-known distinctions that are made between *primary* and *secondary* or *internal* and *external* stakeholders (Clarkson 1995; Freeman 1984). The impact of the different stakeholders on organisational performance and on the decision-making process is in fact very diverse.

Although global stakeholder theories are relevant to performance evaluation and business ethics (Friedman, Parent and Mason 2004), we are concerned here solely with their consequences and implications that can be considered relevant for HRM and for the "change management" perspective that is also a focus of this text.

In spite of the broad range of related players and stakeholders, we believe that the uniqueness of HRM in an OSO stems essentially from three critical stakeholder groups and from the way their peculiar relations are structured. These stakeholder groups are

1. the participants (especially the competitive athletes) as the key group of clients;
2. the volunteer workers; and
3. the paid professionals.

All three forms of human resources—clients, volunteer workers and paid workers—are critical to the effectiveness of an OSO, and the rest of this chapter focuses on them. Responding to the varying demands and preferences of these groups is often a challenge. Therefore, any programme for monitoring organisational performance should include specific indicators that measure the perception and satisfaction of these important constituencies of OSOs (Bayle and Madella 2002; Chelladurai et al. 1987; Papadimitriou 2001). Apart from the conventional performance indicators—such as the number of athletes, coaches or voluntary managers; the number of players included in talent programmes; and the number that have been selected for the national teams—OSOs should also evaluate the perception of the primary stakeholders concerning organisational effectiveness. Examples of scales that have been adapted to a specific national federation (the Italian Track and Field Federation) by Esposito and Madella (2003) based on the conceptual model provided by Chelladurai, Szyszlo and Haggerty (1987) are included in tables 1.1, 1.2, 1.3 and 1.4.

Research conducted by Chelladurai et al. (1987) and Papadimitriou (2001) shows that the perception of the organisational effectiveness varies according to the category of stakeholders (e.g., athletes as opposed to administrators). The question is not to determine which perspective is right but to be able to evaluate all of them and use this analysis for making decisions.

Table 1.1 **Scale of Perceived Effectiveness**[a]

Please indicate how effective FIDAL is with regard to each of the following activities by circling the appropriate number on the right.

No.	Item	Scale: Ineffective						Effective
	Input—human resources							
1	Promoting the participation in athletics in Italy	1	2	3	4	5	6	7
2	Increasing the number of registered members	1	2	3	4	5	6	7
3	Increasing the number of participants in programmes supported by FIDAL	1	2	3	4	5	6	7
4	Increasing the number of young participants in track and field	1	2	3	4	5	6	7
5	Increasing the number of adult and noncompetitive participants in track and field	1	2	3	4	5	6	7

(continued)

Table 1.1 ***(continued)***

Please indicate how effective FIDAL is with regard to each of the following activities by circling the appropriate number on the right.

No.	Item	Scale: Ineffective						Effective
	Input—monetary resources							
6	Developing corporate sponsorship of regional, national and international competitions organised in Italy	1	2	3	4	5	6	7
7	Getting subventions from the local municipalities and regions for local promotional and athlete development programmes	1	2	3	4	5	6	7
8	Becoming less dependent on the financing of the Italian NOC	1	2	3	4	5	6	7
	Throughput—promotion of local participation							
9	The two-way communication between FIDAL, its regional and provincial branches and the affiliated clubs	1	2	3	4	5	6	7
10	The technical assistance provided by FIDAL to the volunteers at the club and local levels	1	2	3	4	5	6	7
11	The coordination of participation in activities among FIDAL at the central level, the regional and provincial branches and other related bodies	1	2	3	4	5	6	7
12	The working relationship between FIDAL and the local branches on local promotional programmes and relations with the school system	1	2	3	4	5	6	7
13	Organisational atmosphere for the staff members and volunteers involved in local promotional programmes and relations with the school system	1	2	3	4	5	6	7
	Throughput—elite sport							
14	The number and the competencies of coaches for the elite athletes at the national level	1	2	3	4	5	6	7
15	The training camp and clinics provided by FIDAL for national team members, Olympic club programmes, coaches and officials	1	2	3	4	5	6	7
16	The working relationship between FIDAL and the regional branches on elite programmes	1	2	3	4	5	6	7
17	The degree of consensus among all concerned individuals over the goals and technical processes related to the operations of the national teams	1	2	3	4	5	6	7
18	The financial and other nontechnical services provided to elite athletes	1	2	3	4	5	6	7
	Output—promotion of local participation							
19	The recruitment and the satisfaction of new participants	1	2	3	4	5	6	7
20	The events and competitions organised locally to promote and support participation	1	2	3	4	5	6	7
21	The impact and originality of the communication related to promotional and youth activities	1	2	3	4	5	6	7

No.	Item	Scale						
		Ineffective						Effective
	Output—elite sport							
22	The recognition from the state and the NOC of the international success of FIDAL	1	2	3	4	5	6	7
23	The number of medals won at international competitions	1	2	3	4	5	6	7
24	The number of victories at dual international competitions	1	2	3	4	5	6	7
25	The ranking of national teams or athletes in international standings	1	2	3	4	5	6	7
26	The satisfaction of professional staff with the performance of their national teams at international competitions	1	2	3	4	5	6	7

[a] Used to evaluate the organisational performance of the Italian Track and Field Federation.

Reprinted, by permission, from P. Chelladurai, M. Szyszlo, and T.R. Haggerty, 1987, "System-based dimensions of effectiveness: The case of national sport organizations," *Canadian Journal of Sport Science* 12(2): 111-119.

Table 1.2 **Job Satisfaction Scale**[a]

Please indicate how satisfied you are with each of the following aspects of your job by circling the appropriate number on the right.

No.	Job aspects	Scale						
		Dissatisfied						Very satisfied
1	Clarity of the tasks assigned to you	1	2	3	4	5	6	7
2	Importance of your tasks	1	2	3	4	5	6	7
3	Degree to which your tasks match your expertise and experience	1	2	3	4	5	6	7
4	Amount of autonomy you have over your tasks	1	2	3	4	5	6	7
5	Recognition you receive for performing your tasks	1	2	3	4	5	6	7
6	Sense of achievement you get from your tasks	1	2	3	4	5	6	7
7	Degree to which your tasks enhance your abilities and expertise	1	2	3	4	5	6	7
8	Amount of information you get about what is going on in FIDAL	1	2	3	4	5	6	7
9	Extent to which you have an opportunity to begin and also complete a task	1	2	3	4	5	6	7
10	Extent to which your tasks require the use of a variety of skills	1	2	3	4	5	6	7
11	Opportunities FIDAL provides for you to contribute to its success	1	2	3	4	5	6	7
12	Extent to which your contributions are recognizable	1	2	3	4	5	6	7
13	Autonomy you have in establishing your priorities	1	2	3	4	5	6	7

[a] This scale is intended to be used with the employees and paid collaborators of FIDAL.

Reprinted, by permission, from P. Chelladurai, M. Szyszlo, and T.R. Haggerty, 1987, "System-based dimensions of effectiveness: The case of national sport organizations," *Canadian Journal of Sport Science* 12(2): 111-119.

Table 1.3 **Process Effectiveness Scale**[a]

Please indicate the extent of your agreement with the following statements regarding FIDAL by circling the appropriate number on the right.

No.	Items	Scale: Disagree						Agree
	Organisation							
1	Job responsibilities are sensibly organised in FIDAL.	1	2	3	4	5	6	7
2	Persons in FIDAL know what their jobs are and how to do them well.	1	2	3	4	5	6	7
3	The administrative structure of FIDAL is efficient.	1	2	3	4	5	6	7
4	In FIDAL, the distribution of responsibilities among the administrators is appropriate.	1	2	3	4	5	6	7
5	The operations carried out by FIDAL are smooth and efficient.	1	2	3	4	5	6	7
	Decision making							
6	In FIDAL, decisions are made at those levels where the most adequate and accurate information is available.	1	2	3	4	5	6	7
7	When decisions are being made, the persons affected are asked for their ideas.	1	2	3	4	5	6	7
8	In FIDAL, information is widely shared so those who make decisions have access to all available know-how.	1	2	3	4	5	6	7
9	The administrators make good decisions and solve problems well.	1	2	3	4	5	6	7
10	People in FIDAL share information about important events and situations.	1	2	3	4	5	6	7
	Personnel relations							
11	FIDAL has real interest in the welfare and happiness of those who work in it.	1	2	3	4	5	6	7
12	FIDAL tries to improve working conditions.	1	2	3	4	5	6	7
13	The volunteer and professional administrators plan together and coordinate their efforts.	1	2	3	4	5	6	7
14	The volunteer and professional administrators get along well.	1	2	3	4	5	6	7

[a]This scale is intended to be used with both professionals and volunteers active at the national and regional level.

Reprinted, by permission, from P. Chelladurai, M. Szyszlo, and T.R. Haggerty, 1987, "System-based dimensions of effectiveness: The case of national sport organizations," *Canadian Journal of Sport Science* 12(2): 111-119.

Table 1.4 **Scale of Distribution of Administrative Responsibilities Among the Institutional, Managerial and Technical Subsystems of FIDAL**[a]

Please indicate how effective FIDAL is with reference to the following tasks and activities by circling the appropriate number on the right.

No.	Process	Scale: Ineffective						Effective
	Strategic tasks							
1	Setting policies	1	2	3	4	5	6	7
2	Making annual plans	1	2	3	4	5	6	7
3	Hiring competent professionals	1	2	3	4	5	6	7
4	Drawing up the budget	1	2	3	4	5	6	7
5	Selecting representatives for international organisations	1	2	3	4	5	6	7

No.	Process	Scale Ineffective						Effective
	Planning and development							
6	Developing the quadrennial plan	1	2	3	4	5	6	7
7	Implementing the quadrennial plan	1	2	3	4	5	6	7
8	Implementing the annual plan	1	2	3	4	5	6	7
9	Publicizing and promoting the programmes	1	2	3	4	5	6	7
10	Organising competitions and championships	1	2	3	4	5	6	7
11	Evaluating plans	1	2	3	4	5	6	7
	General management							
12	Coordinating the activities of professional administrators and volunteers	1	2	3	4	5	6	7
13	Evaluating overall FIDAL activities	1	2	3	4	5	6	7
14	Doing performance appraisal of office staff and professional administrators	1	2	3	4	5	6	7
15	Hiring office staff	1	2	3	4	5	6	7
16	Doing performance appraisal of volunteer administrators	1	2	3	4	5	6	7
	High-performance tasks							
17	Appointing national team coaches	1	2	3	4	5	6	7
18	Selecting national team managers and medical personnel	1	2	3	4	5	6	7
19	Handling grievances of athletes	1	2	3	4	5	6	7
20	Scheduling competitions for national teams	1	2	3	4	5	6	7
21	Doing performance appraisal of national coaches	1	2	3	4	5	6	7
22	Liaising with regional coaching chairpersons or committees	1	2	3	4	5	6	7
23	Providing technical assistance to volunteers at the club or local level	1	2	3	4	5	6	7
24	Administering the national coaching certification programme	1	2	3	4	5	6	7
	External relations							
25	Liaising with the school system	1	2	3	4	5	6	7
26	Liaising with CONI	1	2	3	4	5	6	7
27	Liaising with other federations	1	2	3	4	5	6	7
28	Providing office management and supervision	1	2	3	4	5	6	7
29	Liaising with media personnel	1	2	3	4	5	6	7
30	Lobbying government agencies and officials	1	2	3	4	5	6	7
	Resource acquisition							
31	Canvassing business or industry for sponsorship	1	2	3	4	5	6	7
32	Maintaining business or industry sponsorships	1	2	3	4	5	6	7
33	Soliciting funds from government or other sources	1	2	3	4	5	6	7
34	Fund-raising through clubs and individual members	1	2	3	4	5	6	7

[a]In this table, the scale is modified to assess perceived effectiveness. (Note: The items have to be distributed randomly.) This scale is intended to be used with both professionals and volunteers active at the national and regional level.

Reprinted, by permission, from P. Chelladurai and T.R. Haggerty, 1991, "Differentiation in national sport organizations in Canada," *Canadian Journal of Sport Sciences* 16(2): 117-125.

In the following sections, the significance of these major stakeholder groups is explained and discussed with reference to the main management implications.

1.3 The Participants: Primary Clients and Key Human Resources of Olympic Sport Organisations

As noted earlier, the most important reason OSOs exist is to serve the participants in their respective sport, whether they are actual or simply potential members. The delivery of services for sponsors and spectators is possible and can be further developed only if there are participants who are involved and able to participate according to their will, and who can eventually perform up to the requested standards in their respective competitive arena. Thus, all the activities of OSOs, including their HRM practices, need to be focused on the welfare and satisfaction of the participants and on providing the best possible conditions for their practice, according to their needs and level of performance. Modern thrusts in management—such as total quality management (TQM), customer relationship management (CRM) and service quality—all emphasize the importance of consumers or clients and advocate for major changes in the orientation of the organisation to serve their needs. Such thrusts are oriented towards attracting, recruiting and retaining the customers with a view to enhancing corporate profitability, social legitimacy and organisational effectiveness.

This set of considerations is extremely important for OSOs, which in some cases have been criticized because they are sometimes perceived as primarily serving different categories of interests than those of the participants or members (Madella 2003). Already in the early 20th century, Michels (referring to nonsport organisations) had emphasized that all the voluntary organisations, even if formally democratic, tend to give the priority to the needs of their elites compared to those of the members that they officially serve. In this way, voluntary organisations can easily become oligarchies (Michels 1962). This can sometimes improve efficiency, but it can also have the effect of frustrating and demotivating the most interested and committed members.

Therefore, proper attitudes must be developed and suitable tools must be available to the management in order to avoid the situation where a legitimate interest in strengthening the organisation and achieving a greater level of efficiency has the effect of jeopardizing the needs of the membership and their sense of ownership and belonging. The scales used to monitor the stakeholders' perception (presented in the previous section) are examples of possible tools that can be used on this respect. They can also be complemented by more qualitative tools such as interviews and focus groups.

This emphasis on members and athletes does not preclude OSOs from providing services that are universally claimed to be of great benefit to society, as recognized by the recent emphasis on a broader concept of "social responsibility" with reference to sport organisations. This topic is outside the scope of this text. However, the possibility of OSOs generating benefits to the society at large is substantially related to their ability to provide sport services that satisfy the needs of their clients. It is unlikely that an organisation that is not able to serve its members could generate benefits for a larger public.

Satisfying the members while following the spirit and principles of the Olympic Charter is then the founding mission of all Olympic sport organisations, and it is also an essential concern for the wide network of related sport clubs, national and international governing bodies and scientific institutes. All these sport services are normally provided to all segments of the population without reference to race, religion or ethnicity. Of course, the participants may be grouped based on such factors as age, ability and gender for purposes of efficiency and equity, and the OSOs can adopt dedicated measures or programmes to match a wide range of diversified needs. Elite athletes, for example, are an important segment of participants whose needs have to be matched in special ways that may have little or no similarity to the ways in which the needs of clients in mass markets (including sport and physical activities) are usually satisfied. Actually, the compatibility between these two strands—that is, elite and mass sports—is a critical dilemma for all OSOs. The way this dilemma is dealt with and solved has a significant impact on the allocation of all the resources of an OSO.

Another equally important reason to concentrate on the participants is that, being service organisations, **OSOs cannot produce their services without the active participation of their clients in that production.** While client involvement in the production of a service is recognized in every form of services, sports require that clients engage physically and often very vigorously in the production of a service with special motivation and persistence (Chelladurai 1999). For example, a coach's contributions would be futile if the players do not engage in the strenuous drills and practices enthusiastically or do not share a commitment to the long-term plans. Talent development programmes have no impact if the young people they are targeting do not train regularly or do not comply with the required lifestyle. This means that our clients become a kind of "partial employee" of the organisation and therefore become relevant human resources to be managed. This is not unique to OSOs, but certainly the level of involvement and effort required is often higher than for other service organisations.

In addition, the other implications of this relationship between participants' personal involvement and organisation performance are important to understand. For example, the relationship existing between OSOs and elite athletes poses specific management problems because these athletes are at the same time members of a club and licensed by a federation, whose "color" they defend in the most important competitions. Both the club and the federation (or NOC) have an interest in optimizing the relationships with the athletes and exploiting their potential in order to get the optimal performance at the right time. However, what is considered to be the right time can be different for each of these organisations, and this can sometimes turn into a source of conflict and pressure for the athlete. For example, a club may have an interest in obtaining the best possible performance by an athlete as soon as possible, while a national federation may take the Olympic perspective and be more interested in long-term development. Athletes themselves can have conflicting interests with their NOCs or national federations, especially when they compete for professional clubs (domestic or foreign) whose training practices and competitive calendar are not necessarily harmonized with the Olympic calendar and international federation needs.

The main issues related to the relationships of OSOs with leisure participants (and spectators as well) have been thoroughly discussed by Ferrand and Torrigiani (2005), with reference to internal and service marketing. In this work, we will deal with other distinctive aspects for OSOs. The first point to discuss is the concept of **membership** and its implications for HRM practices in OSOs. Certainly, the concept of "clientele" should be applied to the members of an Olympic organisation, since this strengthens the idea that services must be provided and that needs must be continuously monitored. The importance of a client-oriented perspective needs to be constantly kept in mind. There are many examples of leaders and managers of OSOs (especially volunteers) who do not perceive OSOs as proper service organisations and fail to recognize both the importance of satisfying the needs of their clients and the contribution that proper human resource management can provide to this purpose. Sometimes they even fail to recognize that they have clients to satisfy.

At the same time, we should highlight the idea that being a member of an OSO also means something more than being just a client. That is, over and above serving the members, the OSO should also socialise the members into the cultures of the organisation and its values. The culture of Olympic organisations, while not at all monolithic or identical in each OSO, is a distinctive and essential feature for the identity of these organisations and their derived practices. If this perspective is underestimated or forgotten, it is difficult to find a substantial distinction between OSOs and business sport companies or producers of any kind of business entertainment. On the other hand, the latest marketing manuals and jargon of many commercial companies include a lot of emphasis on the creation of a community of customers, value sharing and other similar ideas. So it would be rather paradoxical if OSOs would neglect these concepts in favor of pure managerial efficiency. On this respect, numerous authors have argued that commercialisation, professionalisation and the perception of increased bureaucratization might facilitate a decline in participation and commitment in such organisations (Cunningham, Slack and Hinings 1987)

The Competitive Athlete As a Special Client: The Construction of Elite Performance

Competing athletes are certainly key stakeholders of OSOs, and the satisfaction and appropriate coordination of these athletes should be considered when evaluating the organisational effectiveness of an OSO. Many textbooks and articles dealing with human resource management in sport do not include athletes within their scope. Manuals and textbooks on human resources usually deal only with the workers, and in many cases (probably the majority), athletes are not formally workers or employees of any of these organisations; the athletes usually "belong" to clubs or to equivalent structures that supply technical and other services for the development of athletes' skills. In other cases, the athletes are subsidized by educational institutions (e.g., universities) or regional or local governments. So they are not considered as human resources to be managed, and the topic of athletes' care and development is often left to the technical manuals for coaches, which many OSO managers are not familiar with.

In our view, it is wrong to underestimate the key role of the athletes for OSOs, even if the precise nature of this relationship is not easy to define. Actually, OSOs are confronted with multiple typologies of athletes (e.g., competitive or noncompetitive; national, regional or provincial; young, adult or mature; men or women) who should be taken into account as relevant clients but at the same time as resources for the organisation. A national or regional federation cannot negotiate with sponsors or local authorities if very few athletes are competing, if the competitions or events they take part in are not attractive, or if no people watch those events. On the other hand, international excellence and the consequent media exposure are not achieved if an effective talent development system is not in place and continuously monitored and updated.

When analyzing the management of competitive athletes, from the perspective of OSOs, the role of the sport associations must be properly considered. Within the context of the Olympic movement, the clubs are usually considered the basis of a kind of pyramid going from mass to elite. This **"pyramid"** concept has been extremely popular and is quite recurrent in the analysis of the structure of the sport system. We will come back to the "pyramid" concept later (section 3.2), since it has an impact on sport management practices (especially in the domain of human resources because it influences the practices of talent identification and development). At this moment, however, we should point out that in recent years the idea of the pyramid has been challenged based on growing evidence that in many countries there have been numerous elite athletes and medals without significant mass participation in a specific discipline—and, conversely, huge mass practice without medals or world-class success (Green 2005; Lyle 2004; Madella 2004). This has been documented for many sports in different countries (e.g., fencing, bobsled, women's wrestling, women's cross-country skiing, and so on), and it is evident not only in the scientific literature; the reference to the "shrinking" or "splitting" of the pyramid has become more and more common in the experts' discourse. This poses important questions on the organisation of the sport systems and the allocation of the resources available for the development of athletes.

For an OSO (mainly in connection with national governments), typical key questions include the following: Should we support more elite athletes or mass sport? How can we manage to find the right ratio between the two? How much does supporting mass sport really benefit elite development? Or how much do we need champions and sport stars to promote mass participation?

All Olympic sport organisations are confronted with these problems, and the solutions depend essentially on the way the relations between the two domains (i.e., mass sport and elite sport) are conceived and on the priorities that are set up in each specific national or local situation. When formulating specific strategies concerning athletes' development, a difficult element that must be dealt with is the different time scales of the two perspectives: Investment in talent programmes is typically a long-term one with a high degree of uncertainty and risk of dispersion of resources (e.g., athletes may migrate to another country or club after having been supported for 5 to 10 years or even more), while concentrating resources on a selected number of top performers tends to have more chances of short-term success.

The contradictory nature of these measures is evident. Even if OSOs are responsible for a wide range of services for all their members, sport "stars" cannot be compared to ordinary "clients" such as customers of a commercial fitness centre or of an outdoor sport service. Elite athletes exchange their time and effort not for health- or fun-related benefits but in view of very different kinds of rewards (including financial benefits and personal achievement) in a very competitive environment (Digel 2005). In this environment, many countries compete for more or less the same number of medals (figure 1.2). To be able to achieve world excellence, a large number of services, whose amount has increased significantly both in quantity and degree of specialisation, have to be delivered to the athletes. Athletes can therefore be considered as primary beneficiaries of OSOs. Sometimes the athletes are financed directly by a federation, and even if this is not the case, they are usually subsidized and provided with extensive and specialised services to facilitate the pursuit of excellence. They often receive more than just grants; if included in some kind of Olympic club or excellence programme, they normally have access to high-level medical, psychological and other kinds of specialised services. This is true at all levels of athletes' development. Global packages are being created to facilitate the maximum development of an athlete's talents in order to achieve elite performance. For many years, this support has been characterised mostly by coaching, psychological and medical services, but in recent years, more global strategies encompassing the athletes' needs in the broadest sense (e.g., educational and work placement services) have been worked out and tested.

For this reason, in the nonprofessional sports or in those contexts where monetary rewards are not really abundant for competitive athletes, the relationship with the federation (or the NOC) is often more important for the athletes (in terms of money and career) than the one they have with their club. Clubs are sometimes not "strong" enough to be involved effectively in the process of supporting athletes through a whole range of necessary actions. However, this is quite variable according to the specific nature and positioning of each sport in the market. Nowadays, elite athletes are getting more and more support from sponsors or other actors (e.g., universities), sometimes independently of their

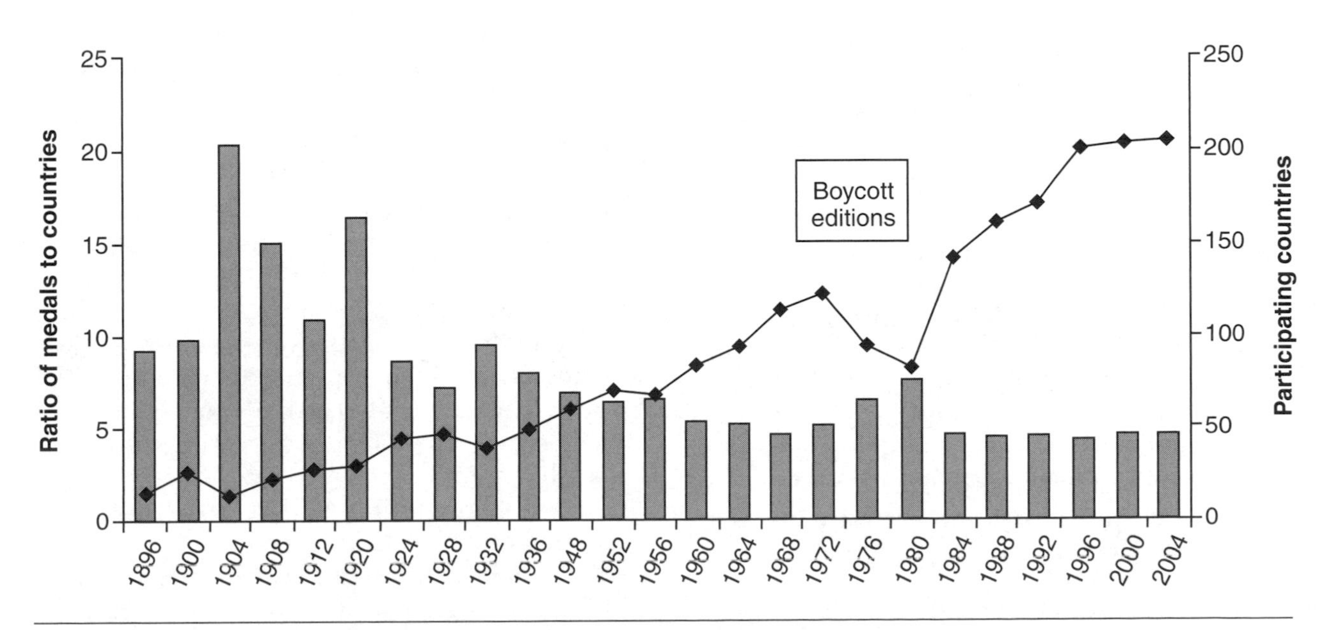

Figure 1.2 Evolution of Summer Olympic Games: participating countries, events and medal chances.

Note: The ◆ represent the number of participating countries and the columns represent the ratio of medals to countries.

clubs or federations and other times on the basis of planned synergies and co-operation.

Today, the competition between countries and federations to attract and retain athletes is based increasingly on the capacity to provide a fully supportive environment to the athletes. This indicates that athletes are being positioned more at the centre of the sport system. The last two decades of the 20th century have been characterised by a significant growth in the importance of the athletes in general and in their negotiating power, following clear indications from the IOC.

As a result, the need to systematically pursue the satisfaction of athletes is being increasingly recognized. Even though this subject is not common in sport management studies, there is some evidence of a persistent lack of satisfaction among elite athletes. We can quote, for example, a study (Papadimitriou 2001) carried out on top-level Greek athletes, within a multiple constituency approach. This study showed a low level of satisfaction of elite athletes (especially those in individual sports) for the services received from their national sport governing body, particularly the training and the competitive conditions: "The low effectiveness rating given by elite athletes to the National Sport Organisation indicates that they are not always ready and capable to meet the needs of their sport" (p. 79).

The "climate" surrounding top-level athletes and teams is clearly extremely important on this respect. Papadimitriou maintained that the climate needs to include a "warm and trusting atmosphere" but especially a network of services and a set of integrated activities inspired by a perceivable "athlete-centred approach". The results derived from the Papadimitriou study can probably be generalised and applied to numerous other OSOs, whose main challenge is to design and implement additional initiatives and programmes in order to satisfy elite athletes as fundamental beneficiaries. This process has also produced an important extension of interest towards the whole life of the athletes and not just in the period while they are competing.

> "It is very unfair that at the end of the career of these brilliant Athletes, who everyone has stimulated to train and reach their best, when they are 30-35, which is mostly the age of their retirement, we would shake their hands and say to them: 'Thank you very much, congratulations for your career, and now you help yourself in future life'. We simply cannot do that. We have the moral responsibility to help them in various ways: To help to find jobs for them, to give them education, and to help them to re-integrate in life" (J. Rogge 2003, Osaka Award Ceremony).

These concepts, now largely expressed within the general idea of an "athlete-centred" approach (Thibault and Babiak 2005), have pushed Olympic sport organisations to develop career transition management processes and services for elite athletes and to integrate this perspective into all their athlete management practices.

Recruiting and Developing Talented Athletes: Phases and Challenges

Although serving the needs and interests of the different categories of participants is essential for all OSOs, the identification and support of elite athletes has a special meaning for their organisational performance. As we have already indicated, we believe that this is a fundamental challenge for OSOs. Even if innate biological factors have an undisputable importance to the development of a talented athlete, there is growing evidence of the dominant role played by environmental factors. It would be a mistake to assign this topic to other fields outside sport management, for example, to the methodology and organisation of sport training or the psychology of sport coaching (Haase 1986). Nowadays, the identification and management of elite athletes and their career itineraries is less and less the responsibility of a single club or an isolated coach. The career of an athlete has to be managed properly, and there is a growing consensus that this should involve the whole organisational system working within clear guidelines inspired by an explicit and controlled strategy. All the main actors of this system must be aware of the challenges posed by this issue, especially considering the globalisation of sport and its inevitable commercialisation.

The importance that Olympic values and the voluntary culture have for OSOs should certainly be emphasized; however, this should not prevent their actors from understanding the deep changes that have affected the way excellence is produced and cultivated in the different countries or geographic and political areas. For example, an increasing number of athletes have changed their nationality in recent years. In the European Union, the impact of the Bosman law on the market of professional athletes has been very relevant, especially with reference to the transfer rules, the freedom of movement of players and the role of the youth clubs. It is not an exaggeration to say that the majority of top-level players in some sports are migrants (Lanfranchi and Taylor 2001). The liberalisation of the transfer market (clubs are no longer always obliged to pay a transfer fee for a new player) has increased competition between the clubs to acquire the best players and has changed the process of introduction in top-level sport. The most recent regulations allow the players to become free at a certain point in their career. FIFA regulations have dealt repeatedly with this issue in recent years because of the frequency with which sport organisations of the richest countries have exploited young children from less fortunate environments. Within this context, agents of players are playing a more important role.

To understand the challenge and to identify the best actions and principles for developing athletes, we must consider in detail the current conditions for the production of success in Olympic sport. In all sports, the process of producing elite athletes is extremely long and complex: Numerous studies have revealed some important differences between the disciplines, but normally a world-class performance cannot be achieved in less than 8 to 10 years (Balyi and Hamilton 2000; Ericsson 1996; Ericsson and Charness 1994; Salmela 1997). Recent studies also show that the process of sport specialisation to reach the elite level begins very early, sometimes when the children are just 5 or 6 years old. However, there are exceptions, especially in the case of athletes with previous experience in other similar sports. These athletes can have a later introduction without necessarily jeopardising their chances of world-class success.

Olympic sport organisations are supposed to provide optimal conditions and support in all the main phases of the athletes' development. Different periodizations of these phases have been proposed in the past (Filin 1978; Matveev 1984) for sport athletes, and they are not very different from the well-known three-step model (initiation, development, perfection) developed by Bloom (1985) with reference to talent in general. These models, however, have been traditionally limited to the period of time when the athlete is involved in competition, and only recently has an additional phase (the transition from sport to a new career) been taken into consideration (Balyi and Hamilton 2000). In our view, a satisfactory conceptualisation should include the following phases:

1. Introductory (or initiation) phase
2. Specialisation phase
3. High-performance phase
4. Postcompetitive phase

The Introductory Phase

In the introductory phase, the young athlete must become interested in the discipline and develop basic skills and attitudes in a supportive environment. The game component is prevailing so that the distinction between sport and play is minimised. This phase is especially critical because the physical, psychological and motor differences among children are very high and the motivation to participate in sport is quite diversified. Family and club orientation surely add to that.

An appropriate combination of school sport systems, sport clubs and local municipalities is considered essential at the earlier stage of youth involvement, together with a precise interpretation of youth needs and a high quality of youth leaders. Unfortunately, this is not always the case because, for different reasons (e.g., status, remuneration), the best coaching professionals usually prefer to work with older and more skilled subjects (De Martelaer et al. 2002). Further problems in this phase derive from the decreasing rate of physical education classes in many countries and from the growing impact of sedentary habits on kids, combined with the decline of traditional youth sports and motivation for intensive training. On the other hand, youth undertaking sport practice at this stage are often subjected to very high training volumes in order to achieve immediate excellence. Pressure from families, club leaders or coaches to achieve short-time success has often been reported as the rule at this age. Excess pressure from families has been frequently reported as one of the main causes of dropout in this phase or in the phase that immediately follows.

The Specialisation Phase

The age of specialisation is different in the various kinds of disciplines, ranging from 8 to 10 years in gymnastics, diving and other disciplines to 13 to 15 years and even later in other sports. Traditional stereotypes concerning the best age for specialisation are currently under strong criticism; for example, very young runners are now able to run incredibly fast, reaching the world-elite level already at 18 or 19 years old, while in the past it was believed that only older athletes could obtain such results and that there was no reason for specialising too early in these disciplines. No clear scientific evidence exists on this; however, experience tells us that there are very different individual itineraries leading to excellence.

The increase of volume and intensity of the training loads is not the only key aspect in this phase. The process of socialisation into sport that had started in the previous phase becomes critical. The young athlete must be fully socialised to the role of athlete; he or she has to learn appropriate rules and behaviors and must enter a systematic competitive activity. Motivation has to be adapted (if not converted) in relation to the new situational requirements and new identity processes that are developing. In these years, the uncertainty is especially high; athletes are not sure of their future, and they are submitted to multiple environmental pressures and competing values (e.g., sport versus school success or perceived competence in social life). The consequence is that the rate of dropout and withdrawal is the highest in this phase.

The majority of OSOs concentrate many of their efforts on athletes who are in this phase, since these athletes must be properly socialised and accompanied, and proper support to the role of competitive athlete must be provided. This is essential because investments in this phase are long term and quite uncertain; therefore, they must be conveniently secured. Recently, the most developed clubs have also taken care of this aspect. This is the role, for example, that is played by the football academies in the United Kingdom (Richardson, Gilbourne and Littlewood 2004) and in many other countries. OSOs often run their own academies or excellence programmes, investing a lot of resources and efforts in this phase of the sporting life in order to provide systematic advice on competition planning, career and educational choices, and occasionally financial compensation.

Typical successful academies or excellence centres strive to meet the following criteria:

- Incorporation of a dedicated staff with large and diversified competencies (coaches, physicians, psychologists, educational consultants, and so on) with a precise and rigid age or level of specialisation. This is a critical area because many federations have scarce financial and human resources to allocate to this task.
- Integration of all the aspects of the individual curriculum (sport, school, vocational training, and so on) to avoid one aspect taking precedence over the others. For example, some organisations reduce or cancel the support or force an athlete to leave the academy if academic results are not satisfactory or a proper lifestyle is not adopted. Academic time requirements and itineraries for scholarship are normally provided. Global monitoring is usually the responsibility of the director.
- Synergies with the national technical direction.
- Co-operation with the external environment (especially schools, local municipalities, and so on).
- Creation of a large database of information on the followed athletes and on the long-term impact of the activities. This normally directly involves the federation staff who are responsible for talent identification and support.

In some cases, especially in team sports, special relations with local clubs or satellite organisations are developed to optimize the results; in other cases, all the athletes belonging to an academy or an excellence centre may compete for the same club.

Through similar approaches, the sports training programmes and the social support programmes have a better chance of integration and success.

The High-Performance Phase

As we have already mentioned, the high-performance phase is characterised by very high physical and emotional loads. It is evident that the competition level and training complexity require the Olympic athletes to be involved on a full-time basis. Elite sport can correctly be considered as a "total institution" (Goffmann 1961) that totally absorbs the participants and reduces the opportunities for external contacts with competing "social worlds" that have other constellations of meanings, rewarded behaviors and values. This makes it almost impossible for these athletes to carry out a normal study itinerary while training. They have to either quit the educational system or apply to dedicated educational services that are specially designed for athletes.

Once they reach the top performance, athletes need a specialised and dedicated system that is able to reduce risks and optimize the performance. As Papadimitriou has indicated, "this necessitates the provision of financial assistance to promising athletes, as an important means to retain and motivate them to achieve their potential" (2001, p. 79). It is not just a question of money; athletes with high potential need a series of sophisticated services that involve coaches, managers, doctors and many other consultants (Koski and Heikkala 1998). Social security is another sensitive topic that not many organisations cover. These athletes are involved daily in choices concerning the planning of their careers; for example, they often look for the best compromise between the needs of ensuring a long-term career and the access to maximum benefits (financial and prestige) during a single year of outstanding fitness and performance.

If the support measures fail or are not available at all, high dropout rates or a reduction of training volume can easily occur. Recently, other individual strategies (e.g., the change of nationality) have been tried by athletes in order to pursue better opportunities. Dropouts and changes of nationality can easily damage the perceived effectiveness and legitimacy of an OSO. Also, the risk of illegal practices and doping is probably higher when the future of the athletes is at stake. This means that in addition to sanctions (e.g., bans, withdrawal of medals), support programmes for athletes can be indirectly useful for limiting the risk of deviance.

The Postcompetitive Phase

In the postcompetitive phase, the athletes look for a satisfactory life after sport, with significant professional opportunities both inside and outside the sport world. As we have already mentioned, the attention paid to this phase has grown significantly in the last few years. In chapter 2, we will analyze in detail the most important aspects of career transition management.

Recruiting and Developing Talented Athletes: The Construction of an Effective System

The precise relation and integration between these phases of athlete development is a critical point for OSOs. Isolating one phase from another can damage the overall effectiveness of the system. Numerous recent scientific investigations have highlighted the relevant features of the most successful cases; however, these give only limited hints to sport organisations on the best model to be followed.

We have already argued against the traditional view of the "pyramid"—grassroots to elite sport—which has been increasingly challenged in the last few years (Lyle 2004; Salmela 1997). A simplified view of this pyramid advocates that young boys or girls should be introduced into sport through schools or youth clubs where they practice essentially for fun and socialisation. From this environment, it is assumed that at a certain stage the best performers are "extracted" or naturally "selected" and later introduced to specialised and high-quality training carried out by more qualified and dedicated coaches (usually within more organised clubs or excellence centres managed by NSFs, NOCs, and so on). The level of competition and training would rise accordingly in a good and sustainable progression. The role of the OSOs is substantially passive or just limited to the provision of suitable infrastructure, specialised scientific and coaching knowledge and competent human resources (dedicated coaches).

In many sports and countries, this system is still at least partly recognizable, and for many people and authorities, it is ideologically desirable. But we believe that this picture does not always or fully correspond to the reality of the process of producing elite athletes. In fact, in an increasing number of situations, this process has undergone important changes:

- In many sports and countries, specialised training systems for excellence are operational for athletes at a very young age.
- Dedicated detection and supporting structures are being set up by many national federations to optimize the resources and procedures used to facilitate access to high performance. Training camps or permanent monitoring systems are operated to continuously assess the level of motor skills, abilities and psychological variables of promising athletes. A dedicated integrated network of regional and state programmes or "Olympic clubs" is often activated for this purpose.
- In many sports, there is a clear separation between the production system aimed at the top level and the production system aimed at leisure; in most cases, the participants, coaches and even clubs are different, involving different skills and training. Leisure practices are generally financed directly by the participants (sometimes together with other actors), while the search for excellence is often based on the direct investment of the families, but also by public and private funders.
- Competition between sport organisations is increasing, especially with reference to the recruitment of the few youngsters with outstanding skills and abilities. In fact, even if talent development requires means and skill training that is specific to each discipline, the same general abilities (strength, speed, height, and so on) are equally required for many popular sports.

In a sense, at least for some sports, all these elements can be interpreted as a new kind of pyramid (with a much smaller base) that is already oriented to elite success.

These considerations place a formidable pressure on all OSOs, and not only on them. Most of the national states or regional authorities have in fact developed policies and invested in actions aimed at the increase of youth sport participation. They have done this based on the conviction that this process, assisted by a good supply of services by quality clubs, would automatically produce not just psychological and sociological benefits but also a good amount of proficient competitors (De Martelaer et al. 2002; Oakley and Green 2001).

In the last decades of the 20th century, because of changes in market and cultural conditions and probably the negative impact of some phenomena associated with elite sport (e.g., doping), many countries shifted the focus of their investments and political action from elite to mass sport (Koski and Heikkala 1998; Palm 1991). Other reasons cited for this shift included maximisation of health, social and psychological benefits. Although the interest of the whole population in a physically active lifestyle was considered prevalent, this approach was not necessarily perceived as contradictory with world-class success because of the commonsense conviction that there is automatic correlation between the two. In spite of the high value placed on recreational sport and active lifestyles, many national governments continued to see world sport success as an important component of national prestige. In some cases of insufficient world-class performance, OSOs have been subject to heavy criticism, and their organisational processes have been strongly challenged, with all the imaginable consequences (e.g., reduction of funding, political control).

Therefore, talent identification and all the related athlete development processes that remain fall within the most critical aspects of contemporary intervention of OSOs. The delivery of specific and effective programmes to identify, support and optimize talent development is normally one of the most important and discussed components of the strategies of current OSOs, even if in the majority of countries and federations, talent search is still a casual and unorganised process. **Talent search and support programmes have the task of systematically recognizing and developing youngsters with a recognized potential for becoming elite athletes in different sports** (Borms 1996; Williams and Reilly 2000). At the same time, these programmes should avoid dispersion and waste of resources, which is a difficult task since the predictability of sport talents and the relationships between genetic heritage and trainability in sport are not yet well known. To pursue this goal, the concept of talent identification has become more complex and articulated, encompassing a range of specific phases that include identification and scouting first, followed by selection and systematic support (Ziemainz and Gulbin 2002).

Of course, the way the different kinds of organisations can activate and govern this process is very different; for example, international and continental federations normally are not directly engaged in talent scouting procedures, but they are often willing to provide indirect support to the affiliated organisations for this specific purpose (e.g., training and education, equipment, stages, centres, and so on). Interesting examples include the whole range of initiatives by IAAF (e.g., the Puerto Rico Development Centre), FIFA (through some strands of the Goal Project), ITF, UEFA and numerous others.

The amount of training required to become an elite performer is certainly very high; however, very different approaches in terms of distribution and specialisation in the training workload have been chosen and implemented. In most cases, early specialisation is very common. The procedures used to train potential talents are often very demanding, and in many cases, scientific and political authorities have identified serious risks for the psychological and physical health of the potential elite athletes.

National governments and supranational institutions (e.g., the European Union) have expressed their concern on this aspect, assigning a key role to the question of the protection and integrity of young athletes. For this reason, protecting athletes is also becoming more important in the agenda of OSOs. In fact, federations tend to recognize that athletes are exposed to threats and risks that can endanger their careers and the legitimacy of the organisations to which they belong.

Given the high level of competition between and within countries, the efficiency of the talent development system is critical in order to avoid dispersion of resources and loss of prominent talents. OSOs should be aware of all the factors that can restrain the potential of gifted athletes or limit the effectiveness of the process of identification and support of world-class athletes during the long process that leads to athletic excellence. Reasons for the loss of potential sport talents are multiple and have been described by experts and researchers from very different perspectives—for example, from a psychological, sociological, medical (e.g., injuries) or genetic approach.

Oakley and Green (2001) have identified a common trend across those countries that are making significant efforts to develop their athletic elites. In their view, this trend leads towards a homogeneous model that is essentially based on the creation of a network of institutes and dedicated facilities in each country. The Australian Institute of Sport is often identified as a paramount example of an effective specialised institute that is able to facilitate the pursuit of excellence. Following this example, similar institutes have been created recently in numerous countries (e.g., United Kingdom, Canada, Belgium [Flanders]) or have been reinforced in those countries where they already existed.

Some further common features of these systems have been listed by Oakley and Green, and they can be interesting for those OSOs that are trying to put similar systems in place (p. 91):

1. Clear understanding and definition of the role of the different participating agencies and an effective communication network able to maintain the system (and avoid duplications and conflict)
2. Simplicity of administration
3. System for statistical identification of talents
4. Provision of sport service to create a culture or environment where all the main individual actors involved in elite athletic production can interact (athletes, coaches, staff, scientists)
5. Well-structured competitive programmes
6. Well-developed facilities
7. Targeting of resources on a reduced number of sports with higher chances to access medals or world success; every country normally carries out detailed studies on its chances of success in the 4-year cycles and then develops specific plans to target specific events and optimize the resources.

8. Comprehensive planning
9. Recognition of costs and appropriate funding
10. Lifestyle support and preparation for life after sport

The analysis made by Oakley and Green garners great interest but does not consider sufficiently the national specificities and institutional arrangements of the respective sport systems. One fundamental variable is the degree of centralisation or decentralisation of the different sport systems. For example, France is an outstanding example of a centralised system, with a main institute in Paris and various regional centres that also depend on the Ministry of Sport. The personnel providing these services also belong to the Ministry of Sport, even though a decrease in public funding and personnel has been noted in the last few years, coupled with an increasing role of the regional initiatives and also of the federations (which are autonomous).

Where regional authorities are more developed, as in Germany or Spain, the functioning of the development system for elite athletes can take a different route, one that is more regionalized. Another aspect is the source of funding for elite athlete development programmes. In the majority of countries, this is public funding, while in others, such as the United States, the supporting networks of services to the athletes and coaches depend mostly on private funding.

In our view, at least **four major models** of talent development can be identified on the basis of different variables such as the degree of centralisation or decentralisation, the source of funding, and especially the role played by the different actors. These models are presented here simply as ideal types, since they take different forms in various social and economic contexts and can even occur simultaneously in the same country or organisation:

- Centralised model
- Network model
- Club-based model
- Individual or entrepreneurial model

The first model is extremely centralised and is based on a kind of monopolistic role taken by a dominant actor (normally the state, through the Ministry of Sport or a related agency). The original version of the model can be found in the former socialist republics of Eastern Europe, particularly in Russia where a systematic process of talent identification was carried out at the school level as early as the 1930s. The talent identification was mostly based on a combination of qualitative and quantitative indicators (usually field and laboratory tests and psychological measures). This selection generally occurred at a quite early age, depending on the sport, with a high risk of exploitation and alienation. For this reason, together with frequent doping use, this model has been subject to strong ethical and ideological criticism. After the dissolution of the former communist states, however, this model has not been abandoned as could have been expected following the heavy criticism of the very early specialisation, the exploitation of young adults and children and the frequent use of illegal drugs. The importance of elite sport for national prestige is still very high, and the major challenges to the further development of the elite development systems are often more financial than political. Many countries have incorporated the old model within their own context, with specific adaptations. China, for example, has refined its existing (centrally administered) talent support programme associated with a huge investment in sport facilities, targeting the Olympic Games of 2008.

Compared to the old communist system, however, many moderating elements are recognizable. For example, the tendencies towards the "new managerialism" in the public sector (Henry and Theodoraki 2000) require more accountability and transparency and a strong ethical commitment by those bodies charged by the state to take the responsibility for young athletes' development.

The network model, which is less demanding in terms of financial investment and control, is based on the co-operation between different actors with different roles and responsibilities. Normally, the major roles in the process are played by the national federations, the state agencies for sport, the Olympic committees and often the school systems. However, the way these actors interact and inject resources in the system can vary widely. Canada is an example of this model, with different centres scattered across the whole country complementing the activities of the national federations and of the provincial sport organisations for the pursuit of excellence (Canadian Olympic Association 1999; Thibault and Babiak 2005). The funding structure reflects the multiple partnerships, with revenues coming from the Canadian Olympic Association, the government (Sport Canada) and numerous local partners (i.e., the provincial government or its representative provincial multisport federation). The wide composition of the stakeholders is reflected in the composition of the board of administrators of these centres. In Spain, there is also a mixed system with substantial support from autonomous communities but also able to attract private funding. Probably the most cited example of this model is the Australian talent identification and development programme "Talent Search" (Oakley and Green 2001; Ziemainz and Gulbin 2002).

The third model is characterised by the dominant role of the clubs. This normally occurs in the strongest and most commercialised sports. For example, in the case of football, the development of the athletes is a responsibility of the clubs that have developed specific organisations, such as the academies, to develop youth athletes (Richardson, Gilbourne and Littlewood 2004). Examples can also be found at the elite level. A.S. Milan, for example, has created the Milan Lab, a structure with the task of monitoring all aspects related to the performance of the players in order to facilitate the decision making by the coaches.

The last model is purely individualistic: Athletes and families invest their own resources to get the necessary support to achieve excellence. This system is typical of all those countries or conditions where there are not enough resources to assist the athletes; many of them are therefore forced to move to other countries and enjoy the superior level of technical expertise and facilities, following an exchange with local organisations (be it clubs or universities).

Common Strategic Components of Talent Identification and Support

Since the choice of a model for talent identification and support should always consider the local specificities and dominant values and policies, a set of core measures can be identified as common strategic elements of such models. First, it is necessary to have very competent personnel, a clear strategy and a correct division of roles to avoid dispersion of resources, lack of coordination and duplications.

Then, all the potential stakeholders to be involved in the process must be identified (federations, clubs, municipalities, regions, the state, schools and other actors), followed by a definition of common goals, areas of common interest and specific responsibilities. Following that, a specific plan can be created for developing a high-quality system of distribution of services to the athletes. Social and emotional support should combine with the more technical in order to build a balanced package of services. On the organisational side, talent development systems tend to perform best if they can profit from the combined effort of multiple institutional actors, such as the following:

- Specialised research centres
- Centres for excellence
- Regional supporting programmes
- Coach support measures and bodies

In some countries (e.g., Australia, Germany), we can find useful examples of a network of partners who collaborate with different roles and responsibilities to optimize the chances of athletes reaching the top level of their potential. In Australia, for example, the Australian Sport Commission co-operates with the National Elite Sport Committee and the States to facilitate the avenue to success. The Talent Search Programme of Australia is a three-phase programme that relies on a powerful network of schools collaborating for its execution (under the coordination of the Australian Institute of Sport). Phase one is essentially a talent identification programme with different rounds of testing that are carried out for an initial screening. A small percentage of the tested subjects (around 2%) are then selected for the second phase, which is aimed at specific sports. In phase two, more precise information is collected on the individual athletes through specific technical tests for each sport. After this phase, a restricted number of promising athletes are accepted into the core of the talent development programme, which requires them to train in specialised institutes throughout the country. Through this networking approach and its multiple steps, it has been possible to avoid the alienating components that were typical of the centralised model of the old communist states, even if the role of the central state remains crucial.

In Germany, a federal state with a strong separation between the state and the sport system (Braun 2000), there is a developed and decentralised system of regional support points (Olympicstuetzpunkte) with the task of analyzing, supporting and controlling the technical and motor development of the athletes, using an interdisciplinary approach. Regionalization is considered the best option for continuity of support and the network. These support points have been major actors in administration and scientific support of elite-level sport in Germany (Haase 1987; Hagedorn 1987).

NOCs usually take a major role in the development and leadership of such plans, acting as supporting organisations that often follow a strategic plan based on the usual analysis of current strengths and weaknesses and the identification of possibilities for the future.

The complexity of the required coordination explains why some organisations have preferred to acquire athletes already at the elite level (through a process of naturalisation for example), following the model of professional sport, rather than invest so much in an uncertain and costly system of talent development. The impact of globalisation has strongly complicated these processes; in less developed or less wealthy contexts, athletes (even at a very young age) often try to optimize their own chances by following a kind of "cherry-picking itinerary" within a variable and planetary market. In these cases, OSOs are often replaced by athletes' agents who negotiate on their behalf to secure the apparently "best" conditions for their development. Agents have sometimes become more important than coaches and the federation in the establishment of the competition calendars for elite athletes in individual sports. The agent profession is not always regulated in the different countries. Some federations (e.g., FIFA, IAAF) have set up a complex set of rules on agents' activities, but normally most of the NFs and NOCs lack a specific policy regarding them. Since agents try to offer the athletes a facilitating global environment, it is evident that in some cases their function can overlap with the one performed by clubs and federations.

Therefore, the role of the agent is a critical topic of discussion within Olympic organisations. In fact, variable views are often expressed, according to which

- in a free market society, agents are a vehicle for the optimization of athletes' performance, which is in the interest of the Olympic organisations for whom they create value;

or vice versa,

- agents reduce the relations between athletes and their reference organisations, and they depotentiate the role of the coaches with a consequent loss of legitimacy and organisational performance in the long term.

In any case, agents constitute a significant and relatively new group of actors within the sport system. Their role has to be considered properly by OSOs, in relation with other stakeholders (e.g., the state or professional associations), in order for the OSOs to design their own policies to identify, develop and support athletes.

1.4 Volunteer Workers in Olympic Sport Organisations

Almost everywhere in the world, sport organisations are largely dependent on the contributions of volunteers (Beamish 1985; Green and Chalip 1998; Mc Pherson 1986; Shibli 1999). Within the Olympic movement, volunteers are especially important, given the values driving such organisations. Apart from athletes (who can also be differentiated between volunteers and professionals), coaches and administrators operating in these organisations are often willing to devote their time, effort and knowledge to the pursuit of the organisational goals without monetary rewards. Many other roles that are essential for these organisations are also commonly covered by volunteers (e.g., referees). The spirit of volunteerism is therefore a key element of the culture and constellation of values for any OSO, and in many countries, it is the true fabric of the sport sector. In spite of this key role, the overall process of modernization is challenging the traditional logic of operation and typical governance of voluntary organisations in many countries. It is not difficult to find texts or public discourse advocating an acceleration of the professionalisation process and the adoption of businesslike operational ways. On the other hand, volunteer shortages, skills gaps, a crisis of "vocations" and recruitment barriers are often reported. In addition, the cohabitation between volunteers and professionals is indicated as a source of continuous tensions inside these organisations.

The reported difficulty of recruitment of new volunteers is not just a problem of insufficient skills or difficult cohabitation between volunteers and professionals; in every country, there is a more or less wide population of non-profit associations (co-operatives, welfare and health voluntary organisations, movements, parties, self-help agencies, and so on) that can attract those who "feel" inclined to volunteer. For this reason, a reflection on volunteerism in sport organisations is essential to the purpose of this text.

In spite of its large use, the concept of volunteer is not the easiest to define. An example of an effective definition is provided by Smith, who defines a volunteer as

> "an individual engaging in behavior that is not bio-socially determined (e.g., eating, sleeping), nor economically necessitated (e.g., paid work, house work, home repair), nor socio-politically compelled (e.g., paying one's taxes, clothing oneself before appearing in public), but rather that is essentially (primarily) motivated by the expectation of psychic benefits of some kind . . ." (Smith 1981, pp. 22-23).

Halba and Le Net (1997) identify five main conditions that are necessary to define the volunteer:

- The commitment (or engagement)
- The free will (notion of freedom) and lack of coercion
- The lack of interest in economic outcomes
- The belonging to a group or organisation
- The service to a common interest

A plethora of dedicated research has confirmed the great importance and value of the contribution of volunteers and voluntary organisations in the sport sector. We will just mention some of the most impressive data, without any claim of being exhaustive in this review. Chelladurai (1999) estimated the economic worth of the volunteer work in sport in the United States to be more than $20 billion. More recent sources based on different methodologies have indicated a value close to $40 billion. In the Canadian province of Ontario, more than 600,000 volunteers assist sport participants of all ages and levels of qualification. In Europe, more than 16 million sport volunteers are active in more than 800,000 associations, bringing added value that has been estimated to be over €100 billion (EOSE 2004). Swedish sport, for example, is strongly based on volunteerism; the Swedish Sport Confederation reports 600,000 volunteers who carry out tasks within clubs without any financial compensation, bringing a contribution with a value of about €1.5 billion per year.

Sport-related volunteering in the United Kingdom has also been the object of multiple investigations. While Kokolakakis (1997) estimated its value to be around £1.5 billion in 1997, according to Sport England, in 2002 there were 5,821,400 sport volunteers in the country, representing nearly 15% of the adult population, who contribute 1.2 billion hours each year to sport, equivalent to 720,000 additional full-time paid workers. The value of the time contributed by sport volunteers in England is estimated at over £14 billion. Volunteers help to sustain over 106,400 affiliated clubs in England, serving over 8 million members. The sporting sector makes the single biggest contribution to total volunteering in England, with 26% of all volunteers citing sport as their main area of interest.

Sport England (2002) has enriched these quantitative figures with a selection of quotations from different sources that also provide an idea of the social representation of the role and functions of volunteers in the country.

> "It remains the bedrock of opportunity in many sports" (Sheffield Research Team).

"Without volunteers there would not be so many choices for people to participate in sport" (Young Volunteer).

"Without them all the activities we do would fail" (Local Authority Sports Development Officer).

"Without volunteers, our clubs would not exist" (Badminton Club Member).

"Without them we wouldn't survive, there wouldn't be any provision" (Local Authority Officer).

"There is no economic substitute for volunteers in sport" (Sheffield Research Team).

The Australian Sport Commission already in 1993 had estimated that almost 1.4 million adults were volunteering in Australian sport (with an equivalent contribution of $1.65 billion AU annually). In 2001, they raised this estimate to 1.7 million, spending 130 million hours. It is interesting to note that this is more or less the same value as for the professional work carried out by 75,000 professional workers.

Even if volunteering is more prevalent in some specific cultures, especially in Northern Europe and Anglo-Saxon countries, impressive figures have been reported for numerous other countries or other geographic and cultural contexts: €3 billion was the value of volunteer work for Italy in 2001 (Weber, Del Campo & Pelucchi 2002), based on 151 million working hours carried out by almost 700,000 volunteers (source CONI); Fr 1.7 billion Swiss is the value estimated by Lamprecht and Stamm in 1997 for Switzerland; and €13 million is the amount for Slovenia. According to Blanc (1999), there were 2.7 million sport volunteers in Germany, serving yearly for 200 million hours; in France, in spite of the large professionalisation of the sport system, more than 1 million volunteers are reported to have worked 300 million hours. For Flanders, Verhoeven et al. (1999) have estimated more than 200,000 volunteers operating in about 18,000 clubs. However, the role and recognition of volunteers can be very different from country to country and even within the same country or sport (Halba and Le Net 1987).

From a different perspective, megaevents such as Olympic Games are only possible because of the major involvement of volunteers. During the Olympic Games in Barcelona, about 45,000 persons were involved in the organisation of the event, and 34,500 of them were volunteers (versus about 9,000 regularly contracted). In Atlanta, 40,000 volunteers were required. More than 62,000 worked for the Sydney Olympic and Paralympic Games, and another 12,000 were employed in related tasks on the same occasion (e.g., drivers or transport coordinators; source www.sydneyolympicpark.nsw.gov.au). Chappelet (2000), based on his study of four Winter Olympics (Calgary 1988, Albertville 1992, Lillehammer 1994 and Nagano 1998), estimates that the volunteer contributions to the staging of a single Winter Olympics would amount to $40 million (10,000 volunteers × 20 days × $200 US). In Nagano, 32,000 volunteers had been active, more than three times those who were involved in Albertville (9,000), according to Chappelet (2000).

The contribution of volunteers is also essential in smaller scale events. Popular local marathons can require up to 1,000 volunteers. The volunteer programme of the Football World Cup involved 12,000 persons in France in 1998 (Bouchet-Virette 1999).

All these reported figures confirm that volunteering turns out to be a significant economic activity when we place a monetary value on the time, energy and expertise people provide in their volunteer work. Equally or even more important is the noneconomic or social significance of volunteering. Volunteers are a source of credibility and legitimacy for their organisations; they provide objective and constructive evaluation of organisational processes, and they serve the public relations functions admirably. These considerations must be kept in mind every time that higher efficiency and professionalism are mentioned with reference to OSOs. Also, caution is necessary when attempting to blindly transfer knowledge and procedures from the business world and mainstream management studies to Olympic organisations. OSOs are often viewed as rather "primitive" organisations, and the volunteers in sport are sometimes addressed as lackeys that simply perform tasks without the need or ability to think about the bigger picture. This not only is unfair to dedicated OSO volunteers and their considerable capabilities, it ignores the important and specific advantages that derive from voluntary commitment.

Actually, volunteers contribute in many ways and at various levels of an OSO. They serve as members of the board that sets policies and makes other strategic decisions for the organisation. In this case, we would refer to them as **policy volunteers.** They also serve as chairpersons of committees and commissions that execute the policy. In many countries, volunteers representing national sport federations sit on the board or on executive committees of confederations of sport federations or national Olympic committees, thus influencing the national policy making in sport. Some of them play a critical role in the interaction with central state and local administrations or participate in the public relations of the OSO.

Volunteers also serve as **grassroots workers** who provide various sport services such as teaching, coaching and officiating sports as well as organising and conducting competitions or running the administration and operations of clubs and facilities. Volunteers at this level can also be involved in other functions such as ticketing, catering, maintenance of equipment or clothing and even fund-raising. It is also common to find volunteers at middle-management levels, taking care of technical direction or coordination of other volunteers. We will also differentiate later (see chapter 2) between long-term and short-term volunteers. Thus, viewing volunteers as one homogeneous group and managing them as such would be inappropriate. However, there is a common feature in any kind of volunteer management policy: Managers of volunteers lack one critical tool applicable to paid workers—monetary inducements. By definition, volunteers are not paid for their work (except to cover their costs when applicable). Lacking this critical motivational tool, managers have to resort to other means of motivating volunteers, as if they don't have the right attitude in this respect. The fact that volunteers and professionals are sensitive to different kinds of incentives and motivation is an additional factor of complexity for the management of human resources in sport organisations.

1.5 Professional Workers in Sport Organisations

The discussion of the functions and management of professionals in sport organisations, especially if it is geared to a comparison with those of volunteers, requires a preliminary conceptual clarification. In fact, **what does it mean exactly to be a professional**? How easy is it to draw the line between professionals and volunteers? Many people would suggest that a professional is one who is being paid. From this perspective, any workers in a sport governing body—including the caretakers, secretaries and executive directors—would be considered professionals because they are all paid workers. All of these paid workers are critical to the success of the organisation, and their importance grows with the complexity of the organisation. Such success is dependent on how well this set of human resources is managed. The literature on human resource practices referring to paid employees is abundant with theories and practical applications, and it could be a significant support for those who carry out management functions within OSOs.

However, we will explore additional considerations here since the nature and product of OSOs and their structural configuration introduce additional problems and challenges. The concept of professionalism goes beyond categorising the workers on the basis of payment. In service literature, the distinction is often made between **professional services** and **consumer services.** Professional services, as the name implies, are those services that are based on expertise and experience, such as the services of an engineer, an accountant or a manager. The expertise is gained after a lengthy period of training in a specific occupation (e.g., accounting, management). In the context of OSOs, the paid managers and the paid coaches are professionals to the extent that they have gained their expertise through training and experience. If the sport governing body is rich enough to hire an accountant or a lawyer, then those persons would also be paid professionals of the organisation. In sum, a paid professional has the knowledge gained through training and experience, and based on that, he or she is able to provide expert services to the sport governing body or its clients.

Within an Olympic sport organisation, some paid workers at the managerial level would be more professionalised because of their education and expertise, while others would be low on the scale of professionalisation. Morrow and Goetze (1988, p. 94), with reference to the medical profession, have defined the basic conditions for full professionalisation:

- Application of skills based on technical knowledge
- Requirements of advanced education and training
- Some formal testing of competence and control of admission to the profession
- Existence of professional associations
- Existence of codes of conduct or ethics
- Existence of an accepted commitment or calling, or a sense of responsibility for serving the public
- Use of the profession and fellow professionals as a major referent
- Belief that the profession provides an important service to society

A similar approach has been taken by Soucie (1994), with specific reference to the sport management profession, from a North American perspective. He has listed a more restricted set of components:

- Full-time occupation
- Membership in formal organisations (professional associations)
- Advanced education and specialised training
- Scientific (and esoteric) knowledge base
- Service or client orientation
- Professional autonomy restrained by responsibility
- Established code of ethics

Managers of sport organisations may not be as high on the professional status scale as those in medicine or some other professions, and important national and cultural differences can be expected on this subject. But the important point is that the goal of all sport organisation managers should be to become professional in all their activities rather than simply being a recognized or protected profession. Being professional implies that one

- honestly believes in his or her cause and calling,
- constantly strives to improve his or her own knowledge and skills,
- follows the guidelines of professional associations (when they exist), and
- tries to be ethical in all actions.

In this case, professionals can be understood not simply as paid personnel but as recognized and competent experts. It is often discussed which of these elements comes first (expertise or remuneration) in the definition of a professional. In that sense, in several instances the volunteers may indeed be as professional as the paid professionals themselves, both technically and theoretically (Chelladurai 1999). This would be true, for example, of *volunteering professionals,* who are those professionals who volunteer their time and effort towards a particular sport organisation without any remuneration. For instance, one of the volunteer board members of a sport governing body may be a marketing expert from a leading company. Yet another member may be a registered accountant. In these two cases, they are as professional as the paid managers of the sport governing body. Similarly, a volunteer coach of the junior national team may be a qualified and competent coach, and therefore a professional, with the desire of gaining experience and taking part in a network of relations that can be useful for his or her future career.

The *professional volunteers* are those who make a profession of volunteering. Because they volunteer time and effort in a particular cause over a long period of time, they develop sufficient knowledge and expertise about that particular operation. For instance, a longtime volunteer board member of an OSO might have become proficient in the sport as well as in the management of the organisation. Thus, it is inappropriate to suggest that all volunteers lack the necessary professional expertise to be in control of a specified operation. There are examples of volunteers that became employees or paid top managers of an OSO after many years of nonremunerated service, but there are also opposite examples of professionals resigning from their position to become a board member of an OSO. However, we must point out that top positions in a board (or in a local event organisation committee) can usually be associated with a monetary compensation or to other additional reward practices, so the demarcation can become blurred.

By the same token, it is also inappropriate to think of the professional workers as devoid of any altruistic or helping orientation merely because they are paid. The fact that they have opted to work in a sport governing body instead of another organisation (e.g., a bank, a construction company, a business) often implies that they have a liking for sport and the governance of it. Further, since sport governing bodies typically pay less than the going rates for managers, elements of altruism or culture and identification may be motivating factors among professional sport managers. Working time also tends to be more flexible, and working on the weekend is often the rule because of the specific functioning of these organisations. In sum, the personal orientations and attained expertise in specific operations are likely to be shared by both professional and volunteer workers in a sport governing body. Human resource management practices in a sport governing body should tap into these similarities to forge a cohesive unit by providing optimal working environments and motivation.

At the same time, these practices fall in a specific environmental context, where being a volunteer or a professional is not simply a matter of taste or needs, but it is strongly related to external settings, pressures or modifications in the sphere of the dominant values. Local or national authorities, for example, while recognizing the role of volunteers at the grassroots level, require a high level of efficiency and professionalism by national sport organisations. In most cases, this is considered equivalent to the availability of a higher number of paid professionals. In many countries, volunteerism is facing what is often called a crisis of vocations, because of the hegemony of the market and associated ideology, especially in the sport sector. The changes in the system have an impact on the relationship of the people with the system itself. Injection of new and motivated volunteers is becoming more and more difficult. And it is also evident that if an increasing number of persons carry out tasks with remuneration, it becomes increasingly difficult to convince volunteers to carry out similar tasks without being remunerated, especially if other kinds of relevant incentives are not very developed or available. This is especially true in periods of economic crisis, stagnation and unemployment.

In conclusion, even though tension may sometimes exist between professionals and volunteers, this does not mean that the development of professionalism will cancel volunteerism from the sport sector in the long term (as some people believe will occur in the name of modernization and rationalization). A research programme carried out in the 25 countries of the European Union shows, for example, that the rate of volunteers to professionals is extremely variable (see figure 1.3) (Camy et al. 2004). However, it is difficult to dispute that volunteerism requires a convenient environment that cannot be created artificially. The preservation or optimal reinforcement of this environment should be a constant task for OSOs.

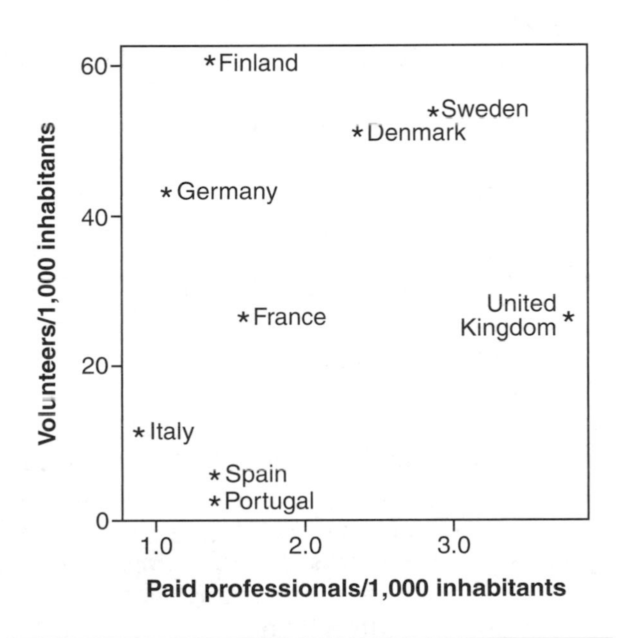

Figure 1.3 Relationship between volunteers and professionals in some European countries.

1.6 Organisational Culture

At the beginning of this chapter, we noted that the specific nature of the OSOs' stakeholders and of their interaction constitutes an important element of specificity of these organisations. In addition, we have also mentioned their distinctive "organisational culture" that derives from their tradition, history, goals, and especially from the values and attitudes that have been developed during the years within the Olympic movement.

Even if we are fully aware of the numerous other factors that in different countries or within a specific sport can influence the organisational culture of OSOs, we think that it is not possible to understand and then to develop effective human resource practices without giving sufficient importance to this aspect.What is an organisational culture? This concept has been one of the most studied and debated in the last few years in the field of organisation theory but also in the mainstream management literature with a practical orientation.

Schein, for example, describes the organisational culture as "a pattern of basic assumptions—invented, discovered, or developed by a given group as it learns to cope with its problems of external adaptation and internal integration—that has worked well enough to be considered valid and . . . to be taught to new members as the correct way to perceive, think, and feel in relation to those problems" (1985, p. 9).

In spite of the different definitions and nuances used to define the concept, organisational culture might be essentially interpreted as a set of values, beliefs, attitudes and expectations as well as symbols, customs and behaviors shared as a system of meanings by members of a specific organisation.

This complex of material and symbolic elements helps provide an orientation to organisational actors on different levels that include behavior, attribution of meaning to the environment, appropriate ways of doing things (Schein 1991) and identity building (Parker 2000). Organisational culture is not static, but rather "an evolving pattern of values and assumptions that reflects the members' shared experience" (Chelladurai 1999, p. 286), and in that sense, its relation with the role and the actions of the leaders of an organisation has been quite often emphasized (Weese 1995). We must also note that some apparently "objective features" of an organisation, such as the organisational structure or the explicit rules and policies, are not at all culture free (Morgan 1986, p. 132) since they can be viewed as "cultural artifacts that help shape the ongoing reality within an organisation".

Focusing on organisational culture is helpful for understanding the differences between organisations operating in different contexts on different dimensions such as tolerance of risk, conflict, importance of individual initiative, reward systems and criteria, modes of control, degree of identification of the employees with the organisation, and so on (Gordon and Cummins 1979). Organisational culture is especially important for managing organisational change, even if there is no clear scientific evidence on the relationship between culture and change. Commonsense views of the problem indicate that a strong organisational culture (in the sense that it is shared by the members and is based on distinctive and visible values) can have a number of advantages, which in some cases have also been analyzed through specific scientific investigation:

- Increases the level of consensus
- Facilitates the commitment and loyalty of employees and especially their retention (Holbeche 2005)
- Increases productivity (Denison 1990)
- Produces clear and unambiguous roles
- Improves organisational performance (Kent and Weese 2000; Smart and Wolfe 2000)
- Enhances the possibility to successfully face external challenges (e.g., a crisis or an enemy)

At the same time, organisations with strong cultures are often seen as reluctant to change and sometimes rigid and incapable of significant innovation—and therefore at risk in very turbulent environments.

Although we are not going to discuss here the validity of these statements and their empirical foundation, we think that managers of OSOs should pay attention to a series of issues related to the nature of organisational culture. These issues can have important implications for human resource management and especially for the choice of associated policies and procedures.

Here are some of the key questions that managers of OSOs should try to answer:

- What are the dominant core values in the organisation?
- To what extent are they shared?
- Are they consistent?

- How is the relation between the dominant culture and other organisational subcultures articulated (e.g., volunteers and professionals; centre and periphery; male and female)? Is there a significant diversity? Is it affecting the overall organisational performance?
- Is there any evidence of conflicts (e.g., role conflicts) that are related to the cultural dimension?
- How consistent are HRM practices (staffing, career management, pay, and so on) with the nature of the organisational culture?

Human Resource Practices

In chapter 1 we discussed the nature of sport governing bodies and the attributes of the three most significant stakeholders (participants, volunteers and professionals). With this as the backdrop, let's now look at human resource management procedures and practices.

Human resource practices

- constitute the essential area of activity of the managers responsible for human resources within an organisation; and
- are the real focus of the attention of the members of an organisation, who usually do not care too much about slogans, ideologies or communitarian rhetoric but constantly analyze the way persons are selected, appointed to different positions, rewarded, and so on.

In the following sections, we outline some of the critical human resource management practices and provide a few selected examples of procedures and policies that have been adopted by different OSOs. Since examples can easily become outdated, given the high rate of change in the sport organisation environment, we will use them more as facilitators of personal reflection and hints for collective initiative rather than as best practices or models to be "copied".

The HRM practices that we will outline and discuss include

- staffing,
- assessment of employees and career management,
- pay and reward systems,
- training,
- empowerment, and
- conflict management.

In our discussion, specific attention will be paid to the ways these practices can be customised to OSOs and especially to the simultaneous management of volunteers and professionals.

We will analyze each individual practice in detail, but managers operating in OSOs must consider the need to integrate these practices in a common human resource strategy. For example, it makes no sense to develop sophisticated staffing procedures if the pay and reward system is not developed enough to satisfy employees with outstanding skills and qualifications. This strategy can be embedded in specific human resource and employment policies regulating the fundamental aspects of the employment practices of a sport organisation. On this respect, no special differences can be identified compared to other kinds of organisations, such as those in the business sector.

Employment policies should normally

- list the basic inspiring principles concerning the relations between an organisation and its employees;
- define the hiring and probation practices and the general terms of employment;
- define the working hours, vacation time and overtime;
- indicate the compensation practices;
- indicate the procedures used to assess employees;

- define the procedures to be used to deal with reclamation and grievances;
- regulate the question of the conflict of interest; and
- indicate how maternity and other kinds of leave are regulated.

To illustrate such policies, a practical example is included in the appendix, taken from the Canada Volleyball Federation.

2.1 Organisational Justice

Before analyzing the major human resource practices, we will spend some time discussing a preliminary area of concern—the concept of organisational justice. We believe that this concept is very inspiring and truly essential for those who are involved with human resource management, and that it should be considered for all the related practices.

A fundamental theme that runs through all managerial practices is the notion of **justice.** Managers should be concerned with being fair and just to all those affected by their actions. Those affected could be employees of the organisation or external stakeholders such as the clients or customers, suppliers, and other people who come into contact with the organisation for different reasons. From our perspective, organisational justice is one of the cornerstones of all human resource management policies and practices. In fact, organisational justice is one of the most essential components in the satisfaction of the members of the organisation.

Many of the problems that are commonly reported in sport organisations are related to violations of organisational justice. These problems include the following:

- Managers' lack of understanding of justice or fairness
- Unfairness, discrimination or nepotism in recruitment or career progression
- Outright ill treatment or abuse of staff
- Controlling policies through informal and inconsistent decision making
- Practice that ignores a previously established formal policy
- Inconsistency of treatment, particularly between a board and staff
- Exclusion of members from key decisions (e.g., budget)
- Conflict of interest or loyalty
- Unfair reward system

Considering the importance of these problems, let's look at the concept of organisational justice in detail.

A critical area of concern in the human resource management of any organisation, including an OSO, is the notion of perceived fairness of management decisions and practices. For instance, when an OSO allots different amounts of budget to the men's and women's national teams, would that be perceived to be a fair distribution? Members may also perceive the procedures adopted by the board to arrive at budgetary decisions to be unfair. For instance, the women may believe that they were not consulted as much as the men on a specific issue. Finally, some members may perceive that the way managers interact with them at an interpersonal level is cursory and crude. These issues are the subject matter of what is termed *organisational justice,* which is composed of

- *distributive justice* (referring to the outcomes for individuals or groups);
- *procedural justice* (referring to the procedures used to come to decisions); and
- *interactional justice* (referring to the manner in which a decision is communicated and eventually explained to individuals).

In the following sections, we discuss the three views of organisational justice more precisely in order to identify the implications for human resource management practices.

Distributive Justice

Distributive justice relates to the fairness in the disbursement of resources to members and groups. The resources may be the salaries and wages distributed to workers, the opportunity for training and competition for athletes, the budgets and facilities provided for the national teams, the allocation of office rooms to the personnel in the office, the possibility to travel with the team to international games for volunteers, and so on. When an OSO pays more for its national coach than for the technical director, the distribution is based on the criterion of *equity* considering the relative contributions of the two individuals to the OSO. The coach presumably has greater expertise, and his or her successful performance (i.e., the team's successes in the international arena) brings glory and status to the OSO. The OSO may also employ the *equality* principle in distributing certain resources. For example, the rates for travelling expenses (e.g., per mile car allowance) may be the same for all employees of the OSO. Finally, there is the principle of *need,* where the resources are distributed on the basis of need. For example, an OSO may buy a desktop computer for its secretary while it may buy a more expensive laptop for its technical director because he or she is required to travel around the country. Athletes with alimentary disorders or study problems may be allowed to practice different training regimens compared to others. Thus, the specific principle used may depend on the circumstances.

What is important is that everyone knows what principle is used in the distribution of a given resource and why. There needs to be a transparency in the decisions made about the rewards being distributed to the members. When it comes to performance-based salaries, bonuses and other perks, everyone should know well in advance what level of performance would lead to what level of rewards. It is not uncommon for OSOs to offer extra bonuses for coaches and players when the national team posts victories in international competitions. The majority of OSOs have specific policies for the Olympic cycles that must be as clear as possible; for example, clear policies regarding access to bonuses can help avoid conflict between individual and team athletes or between athletes who have taken part in the final and those who have competed only in the qualifying rounds.

Procedural Justice

As we have already indicated, procedural justice refers to the whole set of procedures that are used to come to decisions. An OSO could adopt the following guidelines to enhance perceptions of procedural justice:

- Communicate explicitly and clearly what distributive principle would be used in allocating a given resource.
- Be consistent over time and across people in applying that principle.
- Suppress biases in evaluating the contributions and needs of individuals or groups.
- Conform to community standards of ethics and morality.
- Allow for correcting any wrong decisions that have been made.
- Ensure that all procedures are made public in advance of acting on those procedures.

Interactional Justice

Finally, interactional justice refers to how managers and supervisors of an OSO interact with their subordinates and clients. As noted, one area that volunteers may complain about is the way they are treated by paid professionals. Similarly, care must be taken not to hurt the feelings of clients, participants and elite sports persons. This can easily occur in the case of public declarations to the press. A president of a national federation, for example, could forget to thank somebody who contributed to an outstanding success or can use very generic words to identify the responsibility for an unexpected defeat so that many people could be upset and conflictive.

Even though the actual decisions and associated processes affecting a person or group were based on fair criteria, the recipients may be blinded to such fairness if they feel that the managers were not straightforward and warm in communicating the decisions. Selection for a world competition or the Olympic Games is typically one aspect where problems of interactional justice often come to the foreground. Media coverage of sport events is full of reports and news about athletes and teams complaining about interactional justice, even if this term is seldom used.

We need to keep the concepts of distributive justice, procedural justice and interactional justice in mind when we discuss the whole range of human resource management practices. The basic questions that should guide us as managers are the following:

- Are we just in our decisions (e.g., to distribute the rewards or to promote somebody), whatever they may be?

- Have we followed open and fair procedures in coming to those decisions?
- Are we pleasant and honest in communicating the outcomes of decisions and the procedures behind those decisions?

The importance of taking inspiration from the principles of organisational justice is not based only on an ethical perspective but also follows the idea that organisational justice is a basic ingredient of employee morale and loyalty and consequently of high organisational performance.

A concrete way through which the question of organisational justice is dealt with is exemplified by some items of the contract developed by the Canadian Team Handball Federation, which deals expressly with the concept of justice (figure 2.1). It also contains numerous other aspects that are relevant to the perspective of human resource management (e.g., athletes' protection).

The contract shown in figure 2.1 includes many elements that are clearly meant to create a context where organisational justice is pursued: a reference to the publicity of the selection criteria, the establishment of appeal and hearing procedures and the role of the representation. Item c (in part 1) mentions directly the concepts of natural justice and procedural fairness.

Athletes' Contract

The parties agree to the following:

1. Canadian Team Handball Federation's Obligations

The Canadian Team Handball Federation shall

a) organise, select and operate teams of athletes, coaches and other necessary support staff (a "national team") to represent Canada in the sport of team handball throughout the world;

b) publish selection criteria in advance for all national team major competitions (i.e., Olympic Games, Pan-American Games, Pan-American Championships, World Championships);

c) conduct selection of members to all national teams in a manner that is in conformity with the generally accepted principles of natural justice and procedural fairness;

d) nominate all eligible athletes for the AAP and COC programmes and thereafter ensure these athletes will receive all the benefits to which they are entitled under the AAP and COC programmes;

e) organise programmes and provide funding for the development and provision of coaching expertise, officials' development, competitions and training centres in Canada in the sport of team handball in accordance with the budgetary constraints of the CTHF;

f) publish criteria for the selection of athletes to the AAP and COC programmes prior to the commencement of the eligibility cycle for team handball;

g) provide the athlete selected to be a member of the national team with the national team uniform;

h) regularly provide national team programme information regarding training and competitions to the athlete in the form of electronic mail correspondence and the Athlete Guide;

i) provide a formal review of the athlete's annual training programme;

j) provide a hearing and appeal procedure that is in conformity with the generally accepted principles of natural justice and due process, including access to an independent arbitration process with respect to any dispute the athlete may have with the CTHF, and publish the details of this procedure in a prominent manner and also provide details to any authorized person requesting this information on behalf of the athlete;

k) provide funding for the athlete for training camps and competitions in accordance with the budget of the CTHF;

l) protect the eligibility of the athlete by ensuring that a mechanism for the establishment of a trust fund for the athlete exists that is in accordance with the IHF rules and shall advise the athlete of the nature of all payments to and withdrawals from the trust fund;

m) communicate with athletes both orally and in writing in the language of their choice (English or French);

n) assist the athlete in obtaining quality medical care and advice;

o) provide for a representative elected by the athletes to sit as a voting member of the relevant decision-making body of the CTHF.

(continued)

Figure 2.1 Applications of the principles of organisational justice: the athletes' contract of the Canadian Team Handball Federation.

2. Athlete's Obligations

The athlete shall

a) read and agree to abide by the Athlete's Code of Conduct; follow the training and competitive programme mutually agreed upon by the national coach, the athlete's personal coach and the athlete, recognizing the responsibilities of the coaches in coaching-related decisions; and shall avoid living in an environment that is not conducive to high-performance achievements or taking any deliberate action that involves significant risks to the athlete's ability to perform or limits the athlete's performance;

b) provide the national coach or his or her designate, by electronic mail correspondence, with an annual training chart and monthly updates of changes to the chart or any other necessary information that the CTHF may request;

c) subject to paragraph 2(d), participate in all mandatory training camps and competitions as described in **appendix A**;

d) where possible, notify, by electronic mail correspondence, the CTHF of any injury or other legitimate reason that will prevent the athlete from participating in an upcoming event referred to in **appendix A** and ensure in the case of an injury that a certificate from a medical doctor setting out the specific nature of the injury is forwarded to the CTHF within 3 weeks after the injury;

e) dress in the national team uniform and other official clothing, if applicable, while travelling or participating in events and competitions as part of the national team;

f) avoid any action or conduct that would reasonably be expected to significantly disrupt or interfere with a competition or the preparation of any athlete for a competition;

g) during or at national team training camps and competitions, avoid alcoholic consumption to a level that would reasonably be expected to cause impairment in the athlete's ability to speak, walk or drive, perform athletically or cause the athlete to behave in a disruptive manner;

h) avoid the use of banned substances that would be in contravention to the rules of the IOC, the IHF and Sport Canada policy; and shall agree without warning to submit to unannounced doping control tests in addition to other tests with notice, and submit at other times to doping control testing upon request by the CTHF, Sport Canada, the Canadian Centre for Ethics in Sport or any other authority designated to do so by the CTHF;

i) avoid possession of anabolic drugs and human or synthetic growth hormone, and shall neither supply such drugs directly or indirectly to others nor encourage or condone their use by knowingly aiding in any effort to avoid detection of the use of banned substances or banned performance-enhancing practices;

j) participate as may be requested by the CTHF in any doping control and education programme as formulated by the CTHF in co-operation with Sport Canada and the Canadian Centre for Ethics in Sport;

k) be subject to the penalties for dealing in banned substances, including but not limited to trafficking, selling, importing and possession; minimum penalties to be assessed are as follows:

- For athletes—first time: 3 years; second time: life
- For coaches, officials and volunteers—first time: life

(Furthermore, the CTHF Management Committee will decide the length of suspension for the following offences: insubordination, violence, drunkenness, disorderly conduct, disruptive behavior, or any other actions deemed inconsistent with being a member of the national team programme or the spirit of this agreement.)

l) participate in reasonable noncommercial promotional activities as may be requested by Sport Canada, where the arrangements for such activities are made through the CTHF and are not for more than the equivalent of 2 working days for any individual athlete unless compensation is arranged and agreed to by the athlete,

m) participate in the Canadian Centre for Ethics in Sports Health Status Support Programme if requested to do so by the CTHF;

n) utilize the hearing and appeal procedure referred to in paragraph 1(j) for the remedy of complaints and issues, especially where the situation involves the conduct or performance of CTHF employed staff or coaches;

o) be responsible for the full payment of the annual athlete fee of $2,000 or $3,000 as prescribed, payable to the CTHF; athletes who intend to participate in the national team programme must be in good standing with the CTHF;

p) be responsible for fulfilling all obligations required of national team members pertaining to sponsorship or suppliers for the national team or the CTHF;

q) avoid participating in any competitions where federal government policy has determined that such participation is not permitted;

r) be responsible for costs of passports, vaccines, visas and personal insurances.

Figure 2.1 *(continued)*

Reprinted, by permission, from Canadian Team Handball Federation.

2.2 Staffing an Olympic Sport Organisation

After this important preliminary overview of the concept of organisational justice and its HRM implications, we can now turn to the most relevant human resource practices within OSOs. These practices should never neglect the management implications of the concept of organisational justice that we discussed in the preceding section.

A first significant function of human resource management is clearly to identify, recruit and hire the right people. With reference to elite athletes, we have already dealt with the question of **talent identification, recruitment and development.** For the other categories of human resources that we have analyzed in previous sections, this means not only identification and motivation but also assigning them specific jobs and functions within the organisation. This function is traditionally known as **staffing.** Staffing is a key function that can have a decisive influence on organisational performance, especially in a service organisation.

The purpose of the staffing function is to recruit and hire those workers who

- meet the requirements of a job (i.e., person–task fit), and
- share the organisational values and goals (i.e., person–organisation fit).

The first concern is identifying those with the right knowledge, skills and abilities to carry out the tasks associated with the job. For example, if there is a need for a marketing person to promote a particular project of a sport governing body, it is only appropriate to look for a person who has had training and experience in marketing.

The second concern is ensuring that the person with the marketing expertise also shares the values of the sport governing body and the goals of the project. Another important aspect is to evaluate the capacity of a person to work together with the other professionals and volunteers who are already active within an organisation, and to be able to really contribute to an effective and attractive image of the organisation.

Without valuing sport and liking the organisation that promotes it, and without a conviction that the project and its goals are worthwhile, the person is not likely to be engaged wholeheartedly in "marketing" the project. Hence, the emphasis on **person–organisation fit,** which in these cases is strongly related to the sphere of values and organisational culture. As stated in chapter 1, organisational culture means the set of symbols, values, beliefs, rituals and principles that provide a symbolic base for the organisational system. These components support the attribution of meaning to events, actions and goals for the organisation members. When recruiting, managers usually look to reinforce the current level of internal consensus, so the new organisation members tend to have (or at least to exhibit) the same values that are considered typical and distinctive of that organisation. In OSOs, people should be informed about and should understand well in advance what it means to be a member of such an organisation and to work according to a nonprofit logic. They should also understand who the key stakeholders are and what they expect from the organisation and its personnel.

The obvious first step of the staffing process is to identify the number and nature of jobs that need to be filled (e.g., a secretary to handle the affairs of high-performance sport, an accounting clerk for the entire operation, a technical director, a coach of the national junior team). Because most OSOs are relatively small, the number of personnel to be hired at any one time may be rather limited. Organisational functions, on the contrary, can be extremely diversified, with significant impact on working hours, forms of supervision and required qualifications. For these reasons, the process of staffing must be closely connected with the structure of an organisation (see chapter 3). This means that the staffing structures can be very different in the various types of organisations. Further, in many OSOs, the need to hire a person may not arise as often as in a big organisation (such as the International Olympic Committee). However, the processes of staffing need to be thorough whether there are many people to be hired or only a few. The critical steps of staffing are outlined in the following sections.

Job Analysis

Job analysis involves outlining the various tasks associated with a specific job, as well as the operations and responsibilities of the job. Job analysis may be based on observation of an existing position either within the organisation or in another similar sport governing body. It may also be based on the input provided by those who carry out the same or a similar job, or by the supervisors of such a job. Typically, the job analysis would include the following:

- Identification of the job, including the job title, its department or division and titles of supervisors
- A brief description of the job, including its purpose and activities
- Primary, major and other duties and the proportions of time involved
- Responsibility over use and care of equipment or tools, personal safety and safety of others and the performance of others
- Human characteristics required
- Working conditions where the job will be carried out
- A description of health or safety hazards, including special training or equipment needed
- A description of how performance on the job is measured

Job Description

A careful job analysis should yield good information on the job, the operations, the duties and responsibilities involved in that job, the working conditions and other critical elements of a job. Job analysis should be followed by the creation of a job description outlining the specific duties, responsibilities, working conditions and other aspects of the specified job. In an organisation, a job description should be available and known for each position. The description must be especially clear in order to avoid confusion or ambiguity. More specifically, a job description would include information on

- the job title,
- the immediate supervisor of the job,
- the number and type of jobs supervised by the incumbent, and
- the specific activities of the job.

Job Specification

After describing the job, the human characteristics required to carry out the job effectively must also be specified. These characteristics would include experience, training, education, physical demands and social and mental demands. Figure 2.2 shows an example job description for a technical director at a hypothetical sport governing body. It specifies some of the human characteristics that would be required of the successful candidate for the job. In this specific example, the list may be extended to include a degree with an emphasis on coaching and past experience as an athlete or a coach.

Figure 2.3 presents a real example taken from the National Triathlon Association of the United States. This job description is for the position of athlete development and junior programme coordinator.

From these and other examples, we can identify a set of recurrent elements:

- Description of the position and of the required set of competencies
- Description of the organisational supervision
- Specification of duties and responsibilities
- Description of the process to be supervised
- Identification of the qualifications, experience and abilities required
- Specification of place and time requirements (e.g., if a person is supposed to work in different locations)
- List of compensation and benefits

These elements should always be included for all kinds of job descriptions. They can sometimes also be included as an essential part of the working contract, and for this reason, the employee must be fully aware of all the aspects listed above.

Recruiting

After identifying and describing the activities and responsibilities of a specific job (or jobs), and the human characteristics required for that job, the staffing process would proceed to the next stage—recruiting, which is putting

Position	Technical director
Reports to	Executive director
Purpose of the position	Contributes to the mission of the sport governing body by administering and supervising the policies of the high-performance programme. This entails recruiting and recommending to the board suitable candidates for the positions of coaches, managers and trainers for the elite teams at various levels. The technical director is also responsible for supervising the activities of the hired personnel, interacting with the members of the elite teams and communicating with the media.
Number of people reporting to this position	High-performance staff: 5 Athletes: 120 athletes (6 teams)
Specific responsibilities	Personnel • Recruitment (planning and advertising the positions available in high-performance sport) • Selection (screening applications and qualifications, interviewing and recommending to the board) • Orientation (planning and conducting appropriate orientation and social activities) • Training of personnel (planning and conducting appropriate training activities) • Evaluating their performance (providing employees with feedback on performance, support and supervision) Programming • Scheduling the facilities for the national teams • Inventory management (determining equipment and supply needs, securing high-quality equipment and supplies and maintaining them in good repair) • Record keeping (ensuring all information is updated weekly and producing reports as needed) • Programme evaluation (collecting information from athletes and staff both formally and informally; submitting annual reports to the executive director and the board) • Special assignments (completing special tasks assigned by the executive director)
Work schedule	Since the activities of the position are scheduled throughout the week, the incumbent has a flexible work schedule.
Qualifications necessary	The incumbent should possess excellent organisational skills accompanied with strong verbal and written communication skills. Proven leadership abilities, outstanding interpersonal skills and strong computer skills are essential. In addition, he or she must have a solid background of experience in coaching elite athletes.
Discretion allowed	An action plan for carrying out the tasks is to be submitted and discussed with the executive director.
Critical working relations	The executive director, high-performance staff, high-performance committee, the board, and the media.

Figure 2.2 Job description for the technical director in a sport governing body.

together a pool of eligible candidates for a position and encouraging them to apply for a job. For an OSO, this stage of staffing looks similar to what occurs for any other kind of organisation, outside the sport sector. It usually involves advertising the position in several newspapers, journals, trade publications and the World Wide Web. Advertising reaches a large pool of potential candidates. Another approach is the *employee referral,* where current employees or volunteers are asked to encourage qualified friends and relatives to

Athlete Development and Junior Programme Coordinator

Position: The athlete development and junior programme coordinator provides direction and oversight to the coaches—volunteer or contracted regional athlete development coordinators (RADC) and national team programme staff—regarding the youth, junior and collegiate development programmes.

Reports to: National teams programme director

Background: USA Triathlon is the national governing body for the multisport disciplines of triathlon and duathlon in the United States. The national office and this position are located in Colorado Springs, Colorado. Please refer to the USA Triathlon Web site for more information about the organisation: www.usatriathlon.org.

Primary responsibilities:

Youth, junior and collegiate development programme:

- Creation of recruitment and scouting camps and training camps
- Organisation of a regional development system using RADCs, which will lead to the implementation of regional projects to promote participation and development of the athlete development pipeline throughout the United States
- Implementation of a nationwide race series for youth, junior and under-23 athletes
- Implementation of a junior and collegiate camp system nationwide that will eventually funnel talent to the national teams

Athlete scouting and recruitment programmes:

- Provide direction and oversight to the scouting and recruiting of emerging and existing talent within the NCAA, club, NGB, collegiate, high school and other related programmes

Competitions:

- Draft Legal Race Series – annual series for 13-15 years, 16-19 years and under-23 age groups
- Youth Race Series and Collegiate Nationals
- World University Championships – serve as coach for this event that is held every 2 years
- World Triathlon Championships – serve as manager or coach for the national junior team (16-19 year age group)
- Promote international opportunities for junior athletes

Regional development:

- Provide support to regional athlete development coordinators
- Organise annual RADC work session

Qualifications:

- Bachelor's degree in exercise-related field such as exercise science or physical education from a 4-year college or university and 2 years of related experience. Masters degree preferred.
- Strong computer skills (Microsoft Office including Word, Excel, PowerPoint and Publisher)
- USAT Level 2 coaching certification (or equivalent). ACSM certification highly recommended.
- Able to travel to events (up to 50 days per year)
- Strong customer service skills and management skills
- A minimum of 4 years of related experience working with youth and junior athletes

Compensation and benefits: Full-time position. Salary up to $40,000, plus benefits including health, dental, 401(k), disability and vacation/personal time. EOE

Availability: February 2005

Application deadline: January 10th, 2005

Application procedure: Please submit a resume and cover letter to:

Figure 2.3 Job description for the athlete development and junior programme coordinator at the National Triathlon Association of the United States.

Reprinted, by permission, from National Triathlon Association, USA.

apply for a given position. Because a current employee "knows the organization, its goals, and its processes very well, the employee may have a good grasp of who will fit in well in the organization and carry out the job effectively" (Chelladurai 1999, p. 140). Koski and Heikkala (1998), in their study of Finnish NSOs, report that "full time managers are recruited from within the system of sport organizations itself, they are typically former volunteers or former elected officials" (p. 21), and to them, this is an indication of poor professionalisation. This approach respects the nature and the culture of the organisation (e.g., the voluntary identity), which should not be neglected.

An evident disadvantage of this approach is that current employees may recommend persons of similar attributes and orientations such that diversity in terms of gender, race, ethnicity and other demographic characteristics may be restricted. In OSOs, the volunteers (e.g., a member of the board) may also play a role in the identification of possible candidates for a position in the organisation. This also has both advantages (a good knowledge of the requirements of the organisation) and disadvantages (the possibility that "personal" or "political" interests will prevail over the need for a good person–job fit or that recruitment can be used in the political arena to strengthen or weaken a party, a clique or a coalition).

Another approach to recruiting is to search for suitable candidates from among current workers within the sport organisation itself or its regional or provincial affiliates. Searching internally is cost effective because the would-be candidates are a known quantity and, therefore, do not need to be assessed in terms of person–job fit or person–organisation fit. Such an approach would also be motivational in the sense that current workers could aspire to higher and more challenging jobs. But, as noted, internal searches may also restrict diversity in the workplace and limit the possibilities of innovation.

Hiring

Once a pool of potential candidates has been assembled, the next step is obviously to hire the "best" person. What it means "to be the best" in the interest of the organisational performance is rarely evident and should always involve the analysis of different aspects and perspectives. The application form and other documents that outline the educational qualifications, additional training and related experiences would highlight those candidates who would best fit the job. But the concern should go beyond the simple person–task fit and assess the equally important person–organisation fit—that is, the congruence of the personal needs, attitudes and values of the individual and the values and culture of the organisation. The assessment of the required competence goes beyond the simple evaluation of technical skills. People should understand what it really means to have a nonprofit orientation, who the key stakeholders are and what the governing principles are. Interpersonal skills are also a key criterion. Such assessments are usually made based on biographical background, reference letters, interviews and personal judgments (see figure 2.4).

Previous experience (in general and in the specific sector)
Attitudes and interests
Needs
Potential capacities
Knowledge
Skills

Figure 2.4 Key elements to assess in an interview.

During the hiring process, managers should also consider the specific environment of the organisation. Organisations that operate in a turbulent and changing environment—with complex interaction, a wide range of stakeholders and a high degree of "unpredictability"—should look for employees with a high tolerance of uncertainty and ambiguity, a significant degree of creativity and a good inclination towards co-operation and teamwork (see figure 2.5). This is especially important for organisations where multicultural or intercultural management is the rule rather than the exception. Knowledge of the specific sport is generally required.

1. Definition of the working environment of OSOs

(1.1) Identification of the job requirements (job analysis and descriptions)

(1.2) Identification of the organisational requirements (values, attitudes, culture, and so on)

2. Definition of the competences required

(2.1) Identification of the technical, interpersonal and general competences required

(2.2) Identification of the personal characteristics and traits required

3. Recruitment process

(3.1) Choice of the recruitment methods and procedures

(3.2) Communication to the groups targeted

(3.3) Assessment of the applicants (e.g., tests, interviews, and so on)

(3.4) Information to the applicants about human resource policies, career and working conditions

(3.5) Selection

(3.6) Training or other facilitating processes

Figure 2.5 A general model for staffing Olympic sport organisations.

2.3 Recruiting Volunteers

Although the foregoing discussion of the steps in staffing may be applicable in general to both volunteers and paid workers, there are important differences in the staffing process for these two kinds of human resources of OSOs. In the case of paid workers, a job is clearly described, and the salary or wages for the job are clearly specified. Applicants who have an interest in the specified salary or wages agree to carry out the described job under the control of supervisors.

Volunteers pose a different set of issues that stem essentially from the notion that salary or wages cannot be used as an incentive to attract them or control them and that the factors that motivate them to work for an organisation are different. Volunteers offer their time and effort to a sport governing body to satisfy one or more very specific motives. As a consequence, negotiating with them regarding their function and job description is certainly not uncommon, as well as leaving to them the possibility of making some decisions about how their own tasks have to be carried out.

In addition, cultural specificities are especially significant here, because the importance and role of volunteerism are extremely variable across the countries (Salamon, Sokolowski, and List 2003; Shibli 1999) and recruiting policies surely must consider this aspect. Table 2.1 shows some of the reported results of the Johns Hopkins Comparative Nonprofit Sector Project, carried out in 35 countries.

Another problem is related to the attitude of the organisations towards the volunteer recruitment process. This attitude is sometimes passive or just reactive; many organisations just wait until someone expresses his or her will to become a volunteer. A more active approach might be more useful to the modified societal context. Organisations that are aware of the profound modifications in the patterns of leisure time consumption have instituted marketing campaigns or direct marketing actions to ask people to volunteer. To avoid wasting time and resources, an organisation must be able to identify those people who have a potential interest in volunteering, through the proper use of the most appropriate demographic, social and sport participation variables for that specific context.

For all these reasons, the recruitment and retention of volunteers are key components of what is often called "internal marketing" in OSOs (this concept is not limited to volunteers but usually targets all personnel). Relationship marketing principles are usually advocated: needs analysis, segmentation of potential "clients", promotion initiatives, monitoring satisfaction and communicating the value of the experience. This is so evident that in some cases (e.g., recruiting volunteers for a big event) a close collaboration between the human resource management department and the marketing department is considered not only useful but necessary.

Incentives for Volunteers

Managers must consider in detail the nature of the incentives that are significant both for recruiting and retaining volunteers. We will focus here on the main categories of incentives for volunteers and then provide a few examples of actions and initiatives that can be taken to encourage volunteering and facilitate their recruitment. In fact, all OSOs have the duty to develop practices and programmes to properly manage their volunteers. This can be done by offering them not only the best possible incentives corresponding to their current needs and motivations but also to facilitate their personal and professional development. We must emphasize, however, that since volunteering is closely connected to the values that are significant (if not dominant) in a specific society, it is generally very difficult and frequently inappropriate to transfer successful practices from one country to another or from one specific period to another.

For example, in some countries, participating in voluntary organisations is much more usual and rooted in the local or national culture than in others. The Standing Committee on Recreation and Sport of Australia reported in 2000 that at least 4.4 million Australians have served as volunteers. This is a very high proportion of the total adult population that is not easy to find in other countries and cultures (see table 2.1). In such countries, the "spectrum" of voluntary organisations is usually much larger. This also means that actions and procedures that can be activated where volunteerism is less frequent are clearly very different than those documented for Australia or comparable countries.

Table 2.1 **Civil Society Sector FTE Volunteering by Field (35 Countries)**

	Culture	Education	Health	Social services	Environment	Development	Civic/ advocacy	Foundations	International	Professional	Other	Total (in thousands)
	Percent[a] of total civil society volunteering											
Argentina	11.9	17.1	4.4	17.8	3.4	30.6	3.8	0.0	0.0	10.3	0.7	264.1
Australia	37.0	5.8	6.4	31.6	3.6	9.4	2.1	0.4	0.7	1.0	2.0	177.1
Austria						n/a						40.7
Belgium	33.7	0.6	0.4	55.9	0.6	2.5	1.0	0.7	1.0	3.5	0.0	99.1
Brazil	1.1	21.3	15.6	40.0	0.0	17.5	1.4	0.0	0.0	0.9	2.1	139.2
Colombia	1.8	1.8	8.4	31.6	0.6	35.6	2.4	3.3	0.0	14.3	0.1	90.8
Czech Rep.	44.4	3.3	8.9	16.7	10.4	5.6	4.4	2.5	2.0	1.7	0.0	40.9
Egypt						n/a						17.3
Finland	48.2	1.7	4.7	13.6	0.5	1.0	23.6	0.3	0.5	5.4	0.5	74.8
France	46.7	8.9	3.4	15.7	8.7	4.0	1.8	1.1	3.0	6.6	0.0	1021.7
Germany	40.9	1.5	8.7	10.1	5.7	2.0	5.7	2.0	2.9	4.8	15.8	978.1
Hungary	30.8	4.1	5.5	33.5	2.9	2.6	8.5	5.5	2.3	4.2	0.0	9.9
Ireland	27.2	2.8	7.4	45.1	0.7	10.9	0.7	2.8	0.7	0.0	1.6	31.7
Israel	21.5	0.3	28.4	40.0	0.0	0.0	9.2	0.0	0.0	0.6	0.0	31.3
Italy	41.7	6.5	12.8	23.9	2.3	1.4	4.6	1.9	1.2	3.3	0.5	381.6
Japan	12.9	6.1	7.2	19.4	1.6	6.7	1.5	3.7	5.4	5.0	30.5	695.1
Kenya	5.8	8.9	19.4	12.7	3.2	21.4	5.0	0.1	0.0	2.1	21.2	112.4
Mexico	3.8	5.7	9.2	31.3	3.9	2.7	1.8	1.7	0.0	39.7	0.0	47.2
Morocco						n/a						83.4
Netherlands	39.4	15.8	7.4	22.7	3.9	0.2	6.9	0.0	2.2	1.6	0.0	390.1
Norway	57.4	2.7	3.5	7.0	0.8	5.3	8.2	0.2	3.5	10.9	0.5	103.0
Pakistan	12.3	34.4	9.1	15.3	0.8	8.0	17.2	0.0	0.0	2.8	0.0	180.8
Peru	0.1	0.5	0.1	98.5	0.2	0.1	0.0	0.0	0.0	0.6	0.0	80.1
Philippines	7.6	10.5	1.8	8.1	1.7	28.0	2.2	0.4	0.2	39.5	0.0	330.3
Poland	36.9	16.5	4.7	28.2	1.2	0.6	1.4	0.3	2.0	8.2	0.1	32.1
Romania	24.2	12.8	4.8	41.5	3.4	1.4	3.3	1.1	6.1	1.5	0.0	46.5
Slovakia	37.8	1.4	1.9	21.8	14.2	1.1	5.8	7.1	1.0	6.1	1.8	6.9
South Africa	26.8	2.1	5.9	19.1	3.7	16.6	24.4	0.3	0.1	1.0	0.0	264.3
South Korea	4.9	1.7	22.5	36.5	0.0	0.0	34.2	0.0	0.0	0.2	0.0	122.1
Spain	21.7	12.3	7.3	28.8	8.0	5.5	10.7	0.1	3.9	1.7	0.0	253.6
Sweden	51.4	2.4	0.1	8.2	2.2	3.8	12.2	0.0	2.2	15.6	1.9	260.3
Tanzania	10.7	10.3	9.3	18.1	11.2	12.9	7.1	7.7	3.7	3.1	5.7	248.9
Uganda	26.8	1.8	2.1	3.2	0.3	63.6	0.9	0.4	0.1	0.4	0.4	130.3
United Kingdom	31.3	5.1	12.8	19.7	3.9	18.8	3.1	2.0	0.7	0.0	2.6	1120.3
United States	11.8	13.4	13.6	36.7	2.7	0.0	10.2	2.2	0.9	5.5	3.0	4994.2

[a] Percentages add to 100% across fields.

Lester M. Salamon, Sokolowski, S.W., and List, R. (2003). Global civil society: An overview. Center for Civil Studies, Institute for Policy Studies, The Johns Hopkins University.

In addition, age- and gender-related issues should not be ignored. In some life stages, for example, people are interested in volunteering for a short term or to carry out a specific project, while in others more long-term commitments are preferred. Motives and orientations tend to be different (i.e., more or less altruistic or more or less inclined to self-realization or concrete benefits) with age and gender. According to some studies, young adults seem to be especially interested in interpersonal relations (Omotho, Snyder and Martino 2000), compared to older adults for whom volunteerism means essentially commitment to the society, a personal sense of meaning and influence in an age when the loss of the occupational role may cause helplessness and social marginalization. Once again, cultural and social factors can have an important impact. For example, the effect of age or economic status on the volunteering process has been reported to be very different in Australia compared to the United States (Green and Chalip 1998). Also, the situation of the labour market can be influential; people with a solid and secure job usually tend to be more inclined to volunteer compared to young adults who are unemployed or have two or even more precarious occupations.

Some OSOs tend to look only for long-term volunteers because their leaders think that only these could provide a substantial benefit for the organisation. This is surely a restrictive view; in many cases, people who have no interest in volunteering for a long time could share a specific project that is limited in duration, and then the OSO can take advantage of their availability as well. This is often true for young people, students or parents that may have an interest in serving as volunteers for a club during the time their children are playing. This interest should not be disregarded but rather optimized in the interest of the organisation.

The participation of the volunteers and their contributions are not based on any direct material rewards; therefore, those rewards cannot be used as incentives. As a result, the management of the volunteers (i.e., recruiting them, and more important, retaining them and helping them work together with existing volunteers and professionals) in sport and recreation organisations would require different approaches, compared to what is normally done with professionals. This does not mean that the staffing techniques that we described earlier are not useful for recruiting volunteers. Job descriptions, formal interviews or training can have a significant impact on volunteers and also would make the procedures and working systems transparent to the volunteers. But at the same time, managers should be aware that by overemphasizing these aspects, sport organisations could fail to recognize the main factors driving people to volunteer. This would probably increase the chance of not providing suitable working environments for the volunteers. As Green and Chalip (1998, p. 14) have noted, volunteer programmes should not be conceived "as if volunteers are merely staff who are unpaid". In volunteering, "volunteers trade off time, market-valued skills and often money (in the purchase of transportation or child care) in order to gain the benefits they get from voluntarism" (Unger 1991, pp. 71-72). An understanding of the benefits volunteers seek would facilitate effective management. Reasons for volunteering can combine different motives in original ways: competency in a specific skill, socialising with other persons, public visibility and scene, appreciation by the community because of a specific status, power, and so on.

Shibli (1999) has noted that when volunteers perceive a growth in bureaucratization, they can feel that their capacity to express themselves and co-operate with others who share the same value perspective is threatened, thus reducing involvement and time allocation to these organisations (Hedley and Davis Smith 1992). Following sociologist Max Weber's main approach, Adler and Adler (1987) have shown that while intense commitment is facilitated by charismatic leadership, bureaucratization and authority-based leadership forms are not as effective on this respect. This is not limited, however, to volunteers only; in the literature, cases are reported of workers that have accepted lower pay and fewer career opportunities, being loyal to the leaders of their organisations (Leiter 1986). Loyalty also seems to depend on the centrality that working for a specific organisation has in the life of an individual (Adler and Adler 1987).

A first approach is therefore to identify the incentives that impel persons to volunteer their time and effort to a sport governing body and its client groups. Knoke and Prensky (1984) identified three types of incentives labelled as **utilitarian, affective** and **normative.**

Utilitarian Incentives

Although volunteers may not receive any direct monetary payment for their services, their involvement with an OSO may have some utility for them—that is, they may gain something beneficial to them through such volunteering. If, for example, a student volunteers to assist the OSO in its head office, that student may learn something about management, about sport and about sport management. In addition, the student may gain hands-on experience in managing an activity or carrying it out. Contacts can be useful for a future career. Such learning and experience may be the incentive for the student to volunteer with an OSO. For some events, awarding of academic credits has been used to attract students. For example, the organising committee of the Winter Universiade in Seefeld (2005) has targeted the local student population to attract them as volunteers. To this purpose, an agreement was signed with the University of Innsbruck that not only circulated information through the students but also recognized the volunteering experience within the academic curriculum. Through a preliminary survey, the games organisers had verified the level of potential interest in volunteering in the selected population and the kind of benefits and rewards that could be more attractive to ensure an effective recruitment and mobilization.

Cenci and Semprini (2001) have reported similar techniques to motivate high school students to volunteer on the occasion of the Games of the Small States, held in San Marino. In the "volunteer plan" developed for this specific event, two parallel avenues to recruit volunteers were followed: (a) targeting school principals and through them a selected group of teachers and (b) targeting skilled people involved in sport for all those tasks that could not be carried out by students. A preliminary analysis was done to identify the different jobs and then assign them to the two categories of volunteers.

As another example, a parent may volunteer to help with a youth tournament organised by an OSO because the parent has to be at the tournament site in order to take care of a child who is participating in the tournament. These two examples illustrate two different reasons for volunteers gaining experience: opportunities and child care. According to Vaillancourt and Payette (1986), these utilitarian incentives can be explained by two models derived from economic theory—**the human capital model** and **the household production model.** The student enhances his or her human capital (i.e., increasing knowledge and skill), and the parent discharges the household function (i.e., child-rearing and child-minding activities). The concept of human capital also has relevance for adult workers or professionals (e.g., lawyers, accountants). Through volunteering, they can establish contacts (i.e., build a network) with relevant others who could help promote their career. Such networks can be quite local for grassroots volunteers but may reach even continental or global levels for policy volunteers.

Affective Incentives

One of the attractions that an OSO may have for volunteers is the opportunity to interact with other people who share the same interests (e.g., a liking for the sport) and values (e.g., benevolent attitude towards young people). Such networking opportunities may satisfy the interpersonal needs of volunteers and also help to make them feel better and enhance their self-esteem. But, the particular composition of the membership of an organisation, as well as the purposes and processes adopted by the organisation, may affect the degree to which these benefits accrue to an individual volunteer. These social incentives have been cited as reasons for volunteering in sport and recreation. For example, we have seen that older adults have an interest in seeing their competence recognized. This can be a relief from the sense of isolation that in some cases these people can perceive.

Normative Incentives

Individuals may share the organisational goals of an OSO in promoting mass sport and in facilitating the pursuit of excellence in sport. When these beliefs are high and intense, persons may feel that they ought to engage in promoting those goals by volunteering for the OSO. The normative incentives are the satisfactions derived from having done something good as reflected by the organisational purposes.

Any discussion of human resource management in an OSO must take into account the various incentives that might influence the volunteer members. Because volunteers are an integral part of the organisation, human resource management practices should be geared to satisfy these incentives to the greatest extent possible.

Matching Volunteers and Organisational Tasks

Another important dimension to be considered when dealing with volunteers in an OSO is the relation between tasks to be carried out and volunteering. In many cases (more than for paid employees), when people volunteer, they would like to be assigned specific tasks that they prefer.

As Kouri (1990) noted, in creating a person–task fit in the case of volunteers, management should consider

- the skills the volunteer would like to use, not what the organisation wants to be used;
- the level of responsibility the volunteer wants;
- the type of people the volunteer would like to work with; and
- the volunteer's expectations for the job.

This perspective is partly different from the one that is commonly considered correct for professional workers: While professionals in some way should adapt to the organisations, for the volunteers it can often be the opposite; that is, the organisation tries to adapt itself—within certain limits—to the needs and dispositions of the volunteers.

For example, a volunteer may prefer routine tasks such as mailing out letters, registering players or taking tickets at the gates. Another person may prefer to be involved in more open and challenging tasks such as coaching a team, securing a sponsorship or advertising a programme. Given the clear distinction between the two persons and the two jobs they prefer, it would be futile for the organisation to arbitrarily assign them to tasks without considering their preferences, just because they are volunteers. It would be equally frustrating and dissatisfying to the volunteers. One approach an OSO can take is a cafeteria-style approach where all the tasks to be carried out are clearly spelled out and the volunteers are asked to choose the tasks they would like to undertake. Although this approach is meaningful and appealing, we should be mindful of two problems that could arise. First, two or more volunteers may want the same tasks, which would create a competitive situation. Second, it is possible that certain tasks will not be chosen by anyone, even if they are crucial for the daily operations of the organisation and the organisation cannot afford to hire professionals for these functions. In both instances, the managers would have to exercise their interpersonal and communication skills to convince the volunteers to opt for other tasks. But this cannot be done beyond a certain limit because if a volunteer does not like these tasks, the volunteer can be expected to leave the organisation or minimise his or her contribution.

Managers should also provide a good estimate of the time required for the commitment and should clearly identify what can be done by somebody who only has limited time available. This estimate should be honest and clearly communicated to avoid frustrations or a kind of boomerang effect. The workload should be acceptable; if the organisation puts excessive load on a volunteer, he or she will probably leave the organisation. Other questions to address could include the duration of the task, its flexibility to accommodate volunteer availability, the form of supervision, the kind of support that the volunteers will receive from the organisation, and the "good mix" with already operating volunteers (and also the professionals).

Another aspect that is often applicable to the process of recruiting volunteers is that the number of candidates may not be as abundant as it normally is for paid positions. This clearly affects the possibility of selecting a good candidate. Political considerations, loyalty and coalitions are also frequently involved in the selection of volunteers at the middle and higher levels of the hierarchy of OSOs. Therefore, in the case of volunteer organisations, the issue of efficiency, while not negligible at all, should be regarded in a different way compared to profit-making companies. For example, being efficient in a commercial organisation can mean paying one person for a set of tasks if they can be carried out effectively by that single person. On the other hand, for an organisation employing volunteers, it is surely acceptable for that same set of tasks to be carried out by two persons or even a team, provided that their efforts are coordinated and correct responsibility is taken.

To overcome the problem of a shortage of candidates for volunteer positions, OSOs need to make their voluntary positions attractive to people. The organisation itself should be attractive and well "communicated". This means that a positive image of volunteering for each specific organisation should be created and communicated, and that all the "exciting" and valuable features of this positive image (e.g., sharing experience with sport stars, travelling around the world, having opportunities, making new friends, learning useful skills, serving children, and so on) should become important and visible features of the activity. To attract volunteers, managers should always identify not only the rewards and potential benefits, but also the organisational contexts where the voluntary work is to be conducted (e.g., the supervision or mentoring system, the authority associated with a specific position). Knowledge of the evolution of the value systems of the society is clearly useful to understanding the general disposition towards volunteering, but managers should also consider that volunteer programmes can be targeting only specific and relatively small segments of the population, whose value structure could be different from the majority.

Of course, orientation or even training processes can be provided to facilitate the initial insertion of the volunteers, and—where possible—continuous support to personal development can be provided. Volunteers can be sent to training courses specially designed for them, if available. In recent years, many Olympic organisations have dedicated important resources to this objective and have promoted courses whose significance is not only related to skill development but also to the reinforcement of the sense of belonging. We will focus more specifically on this aspect in the section of this chapter (2.8) that is expressly dedicated to training. Proper information has to be circulated in order to ensure that candidates have realistic expectations of the organisation and the job, without anxiety or fears.

Another critical aspect that affects the possibility of recruiting competent people is the internal atmosphere or climate of the organisation. Controlling the factors that can create demotivation is as important as controlling the motivating factors. A high degree of conflict and internal fighting—where the interests of particular groups are perceived to dominate collective interest and the proclaimed mission—clearly has the effect of keeping away potential candidates. Incidentally, this is true not only for volunteers but also for the most qualified professional executives, who will not show any interest in such organisations, or if they do, they will escape at the first opportunity. Positive publicity from previously involved volunteers is always an important contribution and should be maximised.

High-quality volunteers are essential to achieve the goals of any OSO and to serve the interest of the clients in a correct and competent way. The attitude of the clients towards services provided by volunteers has been reported to have changed in the last few years, because of the pervasive impact of professionalisation and the shared belief in the superior effectiveness of professional intervention. Actually, this is an important argument that is often used by the supporters of remunerated professionalism to justify the marginal role of volunteers. A series of steps is therefore advisable to ensure that no harm can come to clients and participants as a result of the initiative and action of volunteers.

Numerous interesting examples of good practices are available on this respect. One useful model is the "10 safe steps" screening programme developed by Volunteer Canada (www.volunteer.ca) in order to provide an easy-to-use method for organisations to ensure that the people they serve are safe (figure 2.6).

1. **Determine the risk.**
Organisations can control the risk in their programmes. Examining the potential for danger in programmes and services may lead to preventing or eliminating the risk altogether.
2. **Write a clear position description.**
Careful position descriptions send the message that an organisation is serious about screening. Responsibilities and expectations can be clearly set out, right down to the position's dos and don'ts. A clear position description indicates the screening requirements. When a volunteer changes positions, the screening procedures may change as well.
3. **Establish a formal recruitment process.**
Whether an agency posts notices for volunteer positions or sends home flyers, they must indicate that screening is part of the application process.
4. **Use an application form.**
The application form provides needed contact information. If the volunteer position requires other screening measures (medical exam, driver's record, police records check), the application form will ask for permission to do so.
5. **Conduct interviews.**
The interview provides not only an opportunity to talk to the potential volunteer about his or her background, skills, interests and availability, but also to explore any doubts about the suitability of the candidate. In other words, the interview will help determine the "right fit".
6. **Follow up on references.**
By identifying the level of trust required in the position and asking specific questions, the applicant's suitability may be easier to determine. People often do not expect that their references will be checked. Do not assume that applicants only supply the names of people who will speak well of them.
7. **Request a police records check.**
A police records check (PRC) is just 1 step in a 10-step screening process. PRCs signal—in a very public way—that the organisation is concerned about the safety of its participants.
8. **Conduct orientation and training sessions.**
Screening does not end once the volunteer is in place. Orientation and training sessions offer an opportunity to observe volunteers in a different setting. These sessions also allow organisations to inform volunteers about policies and procedures. Probation periods give both the organisation and the volunteer time to learn more about each other.
9. **Supervise and evaluate.**
The identified level of risk associated with a volunteer position will determine the necessary degree of supervision and evaluation. If the risk is great, it follows that the volunteer will be under close supervision. Frequent feedback in the first year is particularly important. Evaluations must be based on position descriptions.
10. **Follow up with programme participants.**
Regular contact with participants and family members can act as an effective deterrent to someone who might otherwise do harm. Volunteers should be made aware of any follow-up activities that may occur. These could include spot checks for volunteers in high-risk positions.

Figure 2.6 The 10 safe steps in screening volunteers.

Reprinted, by permission, from Volunteer Canada. © Volunteer Canada. www.volunteercanada.ca.

All 10 steps may not be relevant or applicable in all situations and contexts, but all organisations should consider making similar efforts and developing procedures for this purpose.

2.4 Recruiting Volunteers for Events and Short-Time Projects

As we have mentioned, numerous people who have no interest in long-term volunteering or in leadership positions can be motivated to volunteer on the occasion of a sport event or for short-time projects. Managers of human resources in sport organisations must have a clear understanding of the implications of these different attitudes and motivations and also of the technical requirements of the volunteer staffing process in these diversified situations. For example, sport events typically require a low number of volunteers for a long period of time both before and after the events, while during the events the required number of volunteers is very high. This is a totally different process compared to the recruitment of a small number of competent people as long-term volunteers in the organisation.

Those who have developed short-time projects usually indicate that the main success factors are the comprehension of the needs and a good technical and strategic capacity to build a specific programme of recruitment and coordination for these kinds of volunteers. For bigger events, this normally requires the constitution of a specific organisational unit (e.g., a volunteer department or division), operating in close connection with the human resource department of the local organising committee. For example, in the Olympic Games in Barcelona, the volunteer division of the Coob '92 was operative from the inception to the three months before the Olympics, with a quite stable personnel (Cases Pallarès 2001). The two main goals of the department were to

- identify, train and select the volunteers; and
- maintain the motivation and the commitment and evaluate final satisfaction.

The first objective was pursued at the national level, attracting potential volunteers from all over the country. To cover the most delicate positions, a close relation was set up with different institutions able to provide some of the requested profiles, such as universities, the Red Cross, local administration, youth organisations, and so on. Job descriptions had been developed by the volunteer division and revised after a test competition organised in 1991 to simulate as much as possible the real situation of the Games.

The second objective was pursued through multiple initiatives, including rotations in job assignments, free tickets for selected competitions as a reward and the possibility to access restricted areas. Of course, the usual set of symbols had been employed to reinforce motivation (magazine for the volunteers, cards, gifts, sportswear, discounts on sponsors goods and merchandise). The programme was completed with a specific communication policy that included

- external communication,
- a specific logo for the volunteers,
- a radio programme, and
- dedicated sponsors.

Finally, the satisfaction of the volunteers was monitored, with a very high rate of satisfaction—around 98%.

For less important events, where a dedicated organisational unit for volunteers is not feasible, an OSO should at least formally appoint a person to be responsible for human resource management. His or her responsibilities and tasks are multiple:

- Conceive and implement a plan to recruit and eventually train the volunteers.
- Produce a clear job description for all staff.
- Identify the set of competencies needed.
- Define and communicate human resource management policies (leaves, permits, benefits).
- Create a dedicated information system (database).

The creation of a position of coordinator of volunteers has been reported to be useful in many practical experiences, but once again, this depends on the nature and context of the event.

Schnitzer (2004, p. 30) has described a specific recruitment experience for the ISOC 2005 Games, where the main target group of the recruitment campaign was university students. Key recommendations were as follows:

- Use of common marketing tools to recruit the volunteers
- Effort to avoid creating false expectations
- Involvement of the marketing department for the volunteer job advertisement and recruitment
- Use of specific techniques of mobilization of the volunteers to produce continuous interaction among volunteers and between volunteers and professionals, thus keeping the motivation permanently high
- Volunteer job advertisement through specific initiatives targeting the students (parties, university newspapers, info points, meetings, posters, and so on)
- Large use of the event Web site to communicate with the volunteers and to recruit them
- Good relations with the university staff and direction, especially by taking a direct and active role in university life
- Appointment of highly motivated faculty coordinators of volunteers, with a small monetary provision to play the role
- Use of the best university athletes for testimonials to promote the values of volunteering

A specific effort has been reported by Schnitzer (2004) to develop an affective commitment in the volunteers; for example, a specific brand—"Community 2005"—has been created and promoted for the volunteer team. The brand was aimed at promoting the identification and sense of belonging of all the members.

2.5 Keeping Volunteers Involved

Recruiting effectively is clearly essential, but keeping volunteers involved is equally if not even more fundamental. Occasional involvement should be turned into enduring commitment. As Green and Chalip (1998, p. 20) have noted, "The retention of volunteers is essentially an extension of the techniques for recruitment". In fact, retention is always related to the personal satisfaction of the volunteers' expectations and therefore to recognition and reward systems. Such recognition and reward systems should be very specific with reference to the expectations and the benefits that the volunteers are looking for. However, managers must not forget that the activities themselves as they are carried out by the volunteers ought to be rewarding *per se*. For example, a good level of task achievement or improvement of specific skills that are highly valued by the volunteers can be extremely rewarding, independent of other benefits. This has to be considered properly by the managers so they can provide opportunities to exercise these skills, give feedback and make it clear to the volunteers that these skills are explicitly recognized.

The maximisation of perceived benefits must be an essential goal of the people responsible for volunteer recruitment and retention. The desired benefits are not necessarily the same as those that were decisive in introducing a volunteer into the organisation. New expectations can be generated, new benefits can become interesting and maybe old needs are satisfied and no longer motivating. For this reason, an important requirement for retention is the capacity to create and maintain a sense of identification and belonging. Identification means higher chances of commitment (Adler and Adler 1987; Cuskelly and Boag 1999) and less turnover (Donnelly 1993; O'Reilly and Chatman 1986; Werber and Gilliland 1999). As Mowday, Porter and Steers have indicated (1982, p. 27), commitment to an organisation is "the relative strength of an individual's identification with and involvement in a particular organization". This variable is strongly related to time allocation, absenteeism and innovative behavior. The problem of developing organisational commitment and loyalty is one of the most important in the human resource management strategies of an OSO.

Some specific examples of different programmes conceived to facilitate long-term volunteer involvement in sport are available at different levels and can be used as potential sources of inspiration. But again, they should not be used as fixed or generalisable models given the strong context and cultural implication of this dimension.

For example, the Australian Sport Commission (ASC) has a long and successful tradition of programmes dedicated to the involvement of volunteers. In 1993, a specific programme called the National Volunteer Involvement Programme (VIP) was designed to explicitly increase community awareness of the importance of volunteers in sport and recreation and to provide support and assistance to those who volunteer.

Within this programme, ASC has recognized the necessity to understand the motivation of the volunteers and manage their involvement so that all parties (clubs, athletes, the community at large and the volunteers themselves) could benefit. All the efforts on this respect should be aimed first at the creation of a positive environment. Such actions are complemented by a set of training initiatives in different contexts but mainly aimed at managing and recruiting volunteers and operating clubs.

Other programmes and initiatives have been adopted in numerous countries where the importance of volunteers is significantly recognized. Of course, there are great differences between these programmes, but a few major components seem to be recurrent in these projects as well as in the literature aimed at practitioners:

- Publicity and promotion
- Supply of training opportunities through direct funding of the volunteers' attendance

- Public recognition of the role of the individual volunteers and personal public praise or recognition in newspapers
- Provision of opportunities to increase the volunteers' knowledge or even to empower them, valuing their suggestions, placing some of them in roles of responsibility or giving the clear perspective that they can grow in their job
- Adoption of deliberate procedures for volunteer management
- Creation of a community through extensive teamwork and mechanisms of informal solidarity (meetings, rituals, shared experience, and so on)
- Involvement of the volunteers in the "creation" of information and in the communication process
- Ongoing dialogue and feedback that is fundamental to avoid dissatisfaction or alienation of the volunteers
- Introduction of opportunities to increase benefits (even if only symbolic) for the loyal volunteers
- Efforts to avoid assigning routine work to volunteers (as much as possible) and distribution of unpleasant tasks between many different volunteers

More practical indications are often given by the administrators of these programmes to enhance the recognition of the volunteers; examples include gifts, informal certificates and awards, free admission to events, the opportunity to wear symbols of the organisation (T-shirts, pins, hats or sweaters that nobody else can have or that cannot be bought in a shop), the opportunity to meet top athletes of that sport, event naming, letters of thanks, get well and business cards, parking facilities, and so on. All these elements, however, require that an adequate emotional framework for the experience has been created. As Green and Chalip (1998) have noted, it is not enough to provide a T-shirt to generate involvement and satisfaction. People normally do not volunteer in order to get a T-shirt or a sweater, and at the same time, affective involvement cannot simply be replaced by training only.

In summary, we would like to emphasize the need for OSOs to adopt in an explicit way volunteer management practices and dedicated plans, without which staffing and retention will be less effective. Hager and Brudney (2004, p. 1) have identified nine main areas of volunteer management practices that in our view are extremely significant for OSOs:

- Permanent supervision and communication with volunteers ensuring that information is shared and affective commitment is mobilized
- Liability coverage for volunteers
- Screening and matching volunteers to jobs
- Regular collection of information on volunteer involvement
- Written policies and job descriptions for volunteers
- Regular public and associative recognition activities
- Annual measurement of volunteer impact
- Training and professional development of volunteers
- Training for paid staff in working with the volunteers

As Grossmann and Furano (2002) have indicated, the application of such practices is necessary to reinforce and support the motivation of the volunteers themselves: "No matter how well intentioned volunteers are, unless there is an infrastructure in place to support and direct their efforts, they will remain ineffective at best or, worse, become disenchanted and withdraw, potentially damaging recipients of services in the process."

Table 2.2 contains an example of specific steps to be followed to develop a volunteer management plan. This example was developed in Australia by Sport and Recreation Victoria.

Finally, we would like to note that even though we have analyzed all these guidelines and techniques with reference to the recruitment and retention of volunteers, managers of OSOs should be aware that many of these concepts can be adapted for paid professionals as well.

Table 2.2 **Steps for the Development of a Volunteer Management Plan**

Step	Description	Notes
1	Form a project working group.	Involve people representative of volunteers in your organisation and relevant external key stakeholders.
2	Nominate 1 or 2 people to "drive" the project.	These people will not be solely responsible for the project. They will, however, act as the "whip" to keep the project going. (Having 2 people makes it a less lonely task!)
3	Determine how you are going to involve the membership in the project.	
4	Promote the project within your organisation.	Inform members how they can be involved. Keep general membership updated.
5	Provide project information.	Ensure that people in the working group have a good understanding of this information, and make it available to the membership that want to familiarize themselves more with the project and its value.
6	Assess the performance of the organisation in relation to volunteer development and support.	
7	Develop strategies or actions to address any issues identified.	
8	Appoint a person responsible for coordinating the implementation of the plan.	Once all the hard work of developing the volunteer management plan is completed, it is important that the impetus is not lost. Placing someone (or 2 people) in charge of overseeing the implementation will ensure that the benefits start to flow immediately.
9	Establish review dates.	Establish time lines to review the progress of the plan. The review can be done by the original working group or by the management committee.
10	Include "volunteer management" as an item on the management committee's monthly agenda.	This will keep the plan and volunteer issues generally on the organisation's "agenda". It will also serve to remind incoming committees that the organisation has a volunteer management plan that is integrated into the organisation's operations.
11	Review the volunteer management plan.	The organisation may choose to do this annually, once the strategy has been implemented or on a cycle that is determined by the organisation. The process used will be the same one followed when putting together the original plan—that is, commence at step 1.
		Additional information
12	Develop project briefs (project outlines).	
13	Develop position descriptions (roles and responsibilities).	
14	Develop a listing of all volunteer opportunities.	

Reprinted, by permission, from Australian Sports Commision, Sport and Recreation Victoria.

2.6 Evaluating the Employees

After having spent time and efforts in the staffing process, it would be curious if sport organisations did not recognize the importance of the continuous professional development of the workforce. The improvement of employees' performance is in fact an essential component of organisational effectiveness. However, on this specific topic, as well as on the question of pay and reward systems, it is difficult to find exhaustive data and specific investigations in the domain of Olympic sport organisations. For this reason, we will mostly refer to concepts and guidelines (in some cases even prescriptions) that have been developed for organisations other than OSOs, but that we believe to be of some interest for them.

Professional development can generally be obtained through two main avenues of actions that should be constantly interrelated:

- Evaluation
- Training

The evaluation process enables managers to appraise in an analytic way the performance of the people working for the organisation. If properly used, this process can provide essential feedback to the employees (who can then compare their behavior with available performance standards), identify eventual failures and limitations and reinforce effective behavior. The way the process is conceived and managed is essential; if the performance evaluation is only occasional, not really consistent and not based on the concepts of organisational justice that have been mentioned previously, this can easily unsettle the organisational system and introduce elements of tension. Badly planned evaluation systems often lead to conflict between employees. Therefore, a dedicated manager or a specific organisational unit should take responsibility for the evaluation programme, and the principles and criteria on which the evaluation is based should be communicated and explained to the staff.

The basic concept of evaluation is quite straightforward—trying to determine to what extent a single individual is able to execute the tasks he or she has been assigned and to what extent the person is up to the responsibilities and challenges of the job.

Some basic conditions are necessary to set up an effective evaluation system:

- Evaluation should not be just a way to control the employees.
- Evaluation should be able to enhance people's motivation and co-operation.
- Evaluation should be conceived as a tool to identify needs and to suggest how to match them.
- Evaluation should monitor the achievement of the operational goals.

If the manager responsible for human resources or the evaluation process in general wants to be really effective, he or she should also be aware of the risks associated with employee appraisal:

- Evaluation should always concern the performance and not the individual.
- Evaluation should be constructive and focused on individual and organisational development.
- Employees should feel that evaluation is useful for them and that it is not just a bureaucratic and formal procedure (or a way to mask the impact of friendship or kinship relations or other kinds of social ties).

All these general principles are contradicted if there is a too strict relation between the evaluation process and the reward system or when disciplinary actions are introduced as the result of the evaluation process.

Another important point is that effective evaluation is only possible when its rules have been clearly defined and presented to the employees. This should be done before the initiation of the system; of course, procedures can vary from one organisation to another. One way is to develop a tentative checklist or an evaluation form to be presented to the employees and possibly negotiated or at least discussed with them.

The content of such checklists depends on the organisational strategies and other contingent factors. Organisations may benefit from evaluating their employees with reference to the following aspects:

- Achieved objectives
- Perception of effectiveness
- Critical incidents or experienced difficulties
- Perceived need and possibility for improvement
- Interest in training initiatives or other actions aimed at professional development

Given the "delicate" nature of the evaluation process, managers need to consider the importance of the organisational atmosphere. Beaumont (1993) has suggested that employees should receive positive feedback for their strong points, and that the eventual negative feedback should always be phrased in a constructive and nonemotional way. Great care is needed to avoid an unnecessary defensive reaction or emotional upsurge.

For the same reason, appraisal of employees should also occur in a face-to-face and private situation (not public), and the employee should be asked directly for suggestions for improvement. In sum, the evaluation process should reinforce in the employee a feeling of being part of the organisation and should involve him or her in setting up new objectives.

The various evaluation forms that are collected with reference to a single employee should be filed and compared and used to monitor how the process of professional development is going. Finally, we must note again that this process—to be really useful—should not be occasional and inconsistent. It should be well integrated into organisational routines and highly evaluated within the internal social context of the organisation.

2.7 Pay and Reward Systems

Pay and reward systems are obviously fundamental to regulate the organisational life and to motivate employees. They can strengthen employee co-operation and contribute to organisational effectiveness. People are supposed to produce more if the reward they can access is valuable and is related to their own "real" effort. According to some (often simplistic) views or traditional approaches, pay systems are really the core of human resource management, but certainly other forms of remuneration (material or symbolic) can contribute to the global reward system. Through its global reward system, an organisation can influence and reinforce desirable individual motivations or working systems (e.g., facilitating teamwork or developing specific competences).

However, managers need to understand that the pay and reward system is not just a way to deal with individual needs and motivation but also a reflection of the system of values and the culture of the organisation in general. A good example of that is the **job valuation,** which is the choice of the level of salary that is connected to a specific working position. How much a job is valued compared to others reflects not only the conditions of the labour market and the organisational costs, but also the specific organisational culture and tradition. In the introduction, we described two different approaches to HRM (i.e., the human capital development approach and the personnel administration approach). In our view, each of them has a particular implication on the way the pay and reward system is structured.

Pay and reward systems are usually defined on the basis of a complex decision making process that takes into consideration

- the analysis of the internal and external economic variables influencing the organisation (inflation rate, profitability of the market, economic macrotrends, internal financial indicators, and so on); and
- the analysis of the characteristics of the individual (evaluation of the job, qualifications, past individual results, future potential, and so on).

On this basis, the structure and composition of the pay and reward system have to be decided, especially with reference to the relation between a fixed part and a variable and reversible part. The relative composition of the remuneration can vary across the organisational function and the career.

Compared to the past, when the development of the pay system was essentially related to the number of working years, a wide range of reward systems have recently been observed that try to establish a closer relation between the reward system and the individual or organisational performance. In these systems, the variable part is not only more important but also extremely diversified.

Many organisations have adopted **gain-sharing** or **profit-sharing systems,** or one of the various forms of specialised incentive programmes. These systems are clear examples of a different conception of the relationship between individual motivation and the reward system. Therefore, the determination of the variable part of the pay is becoming more and more important for human resource policies.

Managers should have a good understanding of the impact of such gain-sharing or profit-sharing systems and incentive programmes on the internal hierarchies, structures and value systems (Beaumont 1993). Numerous advantages have been indicated on this respect; for example, incentive programmes are generally more effective for the behavioral control of employees compared to a fixed pay system. Through this kind of dynamic remuneration (Donnadieu 1999), it is also possible to increase the level of personal motivation without demotivating others, since the system can be restarted every year, which helps to achieve the degree of flexibility necessary to adapt to the different organisational areas.

On the other hand, inconvenience has also been reported in specific cases. For example, an extensive use of pay systems that are based on evaluation of the individual performance is likely to increase conflict and decrease co-operation and organisational loyalty (Adler and Adler 1987). Therefore, managers have to carefully consider the real trade-off between potential positive and negative aspects and evaluate the best possible option between pay per individual performance or pay per organisational performance.

OSOs face numerous challenges when developing special reward and incentive programmes based on performance. On this respect, all organisations have to be aware of and answer three main questions:

1. Whom do we want to motivate?
2. Which objectives should be reinforced?
3. What kind of relations should be established between the objectives and the incentives?

To answer these questions, an organisation must be able to list and prioritise its objectives. When doing so, the organisation should first understand the reasons why an objective has not been achieved already. Inappropriate methods used to define the incentive programmes can cause a kind of boomerang effect. For example, a federation can reward the achievement of a specific position in an international competition by athletes, coaches or teams, but this decision can turn into a problem in at least two different ways. On one hand, if the goal is too difficult, nobody will be able to achieve it; on the other hand, too many organisational actors may be able to reach an easier goal. In the second case, if the incentive is distributed among all the achievers, this will probably reduce the appeal of the incentive, and the incentive will have only a moderate effect on the motivation of the employees.

Compared to business companies, OSOs face additional problems in developing performance-related pay systems. While a commercial company can decide, for example, to allocate 10% of the additional volume of sales to a specific incentive programme, this is much more difficult for a sport organisation. What exactly is the value of an improvement of a position in the world rankings? Or of an increase in mass participation? Another problem that is faced by OSOs is the huge amount of administrative work that is usually necessary to review the performance of the organisational members; in some cases, the process of job evaluation, especially the performance assessment, can be not only complicated but also extremely expensive. Another difficulty is to decide who should be included in the incentive programme. For example, while this system is more easily put in place for players and coaches, OSOs usually find more difficulty in identifying a performance-related pay system for administrative positions or technical positions whose performance is not easy to measure. This can often result in the perception of inequity, since people whose "obscure" work contributes to the success of the organisation may feel that they are not rewarded at the same level as those whose performance is more evident and measurable. Chappelet and Bayle (2004) have clearly identified the problems of defining the organisational performance of an OSO; besides that, a manager of an OSO must also be aware that an individual's contribution to the organisational performance can be even more difficult if not impossible to determine. All these considerations have clear consequences for the possibility of developing performance-related pay systems.

In any case, if a similar system is developed, feedback from the actors about the reward system is always advisable since this can probably minimise future conflicts. Employees have to be fully informed through specific events or written communication.

Lawler (1984) has listed nine key strategic issues for designing a reward system that can be of interest for OSOs. Managers responsible for the design of the reward system should be confronted with the following questions:

1. What is the basis for reward (job-based or skill-based pay system)?
2. What is the pay for the performance?
3. What is the market position (what is usually done in other organisations in the same market)?
4. Is the orientation internal or external (related to question or equity)?
5. Is the system centralised or decentralised (only one pay system in an organisation or multiple pay systems with different forms of administration)?
6. What is the degree of hierarchy (egalitarian versus hierarchic pay systems)?
7. What is the reward mix (which combination or range of benefits is provided)?
8. How are process issues addressed (communication on the pay system and decision making)?
9. What is the general reward system congruence (consistency between all the elements)?

These strategic issues are certainly critical for sport organisations, especially because these organisations have particular problems in finding clear indicators of productivity that are valid for both global and individual performance. This is less of a problem for professional athletes and coaches, whose salary can be related to the objective performance of a team or a player. In professional clubs, for example, pay is usually based on a combination of different criteria; a percentage of the salary is normally fixed, and the rest can be variable and measured according to the performance of the club or player. Taking the example of football, there can be bonuses for the appearance on the first team, bonuses for winning or goals, position (success) bonuses, loyalty bonuses or status bonuses (e.g., related to the maintenance of a position in a series or in a continental competition, or a certain level of performance).

Another point is that since it is not possible to establish an entirely objective relationship between individual performance and overall organisational efficiency, forms of nonmonetary compensation should be considered. On the other hand, widely confirmed sociological analysis of organisational control also points to the same direction: If the workers' reward is uniquely based on monetary compensation, the employees will be willing to co-operate only in relation to how much they are paid (Collins 1975; Etzioni 1975). Insurances, company phones, parking spaces, personalized integrative retirement plans, relocation expenses and grants for children are just some examples of the most common nonmonetary benefits. Flexibility of working times or new working forms (e.g., job rotations) have also been included quite often in reward systems. The composition of the final salary can therefore be very different in different situations.

It is not difficult to understand why reward systems are among the most sensitive organisational issues, with a long history of conflicts. To reduce conflict between employees and employers in sport organisations (mostly professional), different ways to regulate a pay system have been identified:

- Collective contracts
- Gentlemen's agreement (in case of financial problems, the professionals show the will to co-operate with the organisation in solving the problem) and continuous consultations
- Salary caps (common practice in U.S. leagues, but considered less effective in other conditions). The salary cap is based on a very simple concept—that the wages paid cannot be higher than a certain percentage of clubs' income. The general idea is that this would preserve the financial health of the organisation. If

this policy is kept, this can guarantee a financial stability for the organisation. However, only a joint approach of all the organisations active in a market can guarantee success on this respect. If one specific organisation or group of organisations (e.g., a national league) does not accept this approach, then the most skilled professionals and athletes will move to that environment. This is the reason why salary caps have been opposed in top European football clubs that prefer a more liberal approach.

In numerous industrial sectors, it is preferred to keep the highest possible ratio of fixed salaries. But for sport organisations, this is not always the case because a large part of the income can be influenced by contingent variables, such as success or media popularity, so that fixed salaries can become problematic if they decrease. On the other hand, the setup of a salary system mostly based on variable pay can be a risk when an organisation sets too high a goal. In this case, critical situations can occur. If the team or the athletes do not perform well, there will be a financial weakness (often lower income than expected); if they perform well, this could create a huge amount of monetary spending because the rewards offered to the players or the staff have been set too high.

To conclude, in our view, variable pay systems can be effective if the employees trust their managers, if they do not feel that external or contingent factors have too much importance for their work performance, and if the indicators used for the calculation are correct and valid or do not generate inequities.

2.8 Training and Professional Development

Even if the staffing procedures are carried out effectively, complex sport organisations are usually confronted with internal and external pressures that require adaptation and change. New systems of production are put in place, and new technologies and new working or governance principles are advocated. For this reason, in order to further develop the organisation and to react properly to the changing environment, organisations must develop the professional skills of the employees. This is done mostly through specific training processes that try to meet the needs of an organisation by improving the people's skills and changing their attitudes. Although training is more and more recognized as a fundamental strategic factor for organisational development, many organisations are reluctant to invest in training programmes. In addition, the need for training is often recognized only when it has become clear that organisational performance has deteriorated. When the driver of training is a crisis, this can put excessive pressure on the process itself. In fact, training normally should not be used as a remedy for short-term problems but rather on a medium- and long-term scale.

In the context of the Olympic movement, the attempt to professionalise the organisations or to develop the potential of volunteers is characterised by a more frequent use of training as a key human resource practice. In recent years, a radical change in the conception of training practices has occurred, and the training process itself is nowadays sufficiently formalized with reference to tools, procedures and methods. In the past, typical approaches to training have been based generally on the acquisition and cumulation of formal or academic knowledge. Now the emphasis is more on the concept of competence, possibly within a concept of lifelong learning. People never stop learning; the question is how to integrate their existing skills and competence with the new ones that are required and how to be sure that this process can lead to visible and effective outcomes in real professional life situations.

In our view, these requirements are more or less the same for all organisations. What is important in OSOs is that training processes not only refer to the improvement of skills that are useful to daily operations but are also in agreement with the specific mission and values of these kinds of organisations. This means that it is not useful to conceive training processes for OSOs that exclusively target technical skills without giving significant attention to the cultural dimension, for example, by paying explicit attention to the communication of the OSO's strategies and principles. If training is to be a powerful driver of organisational development, the professional competences of the workers must be potentiated in agreement with the overall human resource and global strategy of the organisation. Therefore, training plans should always identify in a concrete way the outcomes pursued and their expected impact on the organisation.

Training can be used for at least two different purposes:

- Training of new personnel
- Improvement of skills of existing personnel

These two approaches are clearly not exclusive and can be developed jointly.

In any case, training is a key management process and cannot be improvised. OSOs sometimes do not fully recognize this aspect; effective training requires specialised professionals who are able to conceive, carry out and evaluate the process. Too often mistakes are made on this respect. OSOs often misunderstand the skills needed to carry out the process and often assume that an expert in the specific professional field is the best professional to deliver training. For example, it is often thought that only the most successful coaches can supervise or conduct coaches' training, or that only the best marketeers can teach marketing to professionals. This is not necessarily true. Even if high-reputation professionals are an important resource for any training process, training is a different thing and requires dedicated professionals and methods, or at least competent people who are able to switch from one role to another. A trainer's manual should be prepared for the people responsible for the training process, specifying expected outcomes and the suitable preparatory sessions that are needed to facilitate the process.

For this reason, training is increasingly carried out with the support of specialised agencies or consultants that can deliver services to a single organisation or multiple organisations. A specialised network of professionals responsible for training engineers, consultants and, of course, the trainers) can be mobilized. In some cases, these networks can be subsidiary units or specialised structures within the national governing bodies themselves; for example, in Italy, the Scuola dello Sport of the NOC has the task of conceiving, conducting and evaluating professional training processes on behalf of the NOC and the national federations. To this purpose, training programmes are approved by national federations and carefully evaluated through a dedicated monitoring system.

To carry out effective training, managers must be aware of key principles of training and education of adults. According to such principles, training should enable individuals to redefine their conceptual frame of reference, mostly through a reflective approach based on experiential learning more than through formal lecturing and top-bottom processes that are typical of traditional curricula (Kolb 1984; Kolb and Fry 1972). In this way, the participant should be enabled to find solutions to the classes of problems that are normally encountered in daily working situations. This does not mean that professional training is just "practice". It is more to develop comprehension and an appropriate conceptual and cognitive articulation that are applicable to real-life situations. Even if new knowledge is always useful, training does not necessarily have to target something new, because it could be even more important to assist the trainees in restructuring and mobilizing their cognitive schemes.

This requires the training process to always be centred on

- the trainee and
- the situation where the competence has to be applied.

While it is easy to have a general consensus on such principles, their implications for the management of the training processes must be carefully considered. In fact, for organisational and economic reasons, some organisations may try to standardise the process as much as possible, and at the same time, to reinforce its predictability. This can be a source of problems and eventually ineffectiveness, because this can lead to the temptation to add as many topics as possible to the training programme in order to take maximum advantage of the opportunity.

An additional difficulty is related to the fact that effective learning can be produced through nonformal processes that do not necessarily require classes or lectures but can derive from a guided and supervised reflection on the experience of the participants.

Planning the Training Process

An abundance of methodological knowledge is available concerning the planning of training processes. In fact, a series of recurrent phases have to be planned and coordinated:

1. The analysis of the needs (both of the workers and of the organisation)
2. The development of a specific plan (based on the results of the analysis and compatible with the available resources and time)
3. The implementation of the plan and its supervision
4. The evaluation (in the short and long term) of the process

All four phases have to be coordinated but also designed so that all the significant and pertinent organisational actors (director of personnel or human resources, general director, trainers, and so on) are involved with different functions (Parlier 1999).

Needs Analysis

The needs analysis is a critical phase that should be carried out in a professional way, which means through the use of the most appropriate tools and methods. The first step of the needs analysis should be to consider the weaknesses of the organisation with reference to the specific problems targeted or more generally to its future development. This process can be a combination of qualitative and quantitative techniques, aiming at the identification of those factors that limit the achievement of institutional goals or specific objectives. The second step would be to identify which of these factors can be remedied through a training process. This is essential because some of the factors that can have a negative impact on organisational performance cannot be influenced directly by the action of the people working in the organisation. Another case is when there are no specialised personnel in an area within an OSO. In this case, instead of training existing professionals, new recruitment can be considered as a possible alternative.

This is surely the most difficult part; through the diagnosis, an OSO may identify weaknesses, but it is not always easy to relate them to the tasks and skills of the human resources. For example, the analysis may reveal that sponsors are not satisfied with the product delivered by an organisation, but this is only the starting point for a complex set of questions that should lead to the decisions on the nature of the training plan. Or, alternatively, a national federation may have had a bad performance in different international or regional competitions, and while this is clearly a fact, the identification of the main weak points that have led to this result is certainly problematic.

A specific methodology could include the following steps:

1. What are the weaknesses and problems?
2. What are the reasons for these weaknesses and problems?
3. What kind of skills or competences are related to these weaknesses and problems?
4. What is the current level of competence of the human resources on this respect?

Of course, there can be other reasons to perform a needs analysis, such as when a new working system or a new technology is adopted. But, in general, the needs analysis phase has a great strategic value since it normally ends with an analysis of the required competence and qualifications for the organisation. In this way, training takes the nature of an investment integrated with the development strategies of the organisation. As with any kind of investment, the investment in training is not immune from risks, which are generally related to the real capacity of predicting the future and relating it correctly to the competences to be developed (Parlier 1999).

The substantial difference between professionals and volunteers should be considered during the needs analysis. While training for professionals can often be easily integrated in their working time, and in some cases, can even be an additional motivation, it is more difficult to match the needs of volunteers since they have limited time (because of their other main professional activities). Volunteers often feel that carrying out their tasks in an organisation is more important than attending classes. On one hand, volunteers must be particularly motivated, and at the same time, the organisation of their training should be specifically targeted to their actual availability. Surely, a low level of perceived relation with concrete operational tasks or strategic responsibilities will contribute to a low level of participation of the volunteers in training programmes or to high dropout levels.

The analysis of the training needs of volunteers should incorporate tools such as questionnaires or forms to identify

1. the preferred teaching methods and training format (e.g., distance learning),
2. the specific expectations, and
3. the preferred time of the courses.

On the other hand, we must note that even if they have indicated specific choices, volunteers will not necessarily behave in agreement with them; however, a preliminary understanding of their preferences and barriers can be useful.

When dealing with professional workers, other problems appear that are especially related to the necessity to keep the organisation producing and working while some people are in training. This can be a delicate issue because there is always the temptation to interrupt or postpone a specific learning event because an "urgent issue" needs to be dealt with. This would endanger the credibility of the whole training process, not only the current one but also those that can be planned in the future.

Development of the Training Plan

Based on the results of the needs analysis, normally the concrete training plan can be conceived and then implemented. The first decisions to be made concern the structure, content and format of the training programme and then the personnel to be involved in the delivery phase. All this requires a clear definition of the resources that are currently available for training purposes. After that, the choice of the professionals that will deliver training will take place.

As we mentioned earlier, the traditional approach to training has usually been based on formal lectures in classes where all the participants are present at the same time in the same place. In this case, communication is generally structured with standard materials and handouts given to all participants. There is usually very little potential for personalisation and limited chances of interaction and active "learning by doing".

Recently, some new developments have been strongly influencing the conception and process of training:

- New technologies
- New concepts on training, especially the great attention paid to coaching and mentorship

These two relatively innovative elements have been welcomed with enthusiasm, but their application has a lot of implications that should never be overlooked by OSOs when developing new approaches to training.

First, let's analyze the opportunities offered by new technologies that have been generally understood as a way to facilitate distance training and a decentralised process with higher potential for individualisation. Economic advantages (savings in tuition fees and travel costs) are frequently reported as further reason to embrace such innovations in the training process.

If we go to the second aspect, the shift of importance from a lecturer-centred approach to a mentor-centred approach poses complex challenges to Olympic sport organisations. The supervision process to be carried out through a wide range of tutors and supervisors is in fact quite complex and requires very high professional skills that are not always available within an organisation.

Mentors responsible for trainees' supervision must be able to master the concepts, procedures and technical skills needed for the job, but they must also be experts in adult education and learning and in the creation and evaluation of effective learning experiences. Such a combination is not always easily found within an Olympic sport organisation, so it is often necessary to hire external consultants as learning facilitators. In this case, attention should be paid to the effective competence of the facilitators as far as the specific processes and problems of an organisation are concerned.

On the other hand, if an OSO decides to keep the whole training process in-house, the people responsible for training should not do it just occasionally or as a third or fourth job. Of course, professionals who are experts in a specific area are an important resource in an organisation, and they can have an extremely important role in training. However, their actions should normally be placed within a learning context in which a professional with expertise in training processes has primary responsibility.

Within such a framework, the training plan can then include a variety of formulas, among which are the following:

- On-the-job sessions
- Experiential learning (e.g., through internship or application to real-world contexts)
- Development of individual projects
- Alternate programmes

After that, the training calendar and the learning sequences with their specific contents and forms of evaluation should be designed in a concrete way. If properly used, technologies can make this process more flexible and able to be diversified in accordance with the personal existing skills of the trainees and the objectives of the learning. These objectives should be formulated in a very specific way and should be communicated effectively before the process starts.

Implementation of the Training Process

Implementation concerns the daily execution of the programme. This is essentially related to more or less routine operations that are requested according to the plan. Logistic aspects take a great importance in this phase—ensuring that all the technological equipment works, that the teaching material is delivered to the student, that the teaching environment is available and comfortable and that all the necessary steps are undertaken.

Evaluation of the Training Process

Evaluation is obviously an essential part of the process, since all organisations have a strong interest in the analysis of the cost–benefit ratio. However, the impact of training can be evaluated on very different levels and time scales. For each of these levels and time scales, a specific set of evaluation tools has to be identified and applied.

Evaluation can involve any of the following:

- **Perceived impact on organisational effectiveness** (or some specific working areas or systems).
- **Learning outcomes** achieved (in terms of skills or knowledge improvement and correspondence with the planned objectives). This evaluation requires that in the second phase of the training process (development of the training plan), the objectives of training had been defined in a precise and objective way.
- **Satisfaction of the trainees,** but also of the trainers, with reference to various dimensions.

Clearly, the evaluation process can provide important hints on the necessary changes to be introduced in order to improve the system.

Evaluation methods include

- questionnaires, checklists or forms measuring judgments and degree of importance; and
- interviews and focus groups.

An example of the possible items to be used in a specific evaluation form is shown in figure 2.7, which indicates the main components evaluated during a specific module of the MEMOS programme.

Contents
Themes discussed
Clarity of concepts
Choice of the reading materials
Cases discussed
Value of lectures
Degree of difficulty
Workload
Overall content quality

Organisation
Daily programme
Documents received
Animation techniques
Teamwork
Lecturers' availability for discussion
General spirit or atmosphere
Participants' involvement

Relevance
Practical use in professional life
Learning atmosphere

Overall satisfaction
Objectives reached
Correspondence to expectations
Recommendation to a colleague

Figure 2.7 Specific items to use in an evaluation of training.

Of course, this approach is useful mostly for short-term evaluation; for the long-term impact on organisational effectiveness, more qualitative tools are suggested, including interviews with the different stakeholders, focus groups, and so on. Evaluation reports should then be written and circulated.

TRAINING VOLUNTEERS FOR AN EVENT

Training has a special importance for preparing volunteers for an event. Usually, a preliminary orientation phase is needed where the volunteers can receive information on

- the nature and goals of the event;
- its functioning;
- the key roles, persons and responsibilities; and
- the role of the volunteers and of the specific human resource policies and procedures applying to them.

Of course, this preliminary phase should also be used to create a good atmosphere and to develop ownership in the volunteers with respect to the event.

After this phase, regular training can be initiated. Managers should consider that the traditional and formal approach to training (based on lectures and descriptions of rules and tasks) may not be the best solution for training event volunteers.

An experience-based training with the highest exposure to real and meaningful situations is advisable. Expert volunteers should be regularly involved in the process, not only in communicating experience and information but also as potential mentors. Times and duration of the training sessions should be flexible enough to match the personal life schedules of the volunteers.

Lifelong Learning

The model that we have presented in the previous sections applies to traditional training processes with a specific life cycle (from beginning to end). In the last few years, training agencies and organisations have been confronted more and more with the need to use training to sustain the continuous professional development of their employees. The concept of **lifelong learning** has therefore become increasingly popular, especially in those economies that highly value knowledge to face international and internal competitions. Lifelong learning is essential to cultivate the full potential of the employees.

2.9 Empowerment Practices

Several authors have suggested that a hallmark of good human resource management is the process of **empowerment** and have reported that practices explicitly oriented to empowerment have become extremely popular in the last few decades (Lawler, Mohrman and Benson 2001). Empowerment means essentially accepting and implementing the idea of a participative management—that is, the idea that the quality of work and the opportunities for professional development will be higher if more people "have power" within an organisation. In this way, people will be more committed, and through a proper application of a wide range of organisational practices, an organisation will be similar to a community. We have already made reference to the potential benefit of empowerment in the initial chapter when we differentiated between the two major approaches to human resource management (i.e., personnel administration and human capital development). Within this perspective, through empowerment, the alienating and bureaucratic side of organisations can be effectively contrasted.

Horch (1996) has also made this point in an article that emphasized the advantages of voluntary associations compared to business companies because of their ability to achieve outstanding levels of trust, distributed responsibility and co-operation. In Horch's view, these elements (which he also finds in the Japanese culture of industrial relations) are facilitated not only by the ideology of volunteerism but also by the structural properties of voluntary associations, essentially the low degree of specialisation and formalization: "more trust than control" (p. 26).

Even if this can be interpreted in the sense that in such organisations, efficiency is less important than commitment, this is not necessarily the only possible interpretation of the relationships between organisational performance, empowerment practices and members' loyalty since positive relationships between intense loyalty and effectiveness have also been reported (Adler and Adler 1987). From the perspective of organisational loyalty, voluntary associations are superior to business companies, because they are institutionally used to looking for the commitment of people since they cannot use too much monetary incentive and have to use strategies based on intrinsic motivations (Brown and Yoshioka 2003). Etzioni (1975) had noted that the kind of organisational involvement that can be generated through symbolic and nonmonetary rewards can be higher and more intense.

In our view, the problem is not the necessary contradiction between commitment and efficiency, but it is rather the observation that in spite of their founding ideology, many voluntary organisations fall short of Horch's picture; they are not democratic at all, do not provide opportunities for newcomers and the decision-making power is usually concentrated in one single point. This is exactly what Robert Michels had already described at the beginning of the 20th century, identifying what he believed to be a general law in voluntary organisations, which was the trend towards oligarchy (Michels 1962). In Michels' view, leaders of associations constitute an informal group of people that not only keep their position for a long time, but also leave very few opportunities for the members to speak their voices, since they are able to control the resources, the rules, the procedures and especially the information. Even if Michels' position is supported by numerous studies (Collins 1975) and everyday life observation, in our view voluntary associations differ a lot in their degree of oligarchy. When the degree of oligarchy is higher, the participation, commitment and loyalty of members will probably be low, and this is more likely in bigger organisations with significant geographic dispersion. At the same time, if information and other resources are circulated, the trend towards oligarchy will probably be less apparent (Collins 1975).

If we follow the previous argument, this means that oligarchic voluntary organisations can be neither efficient nor capable of producing commitment and participation. Therefore, managers must identify those components of intense organisational loyalty that can positively influence the organisational performance (McIntyre and Pigram 1992), including the affective and emotional dimension.

Power is clearly one of these components. In fact, power is a highly rewarding compensation, and it is no surprise that when power is shared, people tend to be more identified with an organisation. For this same reason, managers usually feel a stronger identification with the organisation compared to other workers at a lower level and with less power within the organisation.

The Bases of Power

Power is essentially the potential capacity to influence other people in order to achieve the desired objectives and especially the capacity to influence in a significant way the decision-making process (Robbins and Barnwell 1998).

The sources of power are extremely varied. Mintzberg (1983), for example, lists five sources of power:

1. Control of a resource
2. Control of a technical skill
3. Control of a body of knowledge
4. Legal prerogatives (i.e., formal power)
5. Access to those who possess one or more of the above four sources of power

Other similar classifications of the sources of power have been provided by other scholars. For example, French and Raven (1959), Pfeffer (1981) and Daft (2001) have distinguished between

- reward power;
- legal power;
- coercive, or physical, power;
- expert power; and
- reference power.

One of the richest descriptions of sources of organisational power is provided by Morgan (1986). Besides those sources of power already indicated, Morgan adds other interesting perspectives such as the control of organisational structures and rules, symbolism and management of meaning, informal alliances and networking, control of counterorganisations, ability to cope with uncertainty, and so on.

The relative importance of these bases of power is dependent on the direction and targets of influence. For instance, the power derived from legal prerogatives (i.e., the power formally sanctioned by the organisation and backed by its authority) is relatively more important for a supervisor in influencing subordinates. However, "authority delegated within a system usually has little currency in others" (Miles 1980, p. 318). Similarly, the power derived from technical skill is more germane to the exercise of influence internally rather than externally. Thus, different forms of power are critical for the exercise of influence outside the organisation. Particularly, the ability to influence the elements in the external environment requires that the power be based on control over resources or possession of expert knowledge (e.g., legal expertise), or access to those who have such control.

Power is not simply a personal or individual property or characteristic but rather a form of social relation. This means that power is normally related to the possibility of controlling the resources, usually on the basis of a specific position in the structure (formal, of course, but also informal, as occurs in the case of organisations where there are strong kinship or ethnic relations).

Organisational structures are very different in the way power is distributed; in horizontal structures or where empowerment practices (e.g., a high level of project teamwork) are adopted, power will be more distributed with a higher chance that people can speak their voice. Contingent dynamic trends towards greater or lesser centralisation could also be different.

All these forms of power can be equated with political or economic power. In spite of the diffused rational view of organisational functioning, the large use of power and influence to achieve the desired objectives is what gives an inevitable political nature to all organisational systems (Morgan 1986). Many managers have a bad opinion of politics, but they should understand that no organisation could work effectively without the most appropriate political behavior, especially when change is required.

The Nature of Empowerment

In this chapter, we have briefly identified some significant trends in sport organisations that go clearly in the direction of empowering athletes or coaches within OSOs, providing to them, for example, more opportunities to be represented and to have a voice in the decision-making process.

Actually, similar to many mainstream concepts in management disciplines, empowerment is a very broad concept that can be analyzed from different perspectives, even if its basic meaning is quite clear and unambiguous—a wider distribution of decision making across an organisation. Spreitzer (1995) defines psychological empowerment as "a motivational construct manifested in four cognitions: meaning, competence, self-determination, and impact. Together, these four cognitions reflect an active, rather than a passive, orientation to the work role" (p. 1444). These four cognitions combine additively and lead to intrinsic task motivation.

Within this perspective, *meaning* refers to the value of a work goal. It is a fit between the requirements of a work role and one's personal beliefs, values and behaviors. For example, a person who values including everyone in a programme may be comfortable in mass sports but not in an elite programme that tends to exclude the not-so-gifted individuals. *Competence* refers to an individual's belief in his or her capability to perform activities with skill. For example, some people feel competent to work in the recreational setting, while others are competent in the coaching of elite athletes. *Self-determination* refers to an individual's sense of having choice in initiating and regulating actions. It reflects autonomy in the initiation and continuation of work behaviors and processes. For example, individual workers in both the recreational and elite sport settings may be permitted relatively more autonomy to decide on how they will carry out their responsibilities. *Impact* refers to the degree to which an individual can influence strategic, administrative or operating outcomes at work. This attribute refers to whether the volunteers and paid workers are permitted to have a voice in determining the policies and strategies of the sport organisation.

When workers perceive these four cognitions to be high in their work, they feel empowered. With such feelings of empowerment, workers are motivated to perform their tasks more effectively and efficiently. Besides that, they bring their own creativity and imagination into the organisational system. Therefore, managers have often been encouraged to engage in empowering their workers as much as possible. In Bowen and Lawler's (1992, p. 32) view, empowerment can be achieved by sharing with employees four organisational ingredients:

1. Information about the organisation's performance; no information or relevant data should be hidden from the members. Improved and unrestricted circulation of information and data is a key ingredient of empowerment.
2. Rewards based on the organisation's performance and feedback on individual performance produced by different sources, including workers.
3. Knowledge that enables employees to understand and contribute to organisational performance.
4. Power to make decisions that influence the organisational direction, performance and working systems (especially aspects and procedures related to the employees' tasks).

The essence of this sharing is that management strategies and processes should be transparent to all workers; that is, all members in the sport governing body should be made aware of the goals sought and the rationale for those goals. In addition, the proposed processes to achieve those goals should also be made clear to the members. While sharing all of this information with the members, managers should also allow them to participate in making those decisions.

With such transparency in strategy formulation and implementation, members are more likely to feel ownership of those strategies and to implement them more effectively. For example, the empowered frontline workers would

- respond quickly to customer needs during service delivery,
- handle the dissatisfied customers through service recovery,
- interact with customers with more warmth and enthusiasm, and
- feel better about their jobs and about themselves.

Thus, empowered employees can be a great source of ideas for delivering quality service and they can also help the organization by their word-of-mouth advertising. The process of empowerment releases hidden resources that would otherwise remain inaccessible to both the individual and the organisation. We should also recognize the basic assumptions behind empowerment. The basic assumption here is that all members of the sport governing body

- are willing and able to take on more authority and make good decisions, and
- have the ability to effectively execute those decisions.

It is also assumed that managers are willing to

- let go of their decision-making authority in some areas,
- change their orientations and habits, and
- learn to manage the empowered and enlightened workers.

These assumptions may or may not be true in all cases. To the extent these assumptions are invalid, the empowerment approach may not be practical or fruitful. At the same time, empowerment cannot be imposed by the top managers without considering the will and the attitudes of the workers to be empowered.

Also, the production line approach may indeed be appropriate in the case of some types of services and under some circumstances. For example, for organisations that have no special need to react quickly to their public, the empowerment approach might not increase the performance significantly. Bowen and Lawler (1992) identify certain contingency factors that would indicate if the production line approach would be more appropriate. These factors are shown in figure 2.8.

This model can be used, for example, to rate an organisation on a five-point scale on each of the contingency factors. The lower the score, the more of a production line approach. The higher the score, the more of an empowerment approach.

Other barriers to empowerment can also be identified; for example, leaders often feel that they can lose power if they delegate or empower employees, and consequently, they are afraid that somebody else can gain power in this way. Additionally, leaders can also like what they do

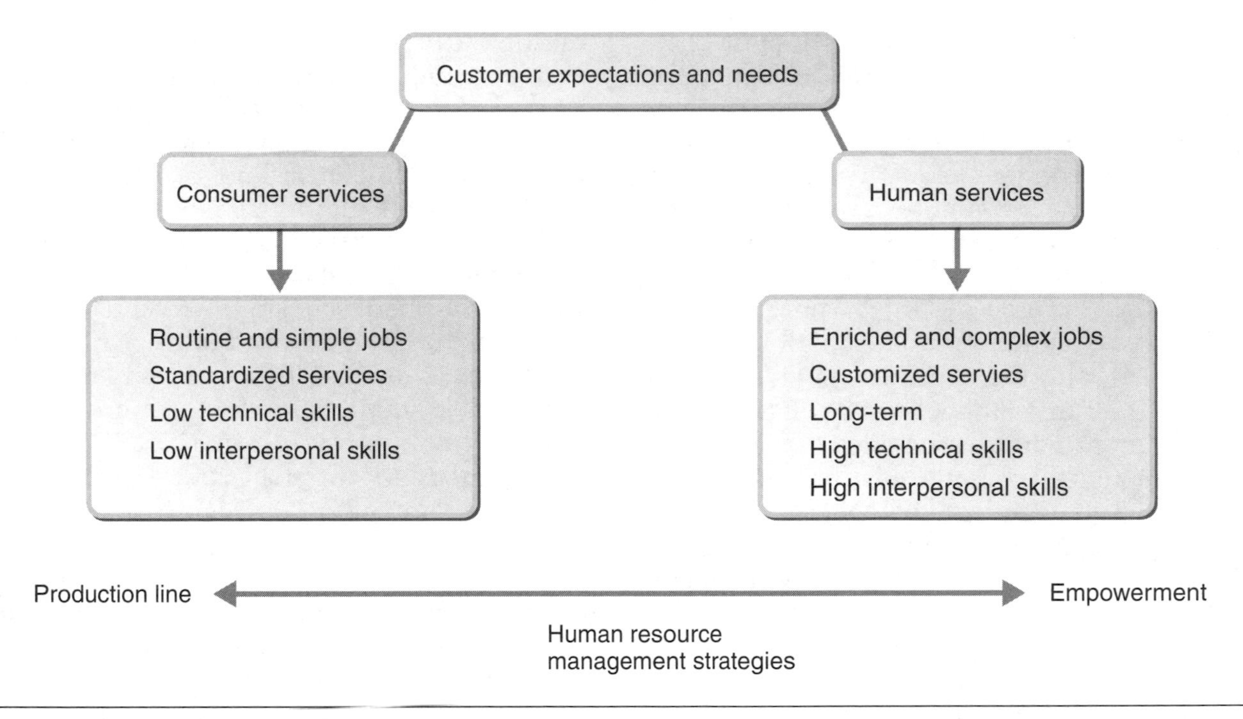

Figure 2.8 Human resource management strategies.

and for this reason be less inclined to delegate tasks. The relationships between managers and subordinates are then critical; if the managers do not trust their employees, the empowerment practices will not be successful.

Structural features can also constitute an obstacle for empowerment. Tall vertical and hierarchic organisational structures tend to be less inclined to empowerment.

When empowerment is attempted in organisations where the cultural and structural conditions are not appropriate, this can provoke a chaotic internal environment, increased conflict and personal insecurity because of the loss of control, and multiplication of informal relationships because of the increase of the power of individual workers. Even in more favorable situations, empowerment always contains an element of risk both for employees and managers.

Hackman (1980) has listed a set of specific indicators of effective application of the empowerment practices in an organisation:

1. Employees are fully aware of organisational goals and contingent objectives.
2. Employees are and feel responsible for the results of their work.
3. Employees continuously evaluate their performance through appropriate indicators.
4. Employees look for new resources when those available are insufficient.
5. Employees take personal initiative to support colleagues.

2.10 Athletes at the Centre of Olympic Sport Organisations: A Specific Case of Empowerment

To what extent are empowerment principles recognizable in OSOs? What are the main challenges for their managers on this respect? As we have already mentioned, athletes' development and protection are currently major challenges for OSOs, which has become more and more apparent following the recent innovation in representation and the general debate about new models of governance for sport organisations. In 2002, the First International Athletes' Forum took place in Lausanne with the participation of athletes belonging to the athletes' commissions of different international federations,

NOCs and, of course, the IOC Athletes' Commission. In fact, following the IOC example, initially started in 1981 but fully developed after 1994, **representation of athletes** has become increasingly common in many federations and national Olympic committees, even if in many cases the function of that representation is still just consultative.

Through this process, athletes have been recognized as a central component of the Olympic movement, and the necessity to give them a voice in the institutional system has become an important point in the strategic agenda of OSOs. Athletes' commissions have been one of the first tools to be developed for this purpose, later complemented by other measures. The definition of who is an athlete is obviously critical. For the IOC, the athletes eligible to be in the athletes' commission are those who have taken part in Olympic Games. Only those NOCs that have a national athletes' commission can submit candidatures for the IOC Athletes' Commission, and this restriction is surely pushing many NOCs and recognized national federations in this direction.

This should not be considered as the simple result of the increasing impact of top athletes on the decision making, but also as a process of democratisation that leads to a stronger "representation" of all the stakeholders, even if the procedures to assure this representation can be very different. Moreover, this is a distinctive feature of OSOs that cannot be identified in professional sport organisations, where representation of athletes in the board of administrators does not take place. Athletes are often in event committees, and their voice is more frequently heard in relation to policy-making issues. Task forces bidding for planetary events such as Olympic Games usually involve athletes as major actors. Athletes' representation usually refers to elite athletes, but there have also been significant examples of larger access to representation. One example is the case of Italy, where a national law in 1999 has determined a fixed representation of athletes (and also coaches) in the sport governing bodies at the national, regional and local level, not only for the NOC and its peripheral branches but also for the national sport federations, including their regional and local committees.

Another significant demonstration of this trend is the growing importance that the employees' representations are taking in the sport industrial relations in many countries of Europe. In France, Netherlands and Sweden, athletes are represented in collective agreements that concern not only world-elite athletes but all the athletes that have some revenues from their activity. The aim of these collective agreements is to clarify and simplify the relations between employers and employees in sport. In France, collective agreements were established initially for equestrian sports, golf and football, and then a more global approach was developed by COSMOS (Conseil Social du Mouvement Sportif), a body set up by the French NOC to deal with industrial relations.

Considering these global trends, it is understandable that the issue of the management of the athletes as a critical resource of OSOs has become more and more important in recent years and constitutes a critical challenge for the policy makers and operational managers in this area. As we mentioned earlier, while in the past the attention was mainly placed on the delivery of optimal services before and during the competition period, and on the creation of award schemes related to world-class results, now it has become critical to provide athletes with a wide range of services. These services have a significant importance to

- avoid fear and demotivation in case of injury or family problems;
- give a life span perspective to the athletes;
- reduce the negative impact of transition that has been demonstrated to have disruptive potential for many individuals, especially because nobody has prepared elite athletes for professional and social life after the termination of their competitive activity;
- facilitate the acquisition of skills usable after the end of the sport career; and
- bring the expertise of the best athletes to the national sport organisation.

Athletes' Career Assistance Programmes

More recently, numerous organisations have conceived and launched **athletes' career assis-**

tance programmes, which have developed a broader approach to the problem.

National Olympic committees, sport confederations or other governmental bodies usually coordinate this process, which can involve a wide range of partners of very different natures (public, nonprofit and private). When the leading role is taken by NOCs, athletes' commissions usually play a major function. Good examples of this approach can be found in a growing number of countries, and we will outline a few of these examples.

In Italy, numerous initiatives have been coordinated by the national Olympic committee in co-operation with working placement companies or with dedicated public agencies for professional insertion and orientation. For example, the "Programma Master 2000" has been made available for the following categories of athletes when they have ended their competitive career:

- National champions (any age group)
- Athletes who have competed at the international level
- Athletes who have competed in any of the following:
  - Mediterranean Games
  - European championships
  - World championships
  - Olympic Games
- Athletes who have played in the first and second division in the team sports

The placement company carried out the following tasks:

- Definition of the professional profiles and inventory of competences of each athlete
- Identification of individual professional potential
- Orientation and provision of information on the labour market
- Definition of a training and professional insertion plan
- Delivery of training in different areas
- Promotion of the project to the business sector

In the period from 2001 to 2004, more than 400 elite athletes have been involved in the project and successfully inserted in the labour market; about 270 of them also took part in a specific training process.

Very similar initiatives have been carried out in numerous countries such as Spain, Norway, France, Sweden, Finland, Switzerland and Denmark, in co-operation with the respective national Olympic committees or ministries of sport. Dutch athletes, for example, are provided with support from NOC and NSF, through professional counselling and dedicated events for 2 years after the termination of the career.

Again in Italy, further training opportunities are currently provided to Olympic or top-level athletes to be involved in coaching and management activities through the National School of Sport of CONI.

One of the most extensive support systems for athletes has been developed in France, where the Institute National du Sport et de l'Education Phsyique (INSEP; www.insep.fr) is the key structure responsible for providing career and non-sport skill development services to the athletes (as part of the state ministry responsible for sport). These services include developing a cluster of vocational qualifications that primarily, but not exclusively, target the sport sector (sport managers, coaches, teachers, and so on). The mission of the institute is then to build the national sport elite, not only with respect to the sport results but also in view of a larger professionalisation process. State agencies support athletes' educational and professional future in many other countries such as Norway (Olympiatoppen) or Canada, where athletes can receive loans to be invested in further education throughout their whole elite sport career, and additional support can be provided for top athletes.

Performance Lifestyle (formerly ACE UK), a service conceived and delivered by UK Sport, provides another example of an individualised support service to help elite athletes in their pursuit of success. Ex-athletes have access to different services around the country that can support the athletes in development of a new career. The most well-known service is "Performance Lifestyle" (www.uksi.net). The aim of this service is to help elite athletes with reintegration after their elite sport career. Currently, there are some 40 advisors around the United Kingdom who work with athletes individually to achieve this goal.

The main idea behind such a programme is to combine the focus on elite performance and associated training with the respect for other key commitments such as the professional career, education, and social and financial support. The programme is based on the strong involvement of coaches and other experts, assembled in an integrated team. Examples of support services provided include financial consultancy, trust funds, relations with the media, negotiation, personal promotion and relations with sponsors. The advisors help athletes optimally combine academic studies and sports training, find jobs with schedules that fit their own training, and facilitate a second career after sport. To achieve this purpose, the British Olympic Association is engaged setting up a network of advisors to work with the athletes. The programme of Performance Lifestyle is available to all athletes in the World Class Performance Programme and those nominated by their respective Home Country Institutes. These athletes can arrange for private sessions with advisors and attend specially organised workshops. The advisors also interact with the staff associated with the sport and design lifestyle management activities consistent with the training programme.

More restricted in its scope compared to Performance Lifestyle is the example provided by Aspire, which is a career assistance for Olympians programme, previously called the Olympic Job Opportunities Programme (OJOP). It has been assisting Australia's elite athletes to achieve meaningful professional careers since 1992. From 1992 to 2000, OJOP placed 325 elite athletes and Olympians in the job market. The Aspire programme is aimed at providing career planning advice and employment opportunities for Olympic and potential Olympic athletes, as well as providing employers with the opportunity to employ Olympians and aspiring Olympians. The programme is quite restricted in its scope since it targets only the following athletes:

- Olympians from the last four editions of the Olympic Games
- Elite athletes who as members of their National Federation Shadow Team have the opportunity to be selected for the Australian Olympic Team

An objective of the Aspire programme is to generate relationships between companies and a selected group of athletes well recognized throughout Australia, emphasizing the benefits that the companies could derive from hiring top-level Olympians. A dedicated Web site and a regular newsletter are used to facilitate the achievement of the programme's objectives. Benefits advertised to the companies are very large and heterogeneous. Here are some from the official document:

- Boost office morale
- Increase workplace motivation
- Share in the successes and journey of an elite athlete
- Take advantage of the unique qualities that Olympians demonstrate when aspiring to be the best in their sport, which include the following:
  - Masters of time management
  - Dedicated
  - Motivated
  - Goal focused
  - Team spirited

  (source http://aspire.olympics.com.au)

This approach is consistent with the results of some studies indicating that sport participation can be more effective than other formal leadership training processes to develop transformational leadership and emotional intelligence (Argent 2005). Aspire and other similar programmes add new ways of facilitating the overall professional development of the athletes (e.g., employment guidance) to the usual psychological, medical, physiological and biomechanical support. This can be facilitated by the great visibility of the elite athletes (who can provide opportunities to partners), by career development and through advice on educational opportunities. In this way, the programme strives to satisfy some of the most crucial needs of the competing athletes—for example, how to properly combine training and study and how to plan for a career (in sport or outside sport) after retirement. To this purpose, a large network of partners must be established at the national and local level.

We must also note that OSOs are not the only organisations developing support to athletic excellence, so their programmes are increasingly confronted with competing initiatives by other organisations. In some cases, athletes can be assisted by different organisations. Universities that have a tradition of supporting their own athletes and teams for intercollegiate athletics are often inclined to provide broader support for their life and career in view of Olympic, international and domestic success. Universities and foundations have developed numerous initiatives in this direction. If this simultaneous support coming from different organisations can be considered as an advantage for the athlete, it is also true that a noncoordinated approach can bring conflict and duplications.

The support to the career of the athletes is just one of the most relevant and lately developed aspects of human resource management concerning athletes as a basic resource for the performance of an OSO.

2.11 Managing Conflict in Olympic Sport Organisations

Of course, the idea of forging a cohesive unit among all the human components of the organisation is a major concern for an OSO, but it is not always easy to put in operation. The main reason is that interests, goals, visions and attitudes can be extremely diversified within each single organisation. This can be true even when there is strong consensus on the *raison d'etre* of the organisation, that is, its founding mission. Even in the most cohesive organisation, goals and driving values always have some degree of ambiguity and indetermination (Martin 1992; Meyerson and Martin 1987; Young 1989) so that the creation of a "coalition of (competing) interests" is almost inevitable.

Aggregated interests have a strong influence on the organisational life and even sometimes on the formal organisational structure itself. Coalitions can be based on division or department affiliation (e.g., marketing department versus production or technical department) or cultural options (e.g., traditional leaders versus leaders coming from another domain) that are often reflected in incompatible objectives, different perceptions of the reality, and a diversity of values. They can also be based on transversal factors such as geographic origin, professional status and even religion. This inevitably generates conflict, which is a constant feature of the interaction between individuals and is therefore also always present in OSOs. The competing views of the large number of different stakeholders and the rivalry between recognized leaders surely add to the problem (Amis, Slack and Berret 1995).

Conflict occurs whenever some organisation members are opposed to other organisation members and the parties involved have the perception that the conflict exists and generate actions or propose goals that are not compatible to each other. The control of the decision-making process is then the main *locus* of conflicts. Conflict can have very different causes and contributing factors of very different order (macroenvironmental, contingent to the specific organisational field and individual). People tend to disagree and create obstacles to other persons or groups essentially because of the scarcity of resources and the divergence of interests concerning their allocation (Daft 2001). The organisational structure can also determine the level of what Slack (1997) has labelled "vertical conflict" that occurs between the central and the peripheral components of an organisation. Decentralised organisations are not less inclined to conflict than centralised ones are, and in some cases, the effects can be extremely disruptive.

Robbins (1990) has identified some sources of organisational conflict that can be grouped in the following categories:

- Task dependencies (especially one-way dependency) so that a unit depends on another to be able to perform effectively
- High horizontal differentiation
- Low formalization, scarce role definition (therefore wide space for ambiguity)
- Common dependence on the same scarce resources
- Difference in evaluation criteria and reward systems
- Heterogeneity of members
- Participative decision making
- Status incongruence
- Role dissatisfaction

- Communication distortions or lack of communication
- Access to information and knowledge

The list could probably be expanded or modified to include other aspects that are particularly valued by managers in OSOs (e.g., insufficient competence of human resources), but the important point is that the possibility of solving conflicts is definitely related to the knowledge of the factors that have caused them. These factors include the reasons for the conflict but also the situation that has produced the conflict (since the individual and group reactions to a conflict are generally related to the sources and to the situation). For each source of conflict, a specific solution should be identified. Unfortunately, these solutions are not always viable; for example, to remedy a conflict related to the common dependency on scarce resources, we may want to increase the resources. But, of course, this is not always possible, so another route may need to be looked for.

In sport organisations, conflicts have been reported repeatedly in relation to workload, lack of human resources to carry out necessary tasks, social and gender factors, power inequalities, poor communication or as a consequence of excessive specialisation. Structural or role conflict can also occur (e.g., elected volunteers that are at the same time on the board of a NSGB and protectors of the interest of their clubs). Violation of organisational justice is another critical factor inducing conflict. This often occurs in the distribution of monetary rewards to employees in relation to their estimated level of productivity. Criteria used in employees' assessments are often badly communicated and very discretionary, and reward distribution can easily be perceived as unfair within the organisation, thus deteriorating the internal climate.

Because of the pervasiveness of conflict—and the reasonable conviction that conflict has a negative influence on organisational performance—the management of conflict is surely an important component of human resource management. Since conflict can easily affect organisational performance, principles and skills related to conflict management and resolution should be an important part of the managers' competence (Danylchuk and Chelladurai 1999). Managers should be able to recognize conflict, to evaluate causes and consequences and to identify possible solutions. In any case, they have to try to regulate conflict and keep it at acceptable levels.

Managers are often afraid of conflict and tend to look for consensus, in spite of the abundant use of competitive metaphors and the idea that life is competition. Conflict is normally feared because it deteriorates internal communication, reduces possibilities of collaboration, produces stereotypes and hinders effective working relationships.

Numerous case studies of conflict in OSOs have been published or have generated reports documenting the nature, the consequences and sometimes the solution of the conflict. But the experience tells us that even if we can identify typologies of organisational conflict and associated causes, their management cannot be derived by simple formulas or generic strategies.

On the other hand, the degree of formalisation or proceduralisation of conflict management processes is very low, and the results of applied research on sport organisations can give quite limited contribution to the development of conflict management skills (Slack, Berrett and Mistry 1994; Verhoeven et al. 1999). The main question for the manager in the field is whether conflict management is always a local and contingent activity whose solutions always have to be "invented" as if for the first time, or if there are general principles that can be usefully applied when confronted with a significant level of conflict.

We have used the term *significant level* because, in spite of the negative connotation of the term *conflict,* today it is frequently acknowledged that a moderate rate of conflict can be useful for an organisation. Conflict can be positive because it allows different perspectives to be discussed and compared (Heinemann 2004). This could improve the problem-solving and decision-making processes. When there is no conflict within an organisation, it means that it is "sclerotized" and autocratic, and this is surely not contributing to innovation or creativity and therefore not contributing to organisational performance (Davidson 1990; Goddard 1986). However, conflict can be useful within an organisation only when enough consideration is given to the representations of the different groups and when it is possible to find solutions based on a co-operative approach and not just based on the personal view of one or a few leaders. On the other hand, conflict often becomes disruptive when personal feelings are significantly touched, and this is an important consideration with very important implications.

Books on conflict management in organisational contexts are very common and quite rich in descriptions of possible or preferable strategies to be used to solve or prevent conflicts. While it is easy to describe these strategies and provide a selective list of the associated pros and contras, it is not easy to anticipate what solution may turn out to be successful in concrete situations.

Here are the main alternatives that are usually listed to handle conflict:

1. Ignoring conflict (i.e., avoiding making decisions, physical separation of the conflicting groups, reduction of interaction and interdependency [Neilsen 1972] or use of verbal tactics to minimise the conflicting views in the name of the superior interest of the organisation)
2. Use of power (unilateral decisions of those who have the authority)
3. Creation of consensus
   - through the search for a common element of interest, thus generating win–win situations or emphasizing the costs of increased conflict;
   - through structured negotiation, where the parties themselves have to decide when and how to stop the conflict; or
   - through the vote by those who are legitimated by the organisational rules
4. Third-party intervention (arbitration)

Normally, ignoring conflict through the different tactics that are available is useful only when the reason for conflict is not very important for the organisational actors. In the other cases, the conflict is not eliminated but is generally only "suspended".

The attempt to create a consensus can be facilitated by a common definition of the situation and, when possible, an emphasis on the common goals, values and perspectives of the conflicting parties. In spite of this commonsense assumption, consensus is not always easy to reach since it requires time and especially involvement and interest by the participants, as well as a minimum level of value and perspective sharing that is not always available within organisations. Nevertheless, the use of a specific method requiring the conflicting parties to openly express their views in a public debate, whatever the final mode of solution will be (vote, decision of the top manager, and so on), can be helpful to preserve an acceptable degree of co-operation and an effective organisational atmosphere and to facilitate innovation, even if the conflicting views will not be overcome. The only problem on this respect is the role that emotion plays when two or more groups are confronted openly on specific issues on which very different views are supported.

Besides these main generic approaches to conflict solution, other initiatives are usually taken to dilute, solve or prevent organisational conflict:

- A more targeted use of communication
- The introduction of new rules to govern the interaction between the conflicting parties and modifications in the organisational structure
- The acceptance of free competition (the best will win)
- The creation of mixed teams (integrating diversity of culture, interest and attitude; sharing perceptions; reducing stereotypes)

The last two strategies have also been indicated as useful for those organisations in which the level of conflict is perceived as too low, thus undermining the capacity of innovation of the organisation.

Different from what occurs in many business environments, in voluntary organisations, competitive situations (facilitated, for example, by the organisational structure itself) are seldom effective because they can easily exacerbate the conflict and the associative ideology does not accommodate well the idea of internal conflicts. This is sometimes displayed in the management of elite teams; for example, when the composition of a team is decided the night before the competition and nobody is absolutely sure of making it, the level of conflict can rise beyond an acceptable level, even if in the short term the high rate of internal competition can benefit the performance.

The creation of mixed collaborating teams composed of persons belonging to different groups or organisational units is frequently suggested as a means to facilitate conflict solutions, since this would improve reciprocal attitudes, reduce prejudice and develop interdependency. However, teams must be carefully constituted, and those who have the responsibility to form them must be well aware of the potential negative consequences of a manifest intragroup conflict.

In addition, it is not always true that conflict can be better solved within a group or a team situation, as sometimes suggested, since negotiation carried out on a one-to-one basis is also possible and can be successful, especially because the negative impact of emotions is easier to control and limit.

Following the principles behind this book, we do not want to review further in depth here the usual concepts on organisational conflict management, since we are especially interested in the specificities of sport organisations. Instead, we want to focus on the conflict that is often mentioned in these organisations—the conflict between professionals and volunteers.

2.12 The Professionalisation Process and the Professional–Volunteer Conflict

Given the nature of OSOs, a persistent area of concern among sport governing bodies is the conflict between the paid professionals and the volunteer workers (Chelladurai 1987; Hinings and Slack 1987; Inglis 1997). While many areas of conflict in sport organisations are quite similar to those that we find in other kinds of organisations, and can therefore be placed in a similar conceptual framework, the conflict between the paid professionals and volunteer personnel is unique to sport organisations and has been an ongoing concern, as it is well documented, for example, in Canada (Canadian Olympic Association 1986) or in many European countries (Chantelat 2001; Madella 2001).

An important source of such conflict is the perceived expertise on the part of the paid or professional workers versus the supposed passionate but unskilled altruism on the part of volunteers. Another source of conflict that has been frequently reported is the perception of inadequate rewards for the volunteers. Differences over the degree of technical expertise and the relative contributions to policy development add to the problem (Inglis 1997). Another important element is that in many cases the turnover of paid professionals in sport organisations is higher than for volunteers, who often have accumulated essential and often tacit knowledge about the organisation, its history and culture and also access to critical information. This is also reflected in the struggles between the two groups of workers over who should control what (Amis and Slack 1996).

Group representations as they are revealed by stories, interviews and anecdotes by both components of OSOs clearly reflect these reasons for conflict; for volunteers, professional administrators are often not loyal and not really able to understand sport and its needs, and in many cases, do not accept being simple "executors" of the policies that volunteers decide. For the staff, volunteers are often considered conservative and not capable of innovation, and they are often believed to lack respect for the division of work and the principle of organisational specialisation. They are also reported to be reluctant to participate in any form of training and professional development, to be too involved in political games and to be inclined to dissolve or dilute responsibility. Moreover, commissions and committees composed of volunteers are believed to generate delays since they slow down the decisional processes, which is felt to be inadequate for the current competitive environment in which sport organisations have to operate.

Another important aspect is the perception about decision-making power; in many sport organisations, volunteers have the feeling that professionals now have a higher level of influence than they had in the past. In some cases, volunteers may agree that this is a necessary trend because they do not have enough competence and time, but in other cases, this is clearly an additional cause of conflict (Auld 1997). This structural trend has become in some ways cultural and psychological, so that the idea that professionals should take control of the organisation can become more and more diffused. Such conflicts, which pose threats and challenges to the management of human resources, have increased with the process of professionalisation of sport organisations that started in many countries in the '70s and '80s.

The professionalisation process can take quite different forms, but usually it is characterised by features such as the following:

- Increasing role of paid administrators and personnel, along with higher influence on the decision-making processes
- Increasing importance of specific skills and competencies
- Adoption of private-sector management criteria (management by results, incentive programmes, and so on) and related techniques and thereby a preference for the concept of effectiveness and efficiency compared to representation, participation and democracy
- Larger use of technologies
- Valorisation of expertise compared to "passion"
- Diffusion of procedures and formal rules
- Introduction of formal measures of output and performance (measurement or benchmarking)
- New jargon characterised by business-oriented concepts or new local concepts (e.g., entrepreneurship of the volunteers, professional volunteers)

The process has been largely accompanied by a general feeling that volunteers are no longer adequate for the new environment and has been widely documented in countries such as Canada (Slack 1997), Australia (Auld 1994; Auld 1997; Hoye and Cuskelly 2003), New Zealand (Collins 1994), France (Chantelat 2001) and Italy (Madella 2001).

Professionalisation can be recognized as a clear trend in the sport sector, but its dynamics and impact are very different in relation to the sport discipline, the size of the market, the interplay of key actors and other environmental and broader cultural factors. In spite of this obvious consideration, the concept has become an important driver of change and therefore of conflict. The process (or even the notion) of professionalisation tends to exacerbate the contrast between professionals and volunteers, since it is often interpreted in a sense that marks the superiority of the first compared to the second. Professionals are often considered not only to be more competent and therefore more skilled—for example, in dealing with customers or in acquiring funds—but also more subject to organisational discipline or social control, because of the prevalence of monetary incentives. Human resource procedures, such as assessment and career scheme, are more formalized and standardised, and this clearly has an effect on the degree of predictability of the organisation and on its rationalization.

Many scholars have described the nature of this process, its important impact on organisational relations and how the conflict between the different organisational components can regulate and influence the professionalisation process itself. The most cited model relating professionalisation, structural conflict and organisational change is surely the one developed by Kikulis, Slack and Hinings (1992). They have identified three general archetypes of sport organisations (figure 2.9) using as criteria of classification the three structural variables (complexity, formalization, and centralisation) that had been originally proposed by the well-known approach developed by the so-called Aston Group (Pugh and Hickson 1976). The three archetypes are labeled as follows:

1. Kitchen table
2. Boardroom
3. Executive office

Consistent with ideas already expressed by numerous organisational theorists (Miller and Friesen 1984; Mintzberg 1979), in these organisational archetypes, the structural elements tend to form an integrated and coherent whole (see figure 2.9).

Kikulis, Slack and Hinings (1992) have also formed a hypothesis about the existence of an evolutionary trend within this continuum for the majority of national sport governing bodies. In agreement with the theory of bureaucratization of Max Weber, specialisation of functions

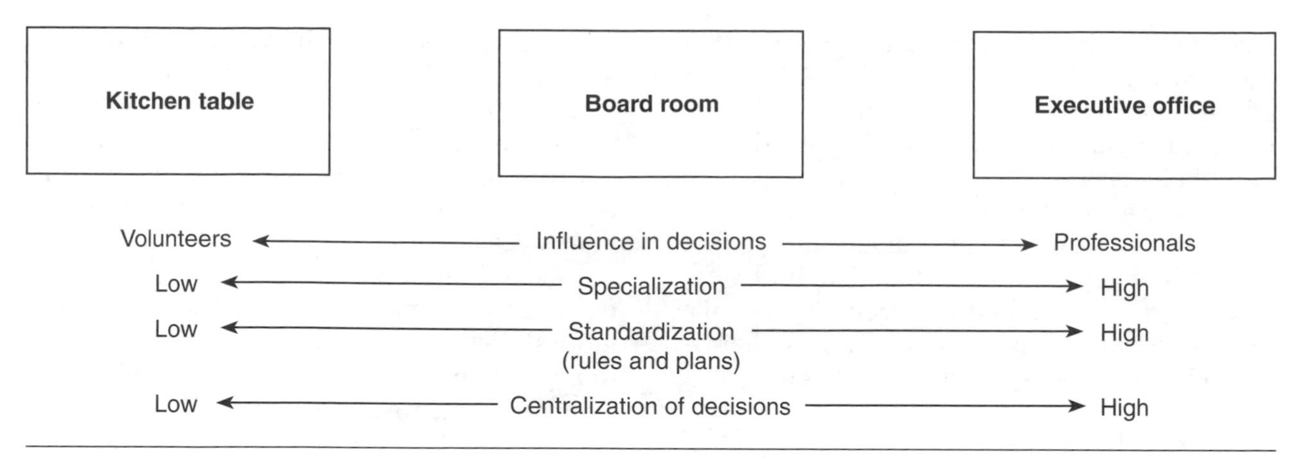

Figure 2.9 Three archetypes of sport organisations and their attributes.

usually seems to be the first change to appear in the simple structures at the kitchen table level. After that, the creation of a vertical hierarchy and the start of a formalization process will follow.

If this hypothesis is confirmed, that would mean that all the large sport organisations should and will follow the same process. This idea is in agreement with previous studies and findings in other kinds of organisations indicating that professionals will become the dominant component in organisations that are sufficiently large, formalized and decentralised (Donovan and Jackson 1991).

The increase of conflict is incorporated within this model; the kitchen table stage is essentially characterised by a low level of centralisation, with a strong control by the voluntary leaders, initially the founding members. In the following phases, decision making becomes more and more decentralised and is progressively transferred to the professional staff, whose power increases because of their superior skills, access to knowledge and the new governance models. A lot of sociological literature demonstrates that any professionalisation process is characterised by a strong tendency of the professionals to gain power and associate it with knowledge and formal expertise. At this stage of development, volunteers only have the symbolic power to ratify and give the final approval to decisions that are made by those who control the resources and especially the information.

These analyses show that interpreting the power relations within OSOs simply as the result of the conflict between volunteers and professionals or between boards and CEOs does not represent the reality of the organisations, which is much more complex. Another important point is that there is no clear scientific evidence of increase of performance associated with this specific transition process from simple to "executive office" organisations.

There are multiple elements of empirical evidence of this transition, even though in many circumstances the supposed linear transition between "kitchen table" organisations and "executive office" organisations controlled by professionals is far from being automatic and fully achieved (Madella 2001). Auld (1997) notes that the full extent of these changes in the Australian situation is not clear: It is true that the current situation is a sort of mixed one where sport organisations are jointly managed by volunteers and professionals, but the balance between the two is very different since there are variable levels of "decision-making power" (p. 20). Kikulis and associates have recognized that the professionalisation process is far from being uniform (Kikulis 1989; Thibault, Slack and Hinings 1991); they have also noted that the relative speed of this change process is often very different and have identified numerous national sport organisations that could have been placed in between two archetypes. According to these Canadian scholars, the decision-making process is the most resistant to the impact of the professionalisation process, probably because of the strong influence of the values driving this kind of organisation.

The variability of the outcomes of the professionalisation process has been confirmed by Murray, Bradshaw and Wolpin (1992), who have classified organisations (or specifically, their boards) on the basis of the relative distribution of the power between the board and the executive management. They have distinguished the following:

- An executive-dominated board, where the main decisions are made by the paid staff (because of the superior knowledge and expertise)
- A chair-dominated board, where power is concentrated in the hands of a charismatic president
- A fragmented-power board (with transversal coalitions)
- A power-sharing board (with a more democratic and participative orientation)
- A powerless board, without effective leadership and communication

Hoye and Cuskelly (2003) have empirically tested this classification on Australian sport governing bodies with good results, thus confirming the heterogeneity of the evolution of the national governing bodies, at least with reference to power allocation. Chappelet and Bayle (2004) have proposed a similar classification differentiating between four main forms of governance: (1) strong presidency; (2) president acting "in tandem" with another executive (usually the CEO, but sometimes the technical director), (3) split presidency (power shared with other managers); and (4) managerial control by the professionals.

Koski and Heikkala (1998), on the basis of the analysis of the evolution of Finnish sport organisations, have concluded that "professionalization in voluntary-based sport organizations is at least in Finnish cases—a specific and context bound process" (p. 11). The research carried out by Nier and Sheard (1999) showed that "the professionalisation of rugby football clubs does not lead automatically to logical, economically-rational business base structure".

Based on all these results, the question can be raised whether the evolution towards the *executive office* model of organisation is really an inevitable trend in the sport sector and what its implications really are for the role to be played by volunteers in the future. Auld (1994) had noted that regardless of the process of professionalisation, in many cases professionals are not allowed to intervene in selected areas of decision making, and this would preserve the role of the policy-making volunteers but at the same time increase the chances of conflict (Amis, Slack and Berret 1995; Koski and Heikkala 1998). Again, Nier and Sheard (1999) have compared the evolution of five elite clubs in different countries. The results of their study show that each organisation, if exposed to the same kind of environmental pressure, responded very differently to the change process, and this was due essentially to the impact of the internal culture and history and to local specificities.

We should also never forget that the professionalisation process does not just occur like an eruption or a hurricane but has social causes and driving forces that are influenced by human agency and deliberate strategies, for example, by national governments, as has been the case in Canada in the past (Harvey, Thibault and Rail 1995; MacIntosh and Whitson 1990; Slack, Berrett and Mistry 1994) and in Flanders more recently. Modernization programmes have been adopted or advocated to facilitate the transformation of structures and culture in this direction. This means that the discussion about professionalisation or the different models of change is not just a scientific dispute on what is going to happen in the near future, but it is also a key question for the development of general organisational strategies and change management. Slack and associates have also emphasized a kind of isomorphic pressure to change acting on organisations in the same sector. According to this view, which essentially follows the concepts formulated by Di Maggio and Powell (1983) and Meyer and Rowan (1977), organisations operating in the same sector tend to take the same organisational configuration, either because of external pressure (e.g., the government) or other internal factors (imitation, reciprocal adaptation or the need for legitimacy). Digel (2005) has made the same point in his comparison of elite sport structures in different countries.

2.13 Managing the Professional–Volunteer Conflict

The previous analysis of the process of professionalisation has revealed that in spite of its variable forms, the potential for professional–volunteer conflict is very high. For this reason, the management of this specific conflict is one of the most recurrent preoccupations for an OSO's leaders and managers. Given the importance of collective representations and group identity, one preliminary step in dealing with the professional–volunteer conflict could be to identify the common elements that underlie professionalism and volunteerism, respectively. Professionals are characterised by a great need for

- *knowing* (mastering the knowledge unique to the field),
- *doing* (application of that knowledge to solving the problems on hand), and
- *helping* others (Merton 1982).

This concept should be conveniently managed and exploited in management practice. When we consider that volunteers join a sport organisation to *help* others, that they want to *learn* (i.e., to *know*) how best to serve their clients, and that they actually *do* things for their clients, we realize that the fundamental bases of both professionalism and volunteerism are not that different.

Gidron (1983) has compared the reasons for job-related satisfaction for both volunteers and professionals and has concluded that in many cases the key components for satisfaction are essentially the same, from the appreciation of the work per se, to task achievement and a non-stressful environment. This concept should be exploited and managed properly. Obviously, in managing professional–volunteer conflicts, an immediate problem is identifying who has the responsibility. Managers in charge of that should help the parties in conflict to identify common drivers of their action and the potential for synergies, at least up to a certain point. Besides that, managers of such organisations should be able to think and analyze the situation simultaneously from the point of view of the volunteers and eventually of other stakeholders. This is well represented by the concept of "organisations of mixed rationales" that Koski and Heikkala (1998) have coined for the Finnish sport organisations, but that can easily be adapted to many others in different countries. Mixed rationales means that voluntary sport organisations integrate at least two perspectives and logics: the one of the volunteers and that of the professionals.

Another useful way to deal with the structural conflict between these two components is to make efforts to understand the problems, characteristics and social influences of volunteers. This means essentially viewing problems from a different perspective. Also, the psychological implications that derive from the professionalisation process for the volunteers should be taken into consideration. Translated into management terms, this means that volunteers (as well as other components) should have **formal opportunities** to express their opinion in planned contexts, and that these opinions should be considered for action.

We would like to stress again these aspects:

- The organisation should put in place events and meeting places where the volunteers are recognized and can give their contribution.
- These actions should never be just formal; volunteers cannot become simple lackeys but must perceive clearly that they are an essential resource of the organisation.

If these opportunities are lacking, volunteers can easily become apathetic or use their remaining power to marginalize the professionals. In organisations of mixed rationale, conflict can be prevented or at least attenuated if, for example, mixed teams are set up, encouraged and rewarded. Professionals could be integrated in bodies usually constituted by volunteers and be more exposed to the specific organisational culture. This would increase interaction, share responsibility and possibly develop new social relations.

Organisational Design and Human Resource Management in Olympic Sport Organisations

In numerous textbooks dedicated to the management of human resources, organisational structures and design are not included because they are not considered a pertinent topic. We believe, however, that the way the work is divided and coordinated in an organisation has a great impact on people's action and co-operation and on their individual and collective performance. Therefore, it must be analyzed from a specific HRM perspective. However, caution should be suggested to the managers of OSOs to avoid concentrating too much on formal structures, therefore underestimating the role of human agency and individual and group strategies within a specific organisational environment (Child 1972; Crozier and Friedberg 1977). Whatever the organisational structure, managers always have a certain degree of autonomy and discretion.

3.1 Organisational Structures, Design and Configurations

The structure is an important means to achieve the organisational goals within a specific environment. The organisational structure includes essentially the allocation of the different tasks, the authority and formal communication lines and the mechanisms that are put into function to ensure effective coordination. Coordination is obviously necessary to avoid duplication of work, to improve synergies, to monitor plans and therefore to ensure the achievement of the goals. Organisational structures can differ a lot on many respects. They can be classified according to many different criteria, which usually can be grasped through the analysis of the specific organisational chart.[1] The most

1. However, all managers (regardless of the sector, size and scope of the organisation) should be aware that, in spite of the precision with which the organisational structure is defined through the organisational chart, organisations always incorporate **informal systems of relations** (i.e., the **informal structure**). Informal structures are characterised by forms of cross-communication or power exercise that do not usually correspond to those predictable on the basis of the formal organisational chart, but that sometimes can be extremely influential to preserve the efficiency and the speed of reaction of the organisation.

cited classification that is explained in all the management manuals is based on the nature of departmental structures (classified by function, clients, geography or process). With reference to the distribution of the authority, organisations are also usually differentiated between tall vertical structures, where we find numerous hierarchic levels, and flat structures, where the hierarchy is less developed. Management textbooks on sport organisations provide abundant technical information and scientific evidence on all these organisational forms, and we refer interested readers to these sources (Chelladurai 2005; Slack 1997).

Other important factors can also be used to group organisations; for example, we have already referred to the following three "**structural variables**" (Pugh and Hickson 1976) as an important way of looking at and differentiating organisations:

- **Specialisation or complexity** (the degree of organisational differentiation; that is, vertical, horizontal or geographic differentiation)
- **Formalization** (the extent to which the organisational life is governed by formal rules, procedures and policies)
- **Centralisation** (the degree to which authority or decision making is concentrated in one or a few points of the organisation or dispersed across the different levels)

What is especially interesting for the purpose of this book is not a general analysis of the differences between the various categories of these classifications, but rather their eventual consequences in terms of human resource management, which we will outline here.

Designing an organisation involves the setup or the change of the systemic relations between the different parts that are critical to its functioning and to the delivery of its distinctive products and services. We must note that even if the preoccupation to build an effective structure is very strong in all OSOs, it is very difficult if not impossible to demonstrate a clear and objective relationship between organisational structure and performance. In other words, different structures can be equally successful in different situations and contexts.

The importance of the context must not be underestimated. In fact, it is useful to think of organisations as systems with an important degree of interaction with a relevant environment (see section 3.2). When talking about organisational structure, the reference to the context has to be especially emphasized. A first influence of the context on the organisational structure has been indicated by Child (1972). He has shown that different organisational fields (sectors) are characterised by different organisational designs compared to others, because of the impact of dominating concepts typical of that context, which tend to be imitated, at least to a certain extent. "Isomorphic" pressures to take similar forms are often visible within a specific sector or organisational field (Di Maggio and Powell 1983).

Another point to consider is the relationship between structure and strategy (Robbins 1990; Slack 1997). We do not want to provide any prescription on this respect, but it is plausible that starting from the structure and not from the strategy can be a source of organisational mismanagement. In our view, imposing an abstract organisational model without looking, for example, at the external (environment) and internal aspects (i.e., existing human resources and their competence) within the general framework of the organisation strategy can turn out to be a mistake.

All this happens because the setup of the organisational structures is not just a technical issue or the outcome of purely rational design processes. The nature of the environment tends to influence the characteristics of the organisation; for example, turbulent environments seem to be better dealt with by more flexible and less formalized structures (Slack 1997). The influencing factors are not limited to the external environment but also include various internal aspects, such as the specific tradition or the organisational values. Hinings et al. (1996) have found a significant association between a specific organisational structure (or an archetype) and the dominant organisational values (mainly recognizable in the elite of the same organisations). This has an important consequence for a change-oriented management perspective: Changing an organisation should essentially involve the sphere of values. It is true that many cases of major organisational changes have been determined or imposed by external agents (i.e., the government), but the speed and stability of these change processes are significantly increased if a modification in the values of the organisational actors supports the change (Hinings et al. 1996).

Let's go back to the idea expressed previously that it is useful to consider the relationship between the way the work is organised and coordinated and the human resource management practices and problems. First of all, it is quite reasonable to think that different organisational configurations can be characterised by different models of human resource management. Therefore, an OSO's managers must have a good understanding of the possible relationships between organisational structures and human resource management models.

An intuitive example can help clarify this theme: A simple and less formalized organisation is less likely to have developed procedures for staffing or for appraising the employees. In similar organisations, the pay system will probably be simple, and the supervision of the employees is usually quite direct. More complex organisations require more fragmented and decentralised systems of supervision. Flat organisations (i.e., those with less hierarchic levels) are characterised by a higher degree of informal relationships, and this often facilitates the creation of stronger personal relations (e.g., friendship) between the organisational members (Collins 1975). Empowerment practices can have more or less chance of success in relation to the specific organisational structures.

Many authors have tried to develop this idea further. For example, De Coster (1978) has used in an original way the well-known model developed by Mintzberg (1979) to illustrate and understand the relationship between organisational structure and global human resource management. Mintzberg has generated a well-known typology of organisations that differentiates five ideal types, clustering in different ways the basic constitutive elements of organisations:

- Simple structures (i.e., small businesses)
- Machine bureaucracies
- Professional bureaucracies
- Divisionalised structures
- Adhocracies, where decision making does not depend particularly on the authority structure and hierarchy

Numerous scholars have applied this typology to the world of sport organisations with slight modifications essentially to understand the nature and the internal logic of the different sport organisations and sometimes their individual positioning in the professionalisation process. Theodoraki and Henry (1994), for example, have developed Mintzberg's typology in order to classify NGBs in Britain according to six main dimensions determined on the basis of structural variables. Their typology differs from Mintzberg's particularly for the large number of variations on the simple structure. In fact, they have distinguished

- machine bureaucracies,
- professional bureaucracies,
- professionalised simple structures,
- typical simple structures,
- simple bureaucracies, and
- specialised simple structures.

In this chapter, we are not interested so much in the typologies per se. Instead, we want to discuss the concept that this typology can be associated with a set of configurations with specific ways of coordination and suitable modes of managing the human resources. The question is whether organisations with a specific configuration require a specific way to manage their human resources.

In the Entrepreneurial configuration, human resources are managed informally and decisions are made at the apex (e.g., the President of the sport organisation may hire someone without any formal procedures). In the bureaucratic model, there are clear formal and impersonal procedures to manage human resources which are uniformly applied to everyone. In the professional model, the professionals are dominant in making decisions affecting the organisation and the human resources therein. In contrast to the bureaucratic and professional models, the missionary and adhocratic configurations are much less formalized. In the missionary configuration, decisions regarding human resources are most likely to be guided by values and thus less formalized rules and regulations. In the adhocratic form of organisation, the rules are flexible and negotiable, and thus the human resource decisions are likely to be individually based.

In spite of this generic correspondence, however, we must consider that numerous other contextual factors can influence the model used to manage human resource practices within each individual organisation. These factors include the technology, the characteristics of the market, the cultural aspects and the form of regulation (or deregulation) of the global and sectorial labour market. So, once again, no deterministic relationship or best way can be found on this respect.

For example, in a specific market, if there is an abundance of qualified workers with a good level of skills, the organisations operating in this environment will probably prefer to train them for the job using flexible forms of in-house training to be sure that these skills really match the needs of the organisation at that particular moment. On the other hand, if the general level of qualification and competence of the workers is low, then it could be more convenient to outsource the training process.

Other structural variables can influence the nature of the human resource management within an organisation. For example, the size of the organisation is also believed to have a significant influence on the HRM model chosen, being an important element influencing the determination of an organisational structure (Blau and Schoenherr 1971; Pugh et al. 1969). Even if common sense indicates this notion can be quite acceptable, the relation between size and structure is not simple, and some scientists have supported the idea that it is probably more the structure that influences size rather than the opposite (Hall, Haas and Johnson 1967). Another aspect is related to the span of control; in flat, horizontal structures, the span of control (i.e., the number of people supervised by a single individual) is wider, and this often can be a facilitating factor for developing commitment and organisational loyalty.

3.2 Olympic Sport Organisations As Systems

A problem for OSOs is how to find an effective organisational setup for each organisation on the basis of its specific environment, history and vision of the future. Mintzberg does not think that one configuration is necessarily more effective than others; these models can be more or less suitable to achieve the organisational goals according to specific contingencies, the size and the life cycle of an organisation. In spite of this statement, it is useful to reflect on the way the different organisational components are coordinated and on the main issues to be considered to promote organisational effectiveness.

In this regard, Chelladurai (1987) proposed that the typical design of a sport governing body followed Parsons' (1960) three-tiered hierarchy consisting of the *technical subsystem*, the *managerial subsystem* and the *institutional subsystem* (see figure 3.1). The technical subsystem is where the organisation's outputs (goods or services) are actually produced. The *mass* and *elite* sport programmes are examples of technical subsystems of an OSO, but certainly many other kinds of technical units can be imagined. The mass technical unit consists of the leaders, operational managers and other personnel involved

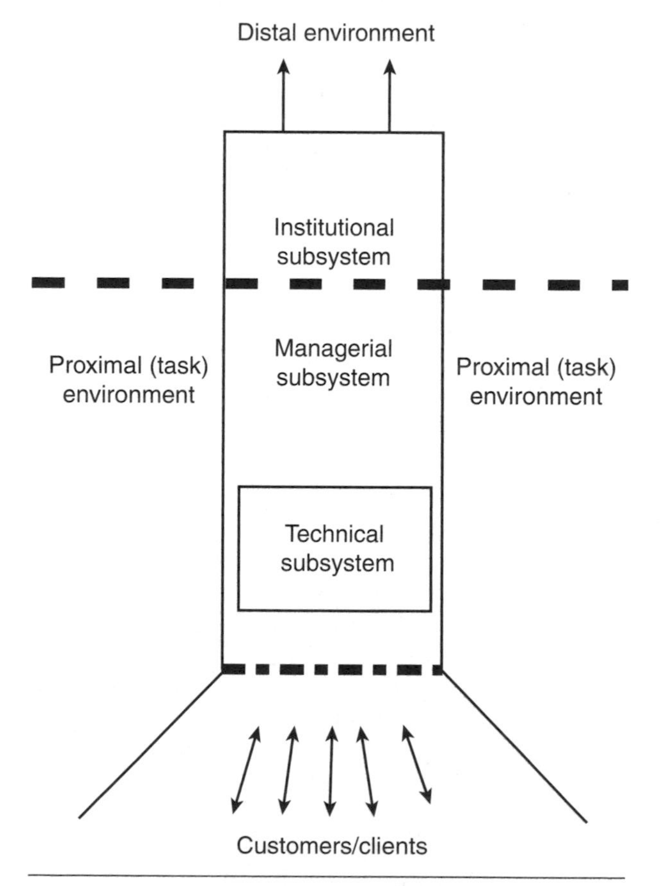

Figure 3.1 Vertical differentiation in an OSO.

Reprinted from P. Chelladurai, 2001, System based organizing. In *Managing organizations for sport and physical activity* (Scottsdale, AZ: Holcomb Hathaway), 219. By permission of author.

in the promotion and selling of the sport to the large public. In a sense, even the clubs and their members are part of this mass unit. The specific task for the mass technical unit of an OSO is the promotion of sport and the provision of recreational opportunities for members of a community. On the other hand, the elite technical unit includes the coaches, the team officials and the athletes of the provincial, regional, national and other representative teams. The task of the elite technical unit of an OSO is to enhance the performance capabilities of the athletes and teams in the pursuit of excellence in sport.

The higher-level managerial subsystem is charged with the responsibilities of mediating between the technical subsystem and those who use its products and procuring the necessary resources for the technical units. The executive committee and the paid administrators of an OSO constitute the managerial subsystem. Their main task is to ensure the smooth operation of the technical subsystems by finding and providing material resources as well as appropriate conditions and facilities, by coordinating their activities and by interacting with external agents (e.g., the national or provincial counterparts; the other OSOs, especially the governing bodies; government agencies; or educational institutions) who have a direct bearing on the activities of the technical subsystems. Another important function of the managerial subsystem is to be a linking mechanism between the technical subsystems and the institutional subsystem at the top of the hierarchy.

Clearly, no organisation can be effective if its operations are restricted to just the production and exchange of its products with its customers and clients. Every organisation needs to respond to and interact with superior agencies representing the larger society and its demands and dictates. Sport is no exception. Thus, every organisation has to design itself in such a way that one of its units will be well equipped to deal with these superior agencies. Parsons would call this unit the institutional subsystem. The board of directors would constitute the institutional subsystem of an OSO. The **institutional subsystem** is responsible for setting objectives and broad guidelines for the OSO, hiring professional staff and providing general supervision of OSO activities. Another more important set of tasks revolve around interacting with significant resource contributors such as the higher echelons in government agencies, corporations, universities, other social institutions and even wealthy and powerful individuals. The successful interactions of the OSO with its international and continental federations, its national Olympic committee and the International Olympic Committee are critical for the effectiveness of the OSO.

In overview, the technical subsystem is mainly concerned with task performance, the managerial subsystem with the facilitation of such task performance, and the institutional subsystem with legitimizing the OSO and its activities. Naturally, it is often difficult to demarcate in a precise way the boundaries of these functions and systems, so real organisational life shows a significant possibility of ambiguity and uncertainty in the relationship between institutions and management. Nevertheless, the principles of the three-tiered hierarchy seem to keep substantial validity.

As noted, these three subsystems are commonly seen in operation. But, the real issue is whether an OSO follows Parsons' principles of

- aligning the differentiated units (particularly the institutional and managerial subsystems) with relevant sectors of the environmental sectors they face;
- insulating as much as possible the technical core from environmental turbulences; and
- securing the independence and autonomy of the three subsystems.

Subsystem–Environment Alignment

Although the need to strengthen the boundary-spanning activities is important, the alignment of the institutional subsystem with the more external (distal) environment and the alignment of the managerial subsystem with the proximal environment of the organisation are even more critical in Parsons' framework (see figure 3.1). The proximal environment refers to individuals and units that are in close relationship to the organisation—those that engage in identical or similar activities, supply the resources for the focal organisation, consume its outputs or in some way directly affect the organisation. In the case of an OSO, elements in the proximal environment (i.e., the immediate task environment) would include other OSOs; the provincial, national or international counterparts of the local OSO; the government agencies with which the local OSO is in direct contact; and public sport departments or ministries. In Parsons' view, the major responsibility for interacting with this proximal environment should be assigned to the managerial subsystem.

The domain of activities for the institutional subsystem of an OSO will be focused on the distal environment. In other words, the interactions of the board of directors of an OSO will be confined to significant elements in the larger society represented by higher levels of government, businesses and industries (i.e., the potential sponsors or benefactors), as well as other individuals or organisations that are not in direct contact with the OSO but can contribute in various ways to its continued growth and stability. Thus, the institutional and managerial subsystems exert their influence in different directions and domains. Their efforts are not dissipated in influencing or controlling each other.

Insulation of the Technical System

Parsons' second prescription is that the organisation should seal off its technical core from environmental turbulences in order to enable the core to continue with the production process without undue interruptions. As noted earlier, the technical units of an OSO are usually its mass and elite programmes. However, the degree to which each of these units—mass and elite sport—should be insulated from the environment is different. By its very nature, mass sport requires that the members of this unit be in contact with that segment of the environment that consists of present as well as prospective partners (i.e., schools, universities, local networks). A broken line in figure 3.1 illustrates the permeability of the boundary marking the mass sport unit. In contrast, the technical core of the elite programme consisting of a limited number of athletes and coaches can easily be (and needs to be) sealed off from environmental disturbances.

Independence of Units

Parsons' central thrust that there should be a clear break in the hierarchy of authority among the three subsystems is contrary to the common belief that a hierarchy is a simple structure involving the continuity of a line from top to bottom of the organisation. However, given the differences in the tasks and the diversity of expertise or abilities required to carry out these tasks, any attempts at direct supervision of the lower system by the higher would only be dysfunctional. Therefore, the authority relationships in the two interfaces—between the board and management and between management and the technical unit—should be structured to ensure that the relative independence of each unit is protected. A specific example of the way the relationships between these two levels are regulated is provided by the Australian Sports Commission in a document listing the main governance principle for NSOs:

> The governance structure should feature a clear separation of powers and responsibilities between the board (mind of organisation) and the CEO and his/her staff (hands of organisation). This clarity of powers and responsibilities must also apply to the various board and management committees. The governance structure should also recognise that individual directors, the CEO (or similar), his/her staff, board committees and management meetings hold no authority to act on behalf of the organisation by virtue of their position alone. All authority rests with the board, which may delegate authority to any person or committee. Each such delegation should be clearly documented in a delegations manual or similar. Normally there shall be significant delegations to the CEO. (Australian Sports Commission 2002, p. 3, item 1.4)

3.3 The Role and the Composition of the Executive Board in Olympic Sport Organisations

How much does the model we have discussed correspond to the real functioning of OSOs? Is the model inspired by Parsons in the '50s still useful and appropriate? Do the prescriptions that can be derived from the model have a real scientific or practical foundation? These questions are strongly related to the latest developments of the concept of **governance** of OSOs. In fact, the recent years have been characterised by a significant ongoing international debate about corporate governance—especially after big scandals such as the ENRON and Parmalat cases—in the domain of profit-making companies. Even if the important reforms carried out in different countries on this respect (e.g., the Sarbanes-Oxley Act in the United States) do not in principle apply to nonprofit organisations, OSOs have not been left outside this debate. This is demonstrated by the ongoing discussion in the IOC and numerous national and international federations that has especially tackled the issues of transparency, communication, social responsibility and accountability.[2]

In this context, we will not be discussing the general issue of the obligations of OSOs towards the society (what has become known as social responsibility) or of governance (which has already been analyzed, for example, by Chappelet and Bayle [2004]) while discussing the concepts and strategies of performance management specifically for this kind of organisation. We would, however, like to mention some important points related to the new concepts of governance that have a special impact on human resource management and on the expectations of the role to be played by the institutional subsystem, according to the previously mentioned Parsons' model. By that we mean essentially the role and the function of the board. Boards are crucial components of good governance and are essential to set the policies and carry on the mission of an organisation, even if a precise relationship between organisational and board effectiveness is very difficult to determine (Hoye and Cuskelly 2003). The board also appoints persons to key positions (e.g., CEOs, directors) and defines the nature and content of their functions. The board is responsible and accountable to the members and has a duty to balance the interests of the different organisational constituencies when designing or approving strategic plans.

For this reason, the nature and functioning of voluntary boards is one of the most popular subjects in scientific and practitioner literature on the management of nonprofit organisations (Connors 1988; Herman and Heimovics 1991).

The size of the board, the competence of the members and its relations with other structural components of the organisation are all critical elements. For example, there is common agreement that a board that is too large, which often occurs in constituent-based governance organisations, may hinder effective organisational performance.

However, the functions that the boards have can be quite different; they can be more or less executive functions, so their grasp of the daily activities of an organisation can be different. This will also vary the importance to the board of accessing information concerning the activities of the organisations and monitoring its achievements.

Board–Management Interface

According to Mintzberg (1983), apart from the overall supervisory and decision-making function (i.e., its internal function), the board has a significant external function. As a tool of the organisation, the board serves it by co-opting external influencers, establishing contacts and raising funds for it, enhancing its reputation and providing it with advice. Accordingly, the focus of the board of directors of an OSO should be externally oriented, thus leaving the control of the internal operations to the executive committee and to the executive director and other paid administrators.

We must note, however, that boards that are too externally oriented might be confronted with significant problems in their relationships with the management and other organisational components (Price 1963). Of course, "real" organisations are very different in size and structural articulation, and this could slightly modify the nature of the relationship between the three tiers, which is also influenced by more external factors such as the culture, the technology and the labour market. Generally, simpler organisational models tend to have more interferences between the levels (Theodoraki and Henry 1994).

2. For example, the First European Conference on the Governance of Sport was held in Brussels, in February 2001. It was organised by the EOC (European Olympic Committees) and FIA (www.governance-in-sport.com).

On this respect, Parsons emphasized that the managerial subsystem should be provided sufficient autonomy and power to discharge its responsibilities, and that it should be able to "negotiate with them [the board] from a position of relative strength, not just to go to them for instruction" (1960, p. 69). Pfeffer (1972) and Provan (1980) have also concluded that the efficacy and efficiency of the board–management interface can only be evaluated by determining how well their respective external environments have been handled.

Management–Technical Unit Interface

Just as in the case of the board–management interface, there should be a clear break in the authority structure between the managerial and technical subsystems. For example, the board should not be involved in the day-to-day management of the operations, which is clearly the task of the CEO (or his or her equivalent) and their staff. The board has the responsibility to recruit, evaluate and eventually dismiss the CEO. In agreement with the CEO, all the other relevant positions should also be chosen by the board. For the CEO and all the other positions of responsibility, the person chosen must have great competence in running complex organisations and wide understanding of sport and interorganisational relationships.

In a high-performance technical unit, the managers (e.g., the coaches) of the technical unit must have almost complete autonomy in their operations—in the selection of the staff as well as the athletes, and in the organisation of activities, including training and competitions. The managerial subsystem (consisting of the executive committee and the professional staff) should ensure the integrity of the team and the autonomy of the coaches and their officials, even from the intrusions of its own institutional subsystem. It would appear from reports of continuing conflicts between coaches and the administrators that some OSOs do not adhere to this principle. This can be surprising since many effective sport organisations, including professional and university teams, permit great autonomy and authority to their coaches.

3.4 Forming a Powerful Board in Olympic Sport Organisations

Differentiation within an OSO refers to both the division of activities (departmentalisation or divisionalisation) based on the environmental diversity faced by the organisation and, equally important, to the staffing of the appropriate personnel to carry out the different categories of tasks. In the present context, those who are assigned to the boundary-spanning roles (i.e., the board members) must possess the necessary prerequisites to be able to influence the relevant units or individuals within their respective environmental sectors. Board ineffectiveness is commonly indicated as a primary reason for the overall lack of effectiveness of voluntary sport organisations at all levels (Hoye and Cuskelly 2003). According to Mintzberg (1983), these prerequisites are some form of power and the *will* and *skill* to exercise that power.

Voluntary organisations are truly political systems; power is continuously exerted by professionals and volunteers to influence decisions and actions in order to satisfy personal or group interests. All the main components of the organisational activity are targeted by the concrete exercise of power (global goals, specific objectives, organisational arrangements, procedures to distribute resources, choice of partners and publics).

The Will

The "will" refers to an individual's predisposition to influence, control and direct others. This type of will is largely a function of personality traits such as the need for dominance and the need for power (McClelland and Burnham 1976). McClelland and Burnham dispel the negative connotations associated with the notion of power by suggesting that there is a "socialised face of power". In fact, they have shown that individuals with a high need for power coupled with a concern for organisational goals are effective and highly respected managers.

The Skill

The "skill" refers to the ability to use the bases of power effectively; the ability to convince other people; the ability to use one's resources, information and technical skills to their fullest in bargaining with other people; and the ability to know where to concentrate one's energies. Skill also includes abilities in communication and persuasion, and adeptness in presenting a case. Special skills are also needed in order to preserve the perception of legitimation of the board, which is an important component of its effectiveness.

Daft (2001) has indicated three sets of tactics associated with power and politics in organisations. The first set of tactics is aimed at *increasing the power* base and it includes engaging in areas of high uncertainty, creating dependencies among peers and subordinates, providing resources to people/units who matter, and satisfying strategic constituents. The second set of tactics is focused on *using the power* one has by building coalitions, creating and expanding networks, controlling the decision processes, portraying legitimacy and expertise and expressing personal preferences without emphasizing personal power. The purpose of the final set of tactics is *to increase collaboration* by creating integrative mechanisms, negotiating and debating, consulting with groups and emphasising the mission and goals of the group/organisation.

The OSO could benefit from following the lead of other organisations and attempting to form "powerful boards" by recruiting individuals of high political, economic or charismatic standing. Respected positions in the local community have been indicated as an important criterion for board performance (Herman and Heimovics 1991; Papadimitriou 1999). As Pfeffer (1973) noted, the more an organisation (i.e., the OSO in our context) is dependent on private donations and sponsorships, the more important it is for the board to have the capacity to raise funds and therefore to have an effective network with the leading personalities of the local community. On the other hand, when the access to financial resources of an organisation is dependent on public funding, the capacity to interact effectively with the politicians or the public administrators is more important. The members of the board should be recruited for their contacts and their ability to generate and raise funds for the OSO.

However, we should never forget that, different from private companies, in all OSOs the formation of the board is normally the result of an election process, where power is conferred to the board by the congress or general assembly (figure 3.2). In this process, apart from competence or positioning in a community, the power and friendship relationship, loyalty and proximity have a substantial importance. This aspect is an essential component of democracy and participation and is often linked to geographical representation or delegation systems with provincial, regional or state elected bodies. Another key element is the typology of the organisation, which is related to its governance structure. Smith (1993, p. 66) has noted that organisations that can be classified as "instrumental (productive for members)" tend to be "more relaxed about effective board policies, caring more for relationships than output".

Normally, the basic structural unit at the decision-making level includes the assembly or congress, the council or board, and a variable number of committees and commissions that are led by those that we have called policy-making volunteers (see figure 3.2).

The challenge here is then how to make compatible two apparently contrary perspectives: (1) the efficiency that is apparently required by commercialisation and elite competition and (2) the voluntary spirit and representation principles. Interestingly, many states or public authorities have simultaneously endorsed both perspectives by placing higher demands

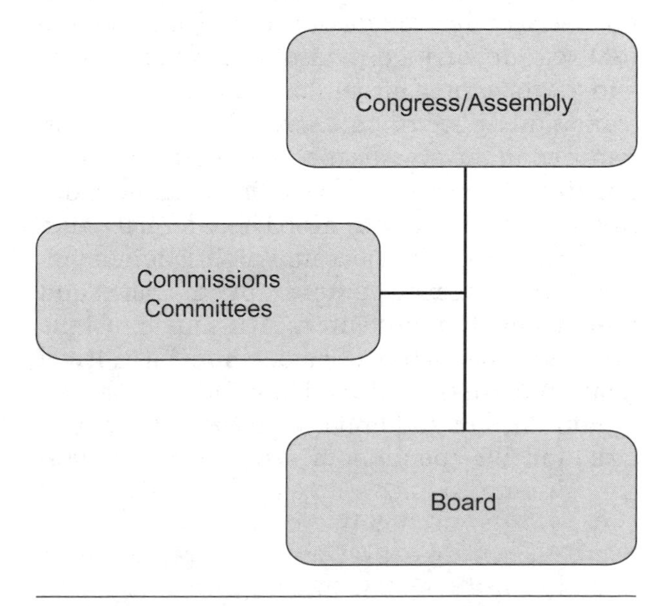

Figure 3.2 The institutional system in OSOs.

on sport bodies (thus requiring higher levels of professionalisation) but at the same time encouraging volunteer recruitment and programmes, without being fully aware of the potential contradiction between these two approaches, especially when not properly managed and coordinated. The third route is that of volunteer professionalisation, which seems to be fascinating but is easier to illustrate than to implement in practice.

We must note that the more powerful the board becomes, the more necessary it is for the managerial and technical subsystems to be strong; that is, the power of the managers below the level of the board should be commensurate with that of the board itself. Such power of the lower managers should be institutionalized within the OSO. Also, the recruitment of the managers should be based on their personal bases of power. This concept goes along with the idea that the board and executive managers should be good partners (an idea that is often found in the practically oriented management literature). This commonsense view, however, is not really supported by any scientific evidence as being a key factor of superior organisational performance (Hoye and Cuskelly 2003).

How is it possible to make compatible these concepts of effectiveness, efficiency, representation and perceived influence? The question of "qualification" and competences of the components of the board has become more and more relevant in recent years as the debate on governance has progressed. To carry out tasks that are increasingly complex and articulated and to develop and control effective policies in a highly competitive environment, passion and enthusiasm are not sufficient anymore. Character and commitment are essential but not sufficient requirements; board members should have comprehension of the sport, experience in managing complex organisations and international or national contacts and prestige. Independence of board members and absence of conflict of interest should also be considered.

Formal tools and procedures have to be developed for this specific purpose; this means that specific candidature forms should be created for all members and that the requirements for specific and diversified positions in the board should be created and communicated. Figure 3.3 provides an example of how the board responsibilities in national sport organisations have been described by the Australian Sports Commission in its document on the principle of governance (2002).

Biographical information about board members should be constantly made public, including information about relations with commercial organisations or other public or private bodies. This is actually an important requisite for transparency of governance.

In addition, other tools can be designed and implemented to assure a smooth outcome of the decision-making process. Such tools can include the formalization of guidelines and principles regulating, for example, the conflict of interest, the adoption of policy guidelines and other directives.

- Set the broad strategic direction of the organisation through appropriate consultation with stakeholders. This includes determining the organisation's purpose, core values and the ethical framework as well as key objectives and performance measures.
- Appoint and direct the CEO, support the CEO's professional development, evaluate the CEO's performance and determine the remuneration of the CEO. Where necessary, the board may be called upon to dismiss the CEO.
- Monitor the financial and nonfinancial performance of the organisation.
- Ensure that financial and nonfinancial risks are appropriately managed.
- Ensure that the organisation complies with all relevant laws, codes of conduct and appropriate standards of behavior.
- Provide an avenue for key stakeholder input into the strategic direction of the organisation.

Figure 3.3 The responsibilities of the board in national sport organisations.

Reprinted, by permission, from Australian Sports Commission, *Governance in Sport—Principle 1 from Sport Innovation and Best Practice.*

four

Managing Diversity in the Workplace

Thomas (1996) noted that the concept of diversity underlies all managerial decisions and actions. All definitions of management point to the coordination of various elements including people and their activities. We noted earlier that the traditional staffing and training processes take into account the diversity among individuals in their talents and abilities—as well as psychological dispositions—and match them with requirements of specific tasks.

However, the traditional managerial concerns with diversity deal with differences in organisationally relevant or task-relevant attributes. For example, when a sport governing body hires a person with a degree in sport marketing over a person with a degree in cultural anthropology, the decision is justified based on the task-relevant knowledge about sport and marketing of sports. The modern concerns, however, deal mostly with diversity in task-irrelevant attributes. The differences in gender, race, language, religion and culture could lead to considerable disturbance and conflict in the workplace. Since every society is fast becoming multicultural, every national and especially international sport governing body is faced with a diverse workforce as well as diverse clients.

4.1 Expressions of Diversity

Some of the task-irrelevant attributes are visible in terms of physique, facial appearance and color. These inherited or biologically determined features cannot be easily altered. Within these categories, there are also differences among people in visibly apparent preferences for certain types of dress, makeup or food, as well as other cultural and religious mores. These mores, customs and preferences that are based on culture and religion can be given up if an individual so chooses. This is what the proponents of the melting pot theory would advocate. But modern approaches to diversity management would hold that the individual should not be forced to give up any of these mores and preferences. Chelladurai (2001) labelled these the *symbolic expressions* of cultural and religious beliefs—those that are identified through symbols such as the unique dresses, the food preferences, religious practices, and so on. These have also been called surface-level or observable differences.

The *substantive expressions* of diversity are based on values, beliefs, attitudes, cognitive functioning, education and experience that are not readily apparent (Chelladurai 2001). These have been labelled deep-level or nonobservable differences. These substantive expressions have ramifications for the functioning of work groups within the sport governing body and the organisation as a whole. Many authors have suggested that the diversity in these respects leads to greater capacity to solve problems and arrive at quality decisions, a better understanding of the market and its segments, good public relations and ultimately to productivity and profitability (Cox and Beale 1997; Robinson and Dechant 1997; Weiner 1997). Now let's turn to the issue of managing these two forms of expressions of diversity.

First, effective management of diversity begins with valuing diversity, which refers to

- a recognition and understanding of diversity,
- genuine acceptance of the inherent worth of diverse elements,
- a recognition of the advantages of a diverse workforce, and
- a clear understanding that the benefits of diversity can be derived only through appropriate managerial practices (Chelladurai 2001; Doherty and Chelladurai 1999; Cox and Beale 1997).

With this philosophy pervading the entire organisation, the aim in managing diversity is to maximise the potential advantages of diversity by using the varied talents and perspectives presented by diversity, and to minimise the potential disadvantages of such diversity (Cox and Beale 1997).

4.2 Strategies for Managing Diversity

Management can employ two basic strategies to deal with symbolic and substantive expressions of diversity respectively—strategies of *accommodation* and *activation* (Chelladurai 2005).

Strategy of Accommodation

The strategy of accommodation simply refers to permitting and facilitating the symbolic expressions of behavioral preferences of diverse individuals (e.g., wearing a saree, praying during lunchtime, ethnic food in the cafeteria). Evidence suggests that the dominance of the symbolic features and expressions in generating negative attitudes fades away when diverse individuals interact with each other on a continuous basis (Sargent and Sue-Chan 2001). The modern-day sport teams are good examples of this process. Players from different countries with different cultural backgrounds and speaking different languages are placed together on a team. Some players artificially set themselves apart from the rest by coloring their hair, tattooing all over their body and piercing various parts of their body. Despite all these differences, they begin to understand each other through constant interactions and task involvement. The apparent differences among them do not have much effect on their performance, although there is some evidence that in the case of crisis or incidents, some elements of differences may be revived and emphasized.

The notion of accommodation has become commonplace nowadays. The basic premise is that the symbolic expressions or features do not matter in the performance of most tasks. However, if the morals and customs would get in the way of performing a task, the task requirements may take precedence. A devout vegetarian would certainly be out of place in a butcher's shop. But for the most common tasks, permitting employees such expressions in the workplace releases the minority members from the burden of suppressing their mores and preferences.

Strategy of Activation

The strategy of activation is the process of deliberately bringing divergent perspectives and competencies to bear on a task or project and facilitating the substantive expressions of values, beliefs, attitudes, knowledge, training, experience and expertise. The interplay of these diverse attributes and perspectives is said to result in optimal decisions on what to do and how to do it (Cox and Beale 1997; Robinson and Dechant 1997; Weiner 1997).

The relevance and utility of the strategy of activation are dependent on the nature of the task. For example, simple and routine tasks such as the locker room operations and ticket taking at sporting events do not require the specialised competencies and different modes of solving problems. In fact, it has been shown that racial and gender diversity does not affect performance of routine tasks (Pelled, Eisenhardt and Xin 1999). Thus, management would be doing the right thing by simply accommodating the symbolic expressions and not worrying about substantive expressions. Further, as noted before, if people of diverse symbolic expressions are exposed to frequent contacts and interactions with each other, the negative influence of such diversity on members' attitudes towards each other would be minimised.

In contrast, complex multifaceted tasks are characterised by an uncertain environment and a lack of information. In this case, there are no prior procedures to guide action. Thus, they require novel approaches and problem-solving skills. Therefore, management should consider invoking employees' divergent competencies, values and beliefs as well as their varied expertise and experience to tackle the problem. Managers should facilitate communication and co-operation among members of the group and should coordinate their divergent orientations and preferences. That is the strategy of activation—bringing the richness of resources and competencies to the table.

The other critical factor related to tasks is the interdependence among tasks. Thompson (1967) described three types of dependence. Pooled dependence is where independent tasks are controlled and coordinated by a supervisor, as in the eight-person crew of a rowing team under the control of the coxswain. Sequential interdependence is where the output of one person is the input for the next person in the chain, as in the assembly lines and relay races. Finally, reciprocal interdependence is where people interact with each other to complete a task. Van de Ven, Delbecq and Koenig (1976) added a fourth type of interdependence labelled "team arrangement" or "teamwork" where group members act jointly and simultaneously on group tasks, as in basketball or football. The impact of symbolic and substantive expressions of diversity progressively increases from independent tasks to interdependent tasks. Thus, the potential for the symbolic and substantive expressions to hinder the smooth functioning of the group also increases. But that need not be the case. With proper management, such negative tendencies can be controlled and minimised.

Most of us are familiar with the "Star Trek" TV series. The men and women in the crew of the Enterprise hailed from different countries and even from different planets. With their expertise in different areas, they collaborated effectively to surmount the dangers they faced and to solve the problems of the universe. In the process, they were blind to all the differences among them. The most diverse person in the group was, of course, Commander Spock. Yet every member of the group respected and admired him, and they all took his opinions very seriously. In essence, the only individual difference that mattered in the spaceship was the relative specialised expertise of each person.

But that is fiction. Let's look at some of the real-life situations in sport. We see many football and basketball teams that are made up of players of different nationalities, different languages, different cultures and different religions. How can persons of such diversity be so effective in coordinating their activities for the good of the team? Chelladurai (2001, 2005) identified the processes that underlie such co-operation among diverse and competing individuals. These processes (listed below) provide a few insights on managing diversity in the workplace.

1. A clear grasp of the task at hand and the processes of accomplishing the task
2. A clear understanding by all members of the relative contributions of each member
3. An acceptance of the pecking order or hierarchy among members based on the relative contributions
4. A belief that the best available talent is being used in the most optimal combinations
5. The realization by every member that he or she will receive his or her personal rewards only if the team is successful
6. The realization that the team will win if, and only if, every member coordinates his or her activities with those of others to enhance team performance
7. The trust that every member will make the most optimal decisions and execute those actions that would benefit the team as a whole
8. The perception that rewards that accrue to the team are equitably distributed based on the relative contributions
9. A belief that personal values, attitudes and behavioral patterns are largely irrelevant to the team and its effectiveness

4.3 Integrity of Individuals and Groups

A critical step in managing diversity is to maintain the integrity of the individuals and groups, including their beliefs and their values. Valuing diversity implies permitting and even encouraging the formation of cliques. But that creates a problem for coordination and integration. It may also lead to prejudice and discrimination (Brickson 2000). These are real threats to group functioning. Effective management of diversity is the art of countering the negative forces of clique formation and channeling the interests of cliques for the common good.

Paraphrasing Sheremata (2000), Chelladurai applied the metaphor of the solar system to effective diversity management. "Gravity pulls the planets toward the sun while the planets' velocity causes them to pull away from the sun. The first type of force is called centripetal, because it is directed inward, toward the center of the circle, whereas the latter is called centrifugal, because it is directed outward, away from the center" (Sheremata 2000, p. 390). The point is that the dynamic equilibrium among the planets and the sun is maintained by the equality of these two forces. If the centripetal force exceeds the centrifugal forces, the planets would be sucked into the inferno of the sun. If, on the other hand, the centrifugal force is greater than the centripetal force, the planets would break loose and be hurtling away from the sun.

In our context, the planets are the individuals and cliques, and the sun is the organisation with its purposes. The centrifugal forces, reflected in the different sets of values and beliefs of the cliques, can impel the individuals and cliques outward, away from the purposes of the organisation.

In contrast, centripetal forces are the organisational structures and processes that integrate the dispersed values, beliefs, ideas, knowledge and information into collective action. They pull the cliques towards the core of the organisation and its purposes. Valuing diversity means recognizing, accepting and allowing the centrifugal forces to operate. Managing diversity requires the creation of the centripetal forces to draw the cliques towards the organisation and its goals, thereby creating the dynamic equilibrium and integration of diversity. It is the balance between the two forces that makes for effective diversity management.

4.4 Valuing Diversity: Gender Issues in the Management of Olympic Sport Organisations

We have stressed that biological diversity is one of the primary sources of diversity within organisations, and surely gender can be regarded as a major factor. In spite of recent changes and a more frequent emphasis on the theme of gender equity (Doherty and Chelladurai 1999; Fink, Pastore and Riemer 2001), ongoing issues on this respect are still evident in national and international sport governing bodies (Hoeber and Frisby 2001; Hovden 2000). Discrimination and underrepresentation still exist in these organisations. In most of the federations and clubs, women are found in lower operating levels more often than in policy-making positions; only a minority of CEOs and directors are women. Despite bylaws and charter statements of NFs and IFs warning against discrimination, very few women are in the top management positions. There appears to be a gender bias in recruitment practices of OSOs.

Since 1990, numerous initiatives have been taken to develop the active participation of women in sport as well as to engage them in managing sport organisations. The 1991 Olympic Charter has clearly indicated that all new sports seeking inclusion in the Olympic programme have to include men's and women's events. In 1994, the same charter encouraged the "promotion of women in sport at all levels and in all structures, particularly in the executive bodies of national and international governing bodies". Trying to analyze the impact of this specific set of initiatives, Rodriguez (2003) found that 67% of NOCs and 43% of IFs had at least 10% of women in their executive committees, and 85% of NOCs and 77% of IFs had at least one woman in the executive committee. With a view to promote

THE EQUALITY STANDARD

The Equality Standard is based on two broad areas of activity and four levels of achievement. All four levels must be supported by relevant evidence, which will be verified through the evaluation process. In defining the equality needs for sport organisations, the Equality Standard has identified two areas of activity:

- Developing your organisation—what your organisation is. This will be a reflection of the culture, policies, leadership and people.
- Developing your services—what your organisation does. This is reflected in the impact that policies, leadership and people have on your organisation's programmes, communications and customer service. Each level has been developed to take account of the different starting points of different sport organisations. The outcomes from each level are as follows:

Foundation

- Your organisation is committed to equality.
- Your organisation has an equality policy that has been communicated and is understood by staff and key volunteers.
- Your organisation is aware of its current profile in terms of equality.

Preliminary

- Your organisation understands the issues and barriers faced by underrepresented groups in sport.
- Your organisation has a robust equality action plan that all staff, volunteers and key stakeholders understand.
- All staff and volunteers within your organisation understand the principles of equality and their role in supporting your action plan.
- Partner organisations and new audiences are aware of, and are engaged in, the delivery of your action plan.

Intermediate

- Your organisation has increased the diversity of its leadership, staff, board and senior volunteers.
- All internal policies pay due regard to diversity.
- You have a staff and volunteer team with a strong understanding and commitment to equality at head office, regional, county and club membership levels.
- You have increased the diversity of people participating in and using your services.
- People inside and outside of your organisation are aware of your success and achievements in working towards equality.

Advanced

- Leadership and staff are reflective of the community your organisation serves.
- Equality is central to the way your organisation carries out all of its work.
- All of your programmes and investments pay due regard to the diverse groups you serve.
- Participants, coaches and officials are reflective of the community.
- All affiliated organisations and clubs are able to engage and develop participants, coaches, officials and administrators from underrepresented groups.
- There is an increase in the number of athletes from underrepresented groups in performance and elite sport.

The advanced level is equal to category two of the modernization programme "Investing in Change" models of good governance. "Investing in Change" clarifies what the modernization process means, identifies the strengths and weaknesses of governing bodies, and offers practical advice on the systems, structures and processes that they can use in order to operate more effectively and more efficiently. Governing bodies that reflect category one of the "Investing in Change" models would be expected to achieve the advanced level of the Equality Standard and to demonstrate that they have both maintained and "excelled" at this advanced level for an entire year. Additional evidence would be required to verify that this work has been maintained for this period, confirming that equality issues are part of the mainstream work of the governing body.

Reprinted, by permission, from Sport England.

gender equity in sport, working groups have been launched, conferences have been organised and strategies have been devised.

Most of these initiatives have been characterised by the adoption of some kind of targets. In 1997, when formulating its Women and Sport policy, the IOC established targets for women's inclusion in NOC executive committees. According to these targets, the IOC expected that women hold at least 10% of the positions in their executive and legislative organs by December 2001, increasing to at least 20% by December 2005.

The IOC carried out an inquiry to track the impact of these initiatives. The results of this inquiry were published in the report "Women and Leadership in the Olympic Movement" and described the impact as follows:

> "The introduction of minimum targets has had a clear and positive impact on the proportion of women in NOC Executive Committees. The rapid growth of the numbers of women in such positions, from a very low base, immediately after the announcement of the minimum targets is clear both in numeric terms from the questionnaire data, and also from the observations made by women and the Secretary Generals during the interviews. Thus the target approach can be said to have had success in raising awareness of gender inequalities, in bringing talented women into the Olympic family, and of improving Olympic governance by setting an example and providing moral leadership to the world of sport in terms of equity in representation" (Henry et al. 2004, p. 8).

However, the use of target systems has been subject to some controversy, not only in the field of sport but also with reference to other organisational contexts. Targets can induce another form of discrimination and even reduce the equality of chances. It is argued that sometimes an effect of the target system (not only in relation to gender discrimination) is that some people who are considered minorities or "discriminated" against are hired or nominated regardless of their real skills and competencies. Another point made is that the target system addresses gender equality only in terms of numbers. And in most cases, inequality is not just inequality in numbers but also in the availability of diverse opportunities for promotions, career advances or other resources. These aspects are much more difficult to address because they reflect more directly organisational ideologies and practices.

With specific reference to the Olympic movement organisations, three other limitations of the target system have been identified in the previously mentioned IOC report:

- The targets affect only the apex of the system (NOCs and IFs) without directly influencing the deep structure of the sport movement (e.g., the clubs) and therefore the global culture.
- Minimum targets are often considered as a goal and not as a means.
- A unique target system such as the one imposed by the IOC does not accommodate the enormous cultural differences existing between various countries.

Gender discrimination can take various forms and result in differences in pay, career perspectives, conditions of work, holidays, recruitment, and so on. Biological diversity is seldom considered a mere biological fact. Social prejudice and stereotypes are common in relation to gender and other sources of biological diversity. McKay (1997) found in his research that the definition of gender inequality varied in different categories of organisational members. We should note that because of social factors, there are times when it is difficult to recruit women for governing bodies since not many women are available for such positions, mostly for family reasons. So, apart from imposed targets, other proactive measures should be taken to promote women in the administrative ranks of OSOs. Practical initiatives similar to the ones proposed in earlier chapters on a more general basis can also be taken on this respect. For example, creating formal job profiles and identifying appropriate criteria for evaluating competencies are surely useful steps in the direction of gender equity. Other initiatives that should be carried out are to ensure that salaries and career opportunities for the same position would be the same irrespective of gender, ethnicity or any other variable. Mentorship and training have been reported (Henry et al. 2004) as important measures not to be underestimated.

All these elements are recognizable in numerous policy documents that have been adopted and implemented by various OSOs in recent years.

Leadership

Management literature and leading sport management and administration manuals devote significant parts of their text to the topic of leadership, since there is a wide consensus on the idea that organisational success depends on how an organisation is actually led. The difficult thing is describing and explaining the ingredients of good leadership and especially how to become a good leader. One of the major reasons for this difficulty is that leadership is simultaneously a function of the wide cultural context, the structure (formal and informal) of the organisation and the personal qualities or character of those who are in a leading position.

Yukl and Van Fleet (1992) define leadership as

> " . . . a process that includes influencing the task objectives and strategies of a group or organization, influencing people in the organization to implement the strategies and achieve the objectives, influencing group maintenance and identification, and influencing the culture of organizations" (p. 149).

We must note the emphasis on *influencing* the various elements in the organisational setting. Every definition of leadership would include the influence aspect of leadership.

5.1 The Multidimensional Model of Leadership

The multidimensional model of leadership (Chelladurai 1993, 1999, 2001) combines and reorients the different perspectives from various theories of leadership in order to gain insight into the area of leadership. Figure 5.1 shows a schematic representation of the model. Briefly, the model envisages three states of leader behavior: required, preferred and actual. The independent variables are those that determine the three states of leader behavior and are classified into macrovariables (i.e., situational characteristics), members' characteristics and leader characteristics. The outputs, or the dependent variables, in the model are group performance and satisfaction.

Required leader behavior is considered to be mainly influenced by the macrovariables, while the preferred behavior is influenced by both the macrovariables and member characteristics. The determinants of the actual leader behavior include all three types of independent variables—the macrovariables, the member characteristics and the leader's own attributes.

With regard to the outputs, group performance and member satisfaction are determined by the degree of congruence among the actual leader behavior, the required behavior and the leader behavior preferred by the member.

Required Leader Behavior

In a typical sport governing body, leader behavior is influenced and bounded by the demands and constraints placed by factors relating to the organisation and its environment (i.e., situational characteristics, or macrovariables as some authors have labelled them). That portion of leader behavior that is influenced and controlled by these situational characteristics is labelled the required leader behavior.

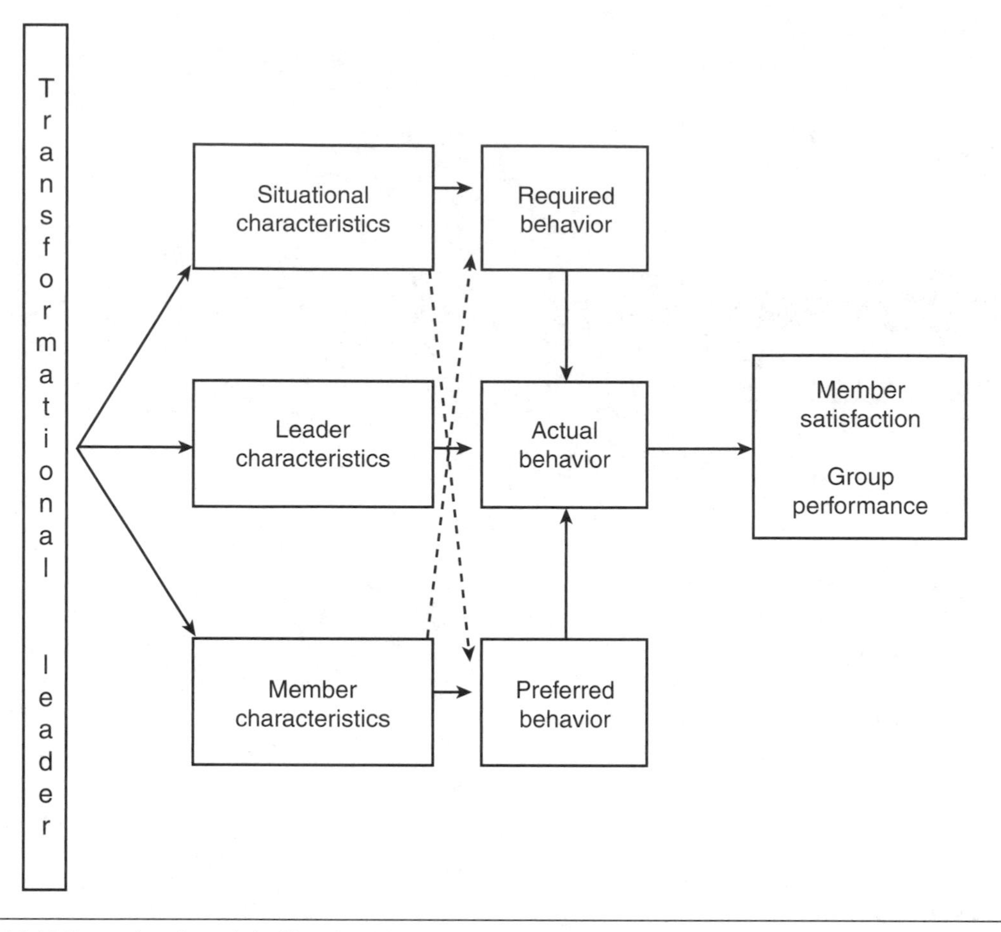

Figure 5.1 Multidimensional model of leadership.
Adapted from P. Chelladurai, 1990, "Leadership in sports: A review," *International Journal of Sport Psychology* 21(4): 328-354. By permission of P. Chelladurai.

Osborn and Hunt (1975) specify the unit's environment, its size, its technology and its formal structure as macrovariables that are common to all group members. We should also include the group's tasks as a situational variable that affects leader behavior. For instance, consider two committees (and two groups) involved in managing the mass and elite programmes of a sport governing body. While all members are oriented towards the overall goals of the sport governing body and its mission and strategy, they are also differentially influenced by the nature of the tasks of their respective groups. Therefore, the processes of leading the members of the two groups would differ from each other to some extent.

We should also consider the goals of the organisation as a situational factor influencing the leadership process. For instance, the leadership process in a professional fitness franchise would be different from the leadership process in a sport club organised for the benefit of its members. A similar difference can be found when comparing professional leagues and a national federation of a specific sport. Other environmental forces are the norms and codes for conduct prevalent (or emerging) in a given social setting (House 1971). Contrast, for instance, the social norms surrounding a coach of an elite team and the leader of a youth recreational team. In general, the leader behaviors required by situational characteristics (unit size, technology, formal structure, group task, organisational goals and the norms and behavioral expectations in a particular social context) tend to be task oriented and instrumental in the realization of the group's objectives (Osborn and Hunt 1975).

Leader Behavior Preferred by Members

The preference of members for specific leader behaviors is considered a function of both the situational characteristics and the individual characteristics of the group members.

Preferences Emanating From Situational Variables

As stated earlier, a portion of a leader's behavior is specified by the macrovariables. Member preferences are also affected by these same macrovariables. As one example, if autocratic and demanding leader behaviors are expected of a coach of an elite team in order to push the athletes towards greater efforts and performance, the same norms would also specify that the athletes accept such behavior from the coach as necessary and fruitful.

Preferences Emanating From Personal Characteristics

Member preference for specific leader behavior is determined by an individual's personality and perceived ability (House 1971; House and Dessler 1974). Ability refers to the current competence of the individual in the performance of a given task rather than innate ability or intelligence. In other words, it reflects the presence or absence of job-specific competence and knowledge. Those who are highly competent in their jobs may prefer not to receive much guidance from the leader. For instance, a volunteer who has been drawing up the tournament schedule for years would actually resent the executive director's guidance in this area.

Attitude Towards Authority

Member preferences are also affected by personality factors such as *attitude towards authority.* Those who have a high regard for authority would welcome some guidance from authority figures. On the other hand, those who are low on this trait would not prefer such guidance. *Cognitive complexity* refers to the way an individual processes information; those high on this trait would not prefer much direction from the leader while those low on it would seek guidance in complex matters. Those high on the *need for independence* would like to be left alone by the leader, and those high in *achievement motivation* would prefer that the leader provide the challenge, responsibility and feedback. While the foregoing relate to task performance, member preferences may also be influenced by their interpersonal needs as the subordinate (e.g., need for affiliation, succor, and so on).

Actual Leader Behavior

As noted, requirements of the macrovariables and preferences by members influence actual leader behavior, but a leader's personality and ability would affect actual leader behavior to a larger extent. According to Fiedler (1967), an interpersonally oriented leader will respond more readily to the needs and desires of the members than the task-oriented leader. In contrast, the task-oriented leader will place greater emphasis on following the dictates of the situation and accomplishing the task. Authoritarianism, dogmatism, domination, cognitive complexity and the need for achievement and affiliation are some of the personality factors that would affect actual leader behavior.

Ability of the leader refers to (a) the specific knowledge and expertise the leader has regarding the various aspects of the group tasks and the processes involved, (b) the leader's capacity to analyze the complexities of a problem and (c) the leader's power of persuasion or interpersonal competence.

Performance and Satisfaction

According to the multidimensional model of leadership, group performance and member satisfaction are generally a function of the degree of congruence among the three states of leader behavior. It is implicit in the model that any of the states of leader behavior can be a limiting factor. For instance, in some sport governing bodies, outdated and dysfunctional policies and procedures restrict performance and reduce satisfaction. Likewise, if members' preferences are not task oriented, performance is likely to suffer. Similarly, if actual leader behavior deviates from the requirements of the organisation or member preferences, members will not be motivated to perform well.

Satisfaction with leadership can be further dichotomized into (1) satisfaction with technical leadership and (2) satisfaction with interpersonal leadership. The technical leadership refers not only to the leader's competence in the technical aspects of the group's task, but also to leader behaviors that facilitate members' work performance. Interpersonal leadership refers to the leader's behaviors that satisfy the interpersonal needs of the member. Thus, the model allows for the possibility that the member may (or may not) be satisfied with either the technical leadership or the interpersonal leadership or both.

In the foregoing description of the leadership process, we emphasized that the manager or leader needs to be attentive to both the requirements of the situation and the preferences of the members. It would appear then that the manager is simply one who juggles the varying demands and constraints. This was the perspective expressed by Carlson (1979) after a careful study of managers:

> "Before we made the study, I always thought of a chief executive as the conductor of an orchestra, standing aloof on his platform. Now I am in some respects inclined to see him as the puppet in a puppet show with hundreds of people pulling the strings and forcing him [her] to act in one way or another" (p. 52).

This perspective is largely true in most organisations most of the time. When a manager is reacting to these demands and constraints, he or she is said to be enacting the *transactional leadership.* The manager is transacting with the members of the group in a process of give-and-take; that is, the manager provides what the members seek in return for their compliance to the manager's directives and the organisational requirements. Although such leadership is an integral part of management, it is based on the assumption that the status quo (in terms of the objectives and programmes) is acceptable. It also envisages that members would engage in carrying out the activities as expected. For example, if management of an OSO is satisfied with the progress it makes with its mass and elite programmes, it can be content with transactional leadership.

5.2 Transformational Leadership

However, occasions may arise where the status quo is not acceptable. Either the programmes are not carried out effectively or the environment has become more challenging. For instance, the government may withdraw its subsidies to the OSOs (which happened in Canada), in which case the OSOs have to alter their mode of operation drastically. Newer and more challenging goals will have to be set, and innovative methods of generating revenues will have to be initiated. When such quantum changes need to be undertaken, it becomes necessary for the manager to enact what is labelled as *transformational leadership.* Transformational leadership refers to

> "the process of influencing major changes in the attitudes and assumptions of organization members (organizational culture) and building commitment for major changes in the organization's objectives and strategies. Transformational leadership involves influence by a leader on subordinates, but the effect of the influence is to empower subordinates who become leaders and change agents also in the process of transforming the organization" (Yukl and Van Fleet 1992, p. 174).

In Bass' (1985) view, transactional leadership is concerned with influencing members' cognitions and their abilities, which in turn would lead to lower turnover and absenteeism, satisfaction and *expected performance.* On the other hand, transformational leadership taps into the emotions, values and beliefs of members and elevates their self-esteem, which in turn leads to higher aspirations, increased efforts and *performance beyond expectations.*

Transformational leadership involves creating a vision for the elevation of the OSO from its current dismal conditions to a higher level of growth and effectiveness. This vision must be clearly explained to the second-level managers and members (including volunteers and clients), and they need to be convinced of the desirability as well as the viability of the new vision. Further, it may be necessary to modify the organisational structure and the operational procedures to facilitate the attainment of the new vision (Yukl and Van Fleet 1992).

Some authors have made a distinction between management and leadership. Some of the differences between management and leadership that these authors describe run parallel to the differences between transactional leadership and transformational leadership that we just outlined. For example, Kotter (1990) views management as coping with *complexity,* planning for *orderly results,* organising and staffing for *precise and efficient operations,* and controlling and correcting *deviations* for *risk-free operations.* In contrast, leadership is seen as coping with *change,* planning with a *vision to serve constituents,* organising and staffing with those who *accept and are willing to implement the vision, empowering them,* and *inspiring and motivating* people to satisfy their *needs for achievement, sense of control and recognition.*

Irrespective of the terminology of transactional versus transformational leadership or management versus leadership, we need to understand that they represent two different but equally necessary forms of leadership. One form is concerned with order and expected performance, and the other is concerned with change (either imposed or self-initiated) and progress through change. Managers of OSOs should be mindful of both forms and emphasize each as the situation warrants.

Change Management and Human Resources: Final Notes

6.1 What Is Change Management?

Change management has become a key topic in management literature (Pettigrew 1985; Hofstede 1991; Quinn 1980). In fact, like living beings, organisations are born, develop, decline and pass away, thus undergoing a common process of change. Multiple-stage or life cycle models have been applied to organisations, but differently from biological entities, organisations of the same "species" or operating in the same sector show very different life cycles. Differences in the stages of organisational life can be related to environmental factors but also to internal and external organisational strategies and individual behavior (i.e., the action of the leaders). Numerous scientific works have investigated both the stages of change and the best ways to augment successful change. Results of these studies have shown that the same stages cannot always be recognized for specific organisations and that the succession of the stages has no relation with the age of the organisation as such.

Studies of sport organisations have also been sensitive to this issue, even if only recently. Strategic management of OSOs is constantly confronted with change, either as a form of reaction to the environment or induced intentionally and proactively, for example, through a strategic plan and the associated change management methodologies. Numerous technical aspects of identifying the required change and the potential of the organisation to face the associated threats and risks are covered in most of the approaches and textbooks on strategic management. However, the relevance and transferability into practice of the concepts contained in these texts are perceived by many sport managers as vague and limited. As a result, they normally tend to rely more on commonsense approaches, personal experience and current success stories in order to develop their own approach to change.

Actually, a methodology for change management is recognized as an important part of the professional competency of a sport manager working in an OSO. The wide range of stakeholders in OSOs with potentially different views creates a further and difficult challenge for the managers involved in the facilitation of the change process. Especially within sport organisations, we find concurrent and competing definitions of the reality and strong subcultures holding very different views of the world. Although a "happy family" view of the organisations may indicate that it would be ideal if all these conflicting perspectives could be reconciled in the superior interest of the organisation, this objective is often very difficult to achieve; therefore, it is more probable that only a reduced and variable degree of integration could be achieved between the competing views.

Defining the meaning of the concept of **change** is a preliminary step for the discussion. *Organisational change* is usually understood to mean the adoption of a new concept or behavior (Daft 2001). The change adopted can concern an organisation or a whole sector (in which case it can be considered a true form of organisational innovation). Organisational changes can be very different in scale; changes may have an impact only on a few units or activities of an organisation, or they may produce significant modifications in all the structures, technologies and organisational processes.

This distinction is usually made in terms of **incremental** or **revolutionary** (or radical) change (Daft 2001). Incremental changes, which are normally the most common (Pettigrew and Whipp 1991), affect only one or a few parts of an organisation and are managed through rather traditional processes and structures. A revolutionary change, on the other hand, has an impact on all the dimensions and elements of an organisation and creates a new structure and new management processes. Mintzberg (1979) has noted that within a certain configuration, all the components tend to become reciprocally consistent, with a specific equilibrium. Revolutionary changes alter this equilibrium and produce new interactions and original internal dynamics. Although this concept does not necessarily provide a clear indication on the best way to drive organisational change, it is enough to warn managers and leaders of OSOs to avoid paying attention only to the modification required in the organisational structure without aligning other essential components. Meyer and Rowan (1977) have described how formal structural changes might be only a tool to increase external or internal legitimacy of an organisation without having any substantial impact on the organisational activity system. For OSOs, Digel (2005, p. 16) has confirmed this finding, concluding that "a separation between the outer formal structure and the inner activity has taken place in high-performance sport institutions".

Very different perspectives on change management are possible, with reference to one or more of the major areas of organisational change. McCann (1991) has listed four main areas that managers can focus on in order to increase organisational effectiveness:

1. Culture
2. Structure
3. Technology
4. Product or services

Change of people, which can be considered a form of cultural change, is also an important intervention strategy that is frequently used by OSOs through recruitment or training.

A big question here concerns the **relation between change and the environment.** Organisations operate in very complex environments and tend to adjust themselves to the changing context in many different ways. Many approaches to change management have recognized the role of context, through specific and quite elaborate models (Pettigrew 1985). In the everyday discourse of sport managers, this relation between context and change is easy to identify. According to this view, change is needed because the external environment is changing: "We have to change, because the world is changing."

Although the contingent dimension of change cannot be denied, the way the context is used to explain or justify the change is sometimes too generic and naive. For example, the role of individuals and of strategic choice is underestimated when change is considered just a necessary product of the environmental pressure. Managers of OSOs always have a certain degree of discretion and autonomy in change-related decisions, even if this discretion naturally varies with the size, degree of legitimacy and financial independence of the organisation or other factors. Smaller and dependent organisations often have less chance to modify and transform their own environment. We should also note that even if the environment of OSOs is often turbulent and the pressure of the stakeholders very high, compared to average business companies operating in a very competitive and globalised market, OSOs seem more protected and resistant to the context for some aspects, at least in the short and medium term. When this perception is shared inside the organisation, it is clear that the willingness to change can be scarce. This may explain why conservatism has often been indicated as a common aspect of these organisations. In some cases, this is confirmed by the long stability of OSOs' governing elites. Actually, this is not a unique aspect of these organisations; different authors (Robbins 1990) have made the point that all managers in general prefer the status quo, or in the best case, as few changes as possible.

Giving the right importance to action and strategic choice should not, however, lead to an opposite mistake—that is, to always consider change as the obvious outcome of a deliberate and rational "planned process". For this rational and anticipatory nature, planning is vastly appealing to the most influential organisational actors. These actors clearly perceive the usefulness of planning for improving the future performances of the organisation through appropriate methods such as SWOT analysis and other strategic planning tools. However, many aspects must be considered that can challenge a too simplistic view of the relation between strategic planning and change, including the following:

- The unpredictability of the external environment
- The reaction of the internal environment (which depends on the nature and evolution of power relations and access to relevant resources)

The combination of these two aspects can easily generate unintended consequences that have not been forecasted in the planning process. Once they become manifest, such consequences are not easily managed by those who are involved in the process. Merton (1936) and Gouldner (1954) are probably the most famous researchers who have dedicated great attention to the unintended consequences of collective actions. According to this perspective, many usual and commonsense ideas and expressions that accompany rational strategic planning—for example, "every detail must be predicted in advance"; "we do not have to leave anything to chance"; "we must strive for total control of the situation"—are not only implausible but can be to a certain extent negative (Delavallée 1999, p. 547), because people (and organisations) sometimes confuse the change process with the plan for changing. Langhorn and Hinings (1987) and Slack, Berrett and Mistry (1994) have demonstrated that the introduction of "rational planning systems" increases the chance of conflict and heightens already existing interpersonal conflicts. This is essentially caused by the impact of planning on organisation differentiation (e.g., creation of new units) and integration (new patterns of interdependency) but also on the cultural dimensions (especially the impact on the values).

Investigations on sport organisations have confirmed this phenomenon. Nier and Sheard (1999), for example, while analyzing elite European rugby clubs in the course of professionalisation, have identified strong tensions and contradictions caused by the change process (in their case, the move towards more formal and professional structures). Incidentally, in their view, this finding confirms the inadequacy of the idea that "members of sport organizations adapt in some mechanical way to external environmental change" (p. 5).

For managers in OSOs, explaining and interpreting change is certainly important, but a key question is how to manage the process and how to avoid as much as possible the unexpected consequences of change.

For this reason, we will concentrate primarily on the internal reactions to the change process, because this aspect is particularly related to human resource management. In fact, significant changes in the structures, products and technologies can only occur if people change with them. They have to learn how to sell the new products, how to use the new communication environment and—even more difficult—how to work with different colleagues and organisational units, on the basis of new principles. Changing people also means modifying the values of the organisational actors, as noted by Cameron and Quinn (1999, pp. 9-10): "Without an alteration of the fundamental goals, values, and expectations of organizations or individuals, change remains superficial and short term duration."

A specific sensitivity to this aspect and to related skills necessary to deal with it is therefore needed within the changing organisations, especially because the organisational actors can be the biggest opponents of change (Delavallée 1999). **Resistance to change** is a common feature of sport organisations. Many organisational actors who in general openly support the need for change and innovation are not pleased at all about changing themselves or accepting changes in their own working conditions. In sport organisations, contrasting views are not limited to the usual dichotomy between employers and employees but concern other components and organisational layers (as we have seen for volunteers and professionals or centre and periphery).

Many different reasons of variable nature for why people resist change have been investigated in the specialised literature. These reasons include the following:

- Fear of losing power or status
- Lack of trust in those who propose change
- Insufficient or divergent understanding of the consequences of change
- Personal or group costs related to change
- External pressures from important stakeholders
- Low personal and psychological tolerance of the change
- Inertia (e.g., voluntary boards have been reported to tend to repeat the same actions and policies, with very little creativity [Middleton 1987])
- Exaggerated attention to monetary costs of change

Open resistance is not the only possibility when change is introduced; concepts such as "ceremonial conformity" or hidden "concealment" have been used to describe those organisational members who in spite of the proclaimed change continue to operate in the same way as before.

Managers cannot just blame those who resist but instead should blame themselves if they do not act proactively to avoid or limit such resistance. Some specific models have clearly incorporated the identification of the sources of resistance within the strategic management model. For example, Chin and Benne (1961) have proposed the following steps to facilitate the production of the required organisational change:

- Perceive and identify gaps and weaknesses.
- Develop solutions and plans for change.
- Identify sources of resistance in the organisation (role system).
- Formulate the strategy.
- Implement the strategy.
- Evaluate the strategy.

Daft (2001) has proposed an integrated set of techniques that are considered useful for a successful change process:

1. Establish a sense of urgency for change (necessary to create a consensus on the problems to be solved and the means to solve them).
2. Establish a coalition to guide the change with the support of the top management.
3. Create a vision and strategy for change.
4. Find an idea that fits the need (this can mobilize participation and interaction between different organisational actors).
5. Develop plans to overcome resistance to change:
    - Adapting to the needs of the actors
    - Communication and training
    - Participation and commitment
    - Use of strength and coercion
6. Create change teams.
7. Foster idea champions, that is, persons with a high reputation who believe in the change process and ensure that all the practical operations are carried out.

Other models (Delavallée 1999) have emphasized further steps, such as the experimentation of change on a smaller scale and the subsequent generalization to the whole organisation.

As we have already noted, there is a risk in the adoption of models that are too mechanic. In fact, change is not a mechanical and predictable process. Organisations are not machines, and to understand the change process, it is probably better to use the metaphor of organisations as **cultures** (Morgan 1986). For this reason, the process of planning and implementing change has a strong political nature; in changing organisations, areas of ambiguity and uncertainty are usually expanded. This is confirmed if we consider some of the actions that have been suggested in the literature in order to facilitate organisational change:

- Using communication and information flows (to inform employees of the perspective of change in order to develop a sense of interest and an understanding of the advantages of change and to produce consensus)
- Involving potential opposition, or using negotiation and co-optation
- Establishing problem-solving teams or transunit activity
- Creating a supportive atmosphere to foster commitment to change
- Spreading change over time (but also "using" crisis to defeat resisters)
- Starting in subunits rather than changing the entire structure (top-down approach)
- Establishing the "institutionalization of change", which should be made visible in structural arrangements, procedures, formal policies and reward systems adopted and communicated by the organisation

To help identify the potential sources of resistance, Pfeffer (1981) has suggested that managers should do the following:

- Identify patterns of interdependence that could be disrupted by the organisational changes.
- Identify the relevant distribution of power across the organisation.
- Hypothesise points of view, attitudes and possible reactions of groups and people in key positions in the organisation, especially considering the impact on careers and reward opportunities.
- Assess the resistant people's real level of control of the situation.

In the change process, the main role of those who are responsible for human resources is to put into operation measures that can facilitate the outcome. Some measures refer to the competence and skills of the people and could include training, new recruitment and even mobility (adaptation needs or resources Delavallée 1999). Other more general measures will target the mobilization of the actors and the integration of their own perspectives into the global process of change.

6.2 The Role of the Change Agents

Change can be facilitated by the action of specific "change agents" or champions who mediate between the organisational context and the strategy. Change agents have the expertise and the influence to make change possible. Important leaders, such as J.A. Samaranch and Primo Nebiolo, have all been considered as true champions of change. Change agents do not simply communicate vision but facilitate a significant learning process by creating step-by-step favorable conditions, fostering the experience of success and rewarding the "new behaviors".

Actually, agents of change can belong to different categories; they can be high officers of the organisation (a president or a CEO) or external consultants. There are interesting success stories of both approaches. An internal leader definitely has more chances and more power to promote the desired change. However, at the same time, reaction and political conflict can be extreme, and this could even disrupt an organisation. An external consultant has the advantage of being more objective and, if really skilled, should be able to identify weak points within the organisation. In spite of this, unless the consultant is unanimously chosen by all the organisational components, there is a high chance that he or she could be considered as serving somebody's interest so that the plan for change will encounter the same kind of resistance and opposition.

The role of the change agent is important not only in the conception of the change process, but also during the implementation phase. This phase regroups the whole set of actions that have to be undertaken when the need for change has been recognized at the highest level of the organisation and a strategic plan to accompany change has been deliberated. Lewin (1951) has made a well-known distinction of three critical phases of organisational change:

1. Unfreezing the organisational status quo (individuals become aware of the

need for change; creation of a feeling of nonsatisfaction and uneasiness that pushes individuals to accept the idea of change[1])
2. Moving an organisation to a new status
3. Freezing the new status quo

Although the demarcation between the three phases is certainly not always easy or even possible, we can see that the role of the change agent is especially important in the second of the three phases. In some cases, it could be useful to have two champions of change, one inspiring the vision to the organisation and the other one protecting and "installing" the vision in the implementation phase.

When trying to facilitate the movement to a new organisational status, the function of a change agent requires special awareness that employees or other organisational members may not accept the new situation and may resist (for any of the reasons that we mentioned earlier).

Therefore, the change agent needs to make the maximum effort to identify the source of resistance, remove the opposing forces (if possible) and encourage in various ways the acceptance of change. In our view, increased resistance to change can be expected when the planned outcome and specific objectives are defined in a very precise and nonnegotiable way. This will probably increase the resistance of those organisational actors who can anticipate negative consequences for them and no way to influence the outcome. This can also be a danger for those who promote the change: If they are not powerful enough to assure the achievement of the objectives in the way it had been described, their reputation and legitimacy could be seriously compromised.

Many methods and tools are available to an organisation to help cope with the resistance to change. A top-bottom approach to change management can be quite ineffective because other actors—different from those who champion change—feel that they have no chance to influence the concrete way that change is put into operation.

On this respect, Kotter and Schlesinger (1979) have listed the following tactics to be considered by the change agents:

- Education and communication to employees (group or individual meetings, short documents, seminars, presentations, and so on)
- Participation (involvement of participants, or some of them, especially the most problematic, in the process)
- Facilitation and support (development of skills, counselling, reduction of anxiety)
- Negotiation (offer of some reward or advantage to those who would resist)
- Co-optation (inclusion of the strongest opponents in the leading team or in the decision-making process)

The following extreme tactics (with significant ethical and power implications) are also sometimes used:

- Manipulation (spreading fears or incorrect information, for example, about an external threat; this can always turn into an unethical behavior)
- Coercion (threatening people with negative consequences in case of resistance)

Obviously, most of these tactics involve an appropriate adjustment of human resource practices. It is therefore surprising that many sport organisations have devoted large efforts, especially in recent years, to modifying organisational structures or developing external strategies (dominated by marketing and public relations concepts) in order to be able to compete effectively in their specific market—and they have devoted much less to setting up and implementing internal strategies aimed at properly training and mobilizing the human resources to accompany the desired change. Of course, this can be related to cost issues and important changes in the structure and functioning of the labour market. But in our view, in many cases, it is the result of the scarce attention paid to human resources in the change management process.

1. Schein (1969) has indicated that this initial phase can be differentiated into three further phases: rupture of the individual perception, anxiety and securisation that makes the idea of change acceptable.

If the actions previously listed (or others that can be envisaged) are not properly carried out, there is a high chance that the change process can be interrupted or that the change will be only formal without real impact on the organisational process. On the contrary, if this phase of mobilization is successful, it is then possible for the change agents to start to refreeze the status quo, giving balance to the organisation and reducing the cognitive uncertainty (and therefore the resistance). New rules and regulations can be enforced and put into practice, and new social norms and patterns of interaction will develop to adapt to the new status quo. In this phase, the role of the change agent is not finished—information is needed, further adjustments have to be made, and most important, what we have called the unplanned or unintended consequences of change must be identified and eventually remedied.

This is a very delicate phase, similar to what occurs to an athlete who has changed a skill; in the most difficult moments of a match, the performance can initially suffer since the new skill is not fully controlled, and this could generate frustration and uncertainty. The same process could occur in an organisation, because it is a very complex system whose complete model of interactions and interacting forces is not easy to identify. This is the moment when some people or groups can suddenly realize that their status is threatened or the workload is unexpectedly increased.

6.3 Redesigning Olympic Sport Organisations to Meet the Transformation of Sport

In recent years, we have seen significant examples of organisational restructuring driven by new long-term visions and change strategies applied in their relevant context. Through a process of reengineering, the usual working systems and business processes are redesigned to produce a simultaneous impact on all the significant organisational dimensions—culture first, and then structures and technologies. In the domain of sport organisations, most of these change processes have followed the path of the "modernization" agenda or the concept of "new managerialism". In Mintzberg's perspective, this essentially is equivalent to the transition from simple structures to divisionalised structures and later from these to highly specialised structures (Theodoraki and Henry 1994). For other approaches, this is characterised by a transition from tall vertical and hierarchic structures to flat organisations more suitable to quick reactions to environmental changes (Henry and Theodoraki 2000; Piore and Sabel 1984).

Analyzing some of these developments in the field of OSOs can help identify potential trends or key elements, even if these models should always be considered specific to the organisations that have developed them (within a specific market and environment and with specific stakeholder groups). A useful example is the case of UEFA, which has developed a specific project on this respect, called Project FORCE (Football Organisation Redesign for the Next Century in Europe). The philosophy of the project has been expressed by the UEFA president Lennart Johansson:

> "It is quite normal for UEFA as a whole to endow itself with modern organisational structures able to respond to current and future (market) demands. It is indeed only with expertise, efficiency and modern successful management at all levels that UEFA can continue to promote and further develop the duality of solidarity and commercialisation for the good of football."

The project needs to be put in its specific context—that is, the series of dramatic changes that had changed football into a commercially oriented activity and that were accompanied by considerable political, social and legal modifications. The project has been prepared through an extensive organisational audit, including business management analysis, interviews with stakeholders and the creation of specific working groups.

From the UEFA documentation, we take a synthesis of the results of the process. For example, when the UEFA was thoroughly restructured in 2000, new organizational priorities were set up, the organizational chart was redesigned where new positions were created and the departments were reshaped. The UEFA's administrative secretariat was renamed UEFA Administration and is headed by a Chief

Executive. It now has seven divisions to deal with Professional Football & Marketing, Competition Operations, Services, Football Development, Professional & Legal Services, Communications & Public Affairs, and Finances. The seven divisions, in turn, comprise a variety of subunits.

The changes adopted were justified on the basis of the following key aspects:

- More businesslike orientations
- New division structure
- Recruitment of top-level professionals
- Reduction of committees (from 30 to 11, a number with a special symbolic meaning in football) in order to achieve greater efficiency with the creation of ad hoc working groups
- New forms of decision making
- More representation of the stakeholders (clubs and professional leagues getting more representation compared to the national federations)

Better Organisational Performance Through New Professional Structures

The international federations surely have an interest in pursuing a progressive professionalisation of the related or affiliated sport organisations. The reasons for this interest can be very different. On one hand, there is the pressure for an increasing legitimacy, which can be achieved only if the organisational structures are up to the standards. On the other hand, there is the need to assure that the "games" are credible, attractive and well managed, and this requires a well-conceived structure that is able to match the needs of the industry and the clients. An interesting example where the process of professionalisation was accelerated is again provided by UEFA with its club licensing system, which was started in 1998 (www.uefa.com).

Although not directly related to OSOs, this model has a relevant interest because it defines standards for professional soccer clubs by providing a model aimed at harmonizing the organisational structure of the clubs and enhancing their quality (on the basis of the inspiration provided by the established ISO 9000 standard). This initiative has produced a manual for the club licensing system that has been adapted to the different national situations (today, all the European national federations have produced national club licensing manuals that have been approved by UEFA). The national regulations regulate the process to be applied by the licensor when assessing the respective clubs. The manuals establish the minimum criteria required for club licensing regulations, which have been regrouped into five main categories of standards. These criteria had to be met in order for a club to be admitted to any of the UEFA club competitions from the 2004 to 2005 season. We should note that one specific group of criteria refers to the human resource dimension; it incorporates 11 different parameters that define the basic organisational setup that is considered necessary for an association to function in an effective way.

For example, clubs have been requested to design their own organisational chart, specifying the roles and functions in a clear way. This may sound obvious in a very professionalised environment, but numerous clubs did not perform well on this respect. These organisational charts have to include some mandatory and distinguishable functions:

- CEO or general director
- General secretary
- Administration, finance and control
- Security
- Press relations
- Youth sport director
- Technical director of the team

Other functions are recommended even if not obligatory (e.g., marketing and communication director, team manager, medical staff leader). UEFA has the responsibility to carry out all the necessary checks to be sure that the new system is correctly applied.

6.4 Conclusion: Learning Organisations and Knowledge Management

In conclusion, we would like to note that organisations that are able to successfully implement changes and integrate them in their daily life are essentially "learning organisations". These organisations are structured around values and practices that are especially suitable to processing, interpreting and making available—through well-designed procedures—the information and knowledge that is generated within the organisation. Learning is dependent on the way knowledge is incorporated within the organisations as their experience progresses. Since organisations generate an incredibly high amount of knowledge (Schon [1983] has defined them as "repositories of cumulatively built-up knowledge" [p. 242]), knowledge management systems are essential to all of them, even if their degree of complexity and structure can be very different. In this way, it becomes possible to adapt to the changing environment without losing sight of the interest and perspective of the constituency, embodied in their accumulated knowledge, which we have repeatedly emphasized in this text. The management of the processes of organisational learning is therefore one of the most important for change management.

However, facilitating and coordinating organisational learning is a difficult challenge. Organisations do not learn in the same way as individuals do, and their learning is not simply the sum of individual learning of the members (Cook and Yanow 1993; Weick and Westley 1996); it is rather a process that looks more like a cultural change process than the cognitive process through which individuals learn on the basis of action, error, feedback and correction. In this case, it can be really helpful to equate organisations to cultures. This means that in conjunction with the change process these organisations have to recognize the value of the production of knowledge and of the people (professionals or volunteers) that contribute to this process. This valorisation is an essential part of the human resource strategies of the organisation. But it must be supported by appropriate methods (i.e., opportunity of reflective practice) and technological environments that make these kinds of best practices and data available to accompany the change process and by the creation of an internal networked structure.

This explains why in the last few years the topic of knowledge management has become more and more crucial for OSOs. For example, the setup of knowledge management systems has been strongly recognized by Organising Committees of the Olympic Games (OCOGs), the IOC and international federations in order to profit from the experience of previous events, without reinventing the wheel every time.

Summary

In this text, we have attempted to highlight the significant aspects of human resource management within OSOs. We began with the discussion of the unique features of OSOs, emphasizing that they are volunteer organisations. We also identified the clients, the volunteers and the professional managers as the significant stakeholders of the OSOs. Focusing on the volunteers and the professionals, we described the salient features of volunteerism and professionalism. We explained how the basic thrusts of both volunteerism and professionalism are oriented towards the welfare of the clients, and thus are complementary to each other. The fundamental thesis of this discussion is that there is no inherent conflict between volunteerism and professionalism. Thus, if there are conflicts between volunteers and professionals, it is mostly a function of how individuals in one set of roles treat their counterparts in the other set of roles. In other words, such conflicts are not a function of the systems of volunteerism and professionalism but a function of the lack of understanding and acceptance of the people in the two differing roles.

We began the discussion of human resource management practices with a description of organisational justice in its three forms—distributive justice, procedural justice and interactional justice. We noted that organisational justice is fundamental to all managerial practices, more specifically to human resource management. Then we described the process of staffing that involves job analysis, job description, job specification, recruiting and hiring. We noted the importance of recruiting volunteers for different levels of hierarchy in the OSO—the institutional, the managerial and the technical systems. We noted that the members of the board should be characterised by one or more sources of power, and that they should have the will and skill to use that power on the behalf and for the welfare of the OSO.

We discussed the concepts of empowerment, especially with reference to athletes, and the strategies for managing diversity. Finally, we used Chelladurai's multidimensional model of leadership to explain the nuances of the requirements imposed on the leader by the situation, as well as the expectations for the leader created by the preferences of the members. We noted that effective leadership is contingent on the congruence among the three states of leadership—required leadership, preferred leadership and actual leadership. We moved beyond this necessary transactional nature of leadership and discussed the transformational leadership where the leader attempts to alter the situational requirements but also change the members' aspirations and self-esteem. A brief reflection on the human resource dimension of organisational change was also illustrated.

In summary, human resource strategies are an essential component of the general organisational strategy and must be consistent and harmonized to the environment. Unfortunately, the place of the human resource function within sport organisations is often subject to questioning. In numerous cases where it is formally present, HRM is typically a staff function with scarce power and resources. By emphasizing the strategic nature of human resource management, we have clearly indicated the need for top or senior managers to be continuously involved in decision making that has an impact on this particular area.

Appendix A

Volleyball Canada Human Resource Policy (January 2003)

1. Goal

1.1 This policy guides the employment practices of Volleyball Canada.

2. Principles

2.1 VC recognizes its employees' right to work in a safe environment which promotes equal opportunity for all, prohibits discriminatory practices and harassment of any kind, and in which all individuals are treated fairly and with respect and dignity.

2.2 VC recognizes that providing for its employees personal, family, and health related needs, will affect their personal well-being and their ability to work effectively.

2.3 VC believes it has a responsibility to encourage the professional and personal development of its employees.

2.4 VC believes that all sensitive and personal employee information must be kept strictly confidential, except where VC is required by law to disclose such information.

3. Field of Application and Authority

3.1 This policy applies to all full-time, part-time and contract employees of VC.

3.2 This policy and the Employment Standards Act of the employee's province of employment shall govern the terms and conditions of employment for Volleyball Canada's employees.

3.3 All parts of this document are supplementary to applicable federal and provincial legislation. In the event of conflict such legislation shall prevail.

3.4 All full-time employees shall enter into a written contract of employment with VC.

3.5 From time to time, VC may hire contractual employees. The terms and conditions of employment for contract employees shall be governed by the terms of their contracts with VC.

3.6 The Director General shall be responsible for the implementation of this policy and for all decisions relating to hiring, firing, and promoting (by way of salary increases) full time employees.

3.7 The Board of Directors shall be responsible for the implementation of this policy and for all decisions relating to hiring, firing, and promoting (by way of salary increases) the Director General.

3.8 All staff members are ultimately accountable to the Director General. The Director General is accountable to the President and the Board of Directors.

4. Definitions

4.1 Full-time employee: an employee who is solely employed by VC works 40 hours per week and received an annual salary and benefits paid.

4.2 Contract Employee: An employee who is employed to complete a specific task or project, for a specific cost, within a specific time.

4.3 Part-Time Employee: An employee who is employed by VC and works less than 37.5 hours per week but more then 7.5 hours per week, and receives an annual or hourly salary and benefits paid.

4.4 Personal Service Contract: is a contract with an individual for that individual to provide specific services to the organization for a specified period, but who is not entitled to employee benefits.

4.5 Senior Staff: All members of the staff who are Directors of specific Program areas.

4.6 Support Staff: All staff members who are Coordinators, Managers and Administrative Assistants.

5. Policy Statement

5.1 VC is committed to fair and equitable practices in employment.

6. Provisions

6.1 Hiring Practices:

- VC employees may be engaged on a full-time, part-time, short-term, or special project contract basis. Personal service contracts shall not be used for full-time employees or part-time employees where the nature of the relationship is that of an employer-employee, as defined in the Revenue Canada Income Tax Act.
- All job vacancies shall be posted in both official languages. The scope of posting and announcement shall be determined by the requirements of the position and the availability of suitable candidates. Advertising or search mediums may include but not be limited to: local newspapers, national newspapers, professional journals, building or centre circulation, executive placement agencies, etc. dependent on the vacancy and the costs involved.
- Any positions funded in part or in whole by Sport Canada revenues will adhere to Sport Canada regulations regarding advertisement and notice of position. Selection Committees will be formed for hiring processes, depending on the position involved.
- All candidates shall be screened against predetermined required minimum criteria. Accepted candidates shall be granted an interview before a selection committee of not less than three (3) people, except in the case of administrative support staff.

6.1.1 Support Staff—Any administrative support staff shall be interviewed and hired by the Director General. Advertising of any available positions shall be at the discretion of the Director General as time and resources permit and dependent on the position. At a minimum, full-time positions will be circulated within Volleyball Canada and the Canadian sport community.

6.1.2 Composition and Role of Selection Committee—a) The Director General (DG) shall be a member of the selection committee for all national office staff, and national coaches. b) The other hiring committee members shall be chosen by the DG, from among but not limited to, the Board, Committee chairs, athlete representatives, and staff, as appropriate to the position being filled. c) The selection committee for senior positions in VC will include the DG, one Board member and for Coaching positions, an athlete representative. d) The Selection Committee shall recommend candidates for the position.

6.1.3 Senior Staff—When a senior staff vacancy occurs, the vacant position shall be reviewed by the DG and the President before advertising.

6.1.4 The Director General Position—Candidates shall be interviewed and selected by the President and the Selection Committee. The outgoing Director General may be invited to form part of the Selection Committee.

6.2 Terms of Employment

6.2.1 Offer of Employment—a) Newly hired staff shall receive an offer of employment in writing from the Director General outlining starting dates, benefits, job description and salary. b) A newly appointed Director General shall receive an offer of employment in writing from the President clearly outlining starting dates, terms and conditions of employment, benefits and salary being offered, and probationary periods and terms. Acceptance of this offer must be received in writing from the candidate, to the VC President. c) The 'offer of employment' will be followed-up with an Employment Contract.

6.2.2 Job Descriptions—a) All job descriptions shall be maintained on file in the national office. b) Job descriptions will be reviewed annually and updated as required by the VC Board in conjunction with the Director General. The Director General's job description will be reviewed annually and updated as necessary by the VC Board.

6.2.3 Probation—a) The first three months of employment shall be considered as a probationary work period for new employees. A performance review will be conducted after this three-month period. All new employees shall be notified in writing at the end of the probationary period of their status. b) During the probationary period of the Director General, the President in consultation with the Board of Directors shall review the work of the Director General and determine suitability for continued employment. Letters pertaining to the Director General shall be written by the President. c) During the probationary period of all other professional employees, the Director General in consultation with the President shall review the performance of such employees and determine the suitability for continued employment. Letters pertaining to professional staff shall be written by the Director General. d) During the probationary period of support staff, the Director General shall review the works of such employees and determine the suitability for continued employment. Letters pertaining to professional staff shall be written by the Director General. Any decision made to terminate the services of a support staff prior to or upon completion of the probationary period must be communicated to the President in advance of the action to terminate.

6.3 Compensation: All employees shall be compensated for their services in accordance with established and previously negotiated rates of pay.

6.3.1 Adjustments—a) Adjustments to salary levels shall be reviewed annually in line with the annual budgeting exercise. Adjustments must be within the set salary range for each position, and are dependent on the availability of funds, and performance and tenure of the incumbent in the position. b) Adjustments to the salary of the Director General are made by the President and/or VC Board of Directors. c) Adjustments to salary levels of other professional positions require the recommendation of the Director General. Adjustments to support positions are the decision of the Director General.

6.4 Employee Benefits

6.4.1 Dental and Medical—Volleyball Canada will provide the following benefits to all full-time, permanent employees and pay 100% of the associated costs: a) Single dental coverage, Single medical coverage, Life insurance, Accidental death and dismemberment, Long-term disability insurance, Short-term disability insurance. b) Employees requiring family coverage must pay the difference in rates between single and family. Deductions are to be made at source. c) No cash shall be given in lieu of benefits for employees not requesting or requiring any of the offered coverage.

6.4.2 Pension—Volleyball Canada provides a pension plan for all full-time, permanent employees. Matching contributions are made directly to a VC Registered Pension Plan on behalf of the employee at a rate established annually by the Board of Directors, upon the recommendation of the Director General.

6.5 Hours of Work and Overtime: Volleyball Canada shall maintain office hours from 8:30 a.m. - 5:00 p.m. Employees are entitled to a one hour lunch break and two 15 minute a day breaks. Given the nature of the activity, i.e., sport, it is understood and accepted by all employees that regular hours are not always part of the job dependent on the position of the employee within the organization. Recognizing this, flexibility is required on the part of both the organization and staff with respect to the hours of work.

6.5.1 Flex Time—Dependent on the position flex hours are possible. A core work day however must be maintained. That core will consist of time between 9:30 a.m. and 3:30 p.m. Flex hours must be approved by the Director General.

6.5.2 Condensed Work Week—Condensed work weeks i.e., 3 twelve hour days, are generally not possible. Exceptions to this may be made at the discretion of the Director General dependent on the position and the positions relationship with other positions within the organization.

6.5.3 Job Sharing—a) Job sharing is possible at the discretion of the Director General and only within certain positions. Details on the split of responsibilities, process, procedures, benefits split, etc. must be acceptable by both the employees involved and Volleyball Canada. b) Employees will be subject to the appropriate salary commensurate with their years of experience, skills in the position and time with the organization. c) Respecting that the job being shared is in effect one position, one benefits package is available, unless an exception is made for valid reasons.

6.5.4 Overtime/time in Lieu—a) Given the nature of our business, i.e., sport, overtime for many positions is inevitable. Employees should be aware of the overtime demands on their position from time to time. b) Where recognized overtime is available as time "in lieu of", equal time for overtime. "Time and a half" is not permitted. Cash "in lieu of" is generally not permitted. Exceptions to this are at the discretion of the Director General and are granted only at the calculated comparable salary "hourly" rate. Overtime being carried over into a new fiscal year must be approved by the Director General. c) Advance permission must be secured for overtime above and beyond the expected, annually occurring overtime demands of the job. d) Employees are encouraged to take the time "in lieu of" immediately following an anticipated event, meeting requiring the overtime, i.e., post weekend meetings and events, in an effort to reduce employee stress and burnout. e) However if this is not possible, employees may not "bank" more than 15 days of annual overtime. Time off must be scheduled in advance with, and at the approval of, the Director General.

6.6 Confidentiality

6.6.1 Employee to Employer—All employees shall respect the privacy of the organization where required agreeing not to compromise the programs and activities of Volleyball Canada in any way by revealing information detrimental to the health or reputation of the organization, i.e., details of confidential sponsorship negotiations prior to closure of deals, etc.

6.6.2 Employer to Employee—Volleyball Canada respects the privacy of its individual employees and members. In keeping with this and understanding the sensitivity of much of the employee/employer relationship, all personnel files will be locked and accessible only to the Director General, his/her appointed agent in his/her absence, and the relevant Board members i.e., President, Executive Committee.

6.7 Conflict of Interest: Recent changes in the sporting system and the external environment have opened new professions, i.e., sport agents, marketing representatives. It is recognized that many of these new professions may at times be in "competition" with Volleyball Canada as it pursues its program and business goals and objectives. In recognition of this, all professional employees shall agree not to engage in paid employment activities outside their Volleyball Canada activities without the permission of the Director General. The Director General shall obtain the approval of the President before engaging in any paid professional activities for other agencies and corporations.

6.8 Performance Assessment: Performance assessment is an on-going process of communication between supervisor and staff member. All full-time and part-time employees are entitled to ongoing performance feedback. The process is a combination of providing periodic feedback to staff on their progress and at least one annual oral review and written evaluation. Performance assessments shall be based on performance goals that are specific, measurable and mutually established at the beginning of the annual review cycle by the employee and the supervisor. If appropriate, feedback will be requested from multiple parties who have personal knowledge of the employee's work. The objectives of performance assessments are: a) To formally review and discuss the staff member's performance with respect to their performance goals; b) Provide the staff member with the opportunity to comment on his/her performance.

6.8.1 Probation Period Reviews—A review of performance during probationary periods will be conducted at the end of the probationary period and prior to making an offer of continuing employment to the incumbent. The results of this review will be communicated to the incumbent.

6.8.2 Annual Performance Review—a) The annual review is a consolidation of the periodic feedback provided throughout the review period. Appropriate notice will be given to the employee of annual review. A minimum of one week's notice will be granted. b) All annual reviews will be signed by both supervisor and employee and retained in the employees personnel file when completed. c) Reviews of the Director General will be conducted by the President and/or VC Board. d) Reviews of the national office staff shall be coordinated by the Director General. e) Reviews of the TCVC senior administrative staff will be coordinated by the Director General, with all TCVC Support Staff reviews coordinated by the Director of Operations. Reviews of the Coaching staff will be completed by the National Team Committee Chair, with required input from athletes, TCVC staff, and the D.G. f) In situations of serious performance problems an oral review and written evaluation should be done at more frequent intervals. g) If an employee's performance is below satisfactory, the Supervisor will discuss with the employee the specific problems, the level of performance that is required, and the time frame for achieving that level. The Supervisor will help the Employee to improve his or her performance through appropriate and corrective action including, but not limited to, daily work review and feedback, further training and/or counselling. All discussions regarding unsatisfactory performance will be documented and placed in the employee's personnel file. If performance does not improve according to the time-frame which has been discussed, the Employee may be terminated for cause. h) If an employee's unsatisfactory performance has no identifiable and correctable reason, the situation will be treated as one of a disciplinary nature. Appropriate disciplinary steps will be taken including a verbal warning, a written warning, suspension without pay and finally dismissal. All disciplinary actions must be supported by detailed written documentation, including the verbal warnings. i) Where an employee disagrees with the performance evaluation, and feels that he/she has been treated unfairly, the employees shall have the right to appeal the decision as specified under Grievances Section.

6.9 Grievances: Should any grievances arise as to the interpretation of personnel or employment policies, such grievances shall be initiated within 10 working days after the circumstances giving to the grievance have occurred. Grievances shall be processed in the following manner: a) By the immediate supervisor who will attempt to resolve the problem within 10 working days. b) By the Director General who will attempt to resolve the problem within 10 working days. c) If necessary the Board of Directors will attempt to resolve the problem within 10 working days. Written records will be kept at each stage. In the case of an unresolved dispute between a volunteer and an employee, the Director General and/or the President must be informed immediately. The Director General and the President will then attempt to resolve the dispute within 10 working days. If the dispute cannot be resolved within that time frame, the VC Board shall be informed and will attempt to resolve the problem within 10 working days. If necessary a conciliator or outside facilitator shall be engaged to attempt to resolve the problem. Grievances related to harassment or disputes involving athletes, coaches, etc. shall be addressed in accordance with established policy.

6.10 Termination: Notice of termination shall not be required for an employee discharged for cause. An employee who breaches the confidentiality of information obtained as a result of employment with VC shall be subject to termination without notice. An employee who knowingly condones or encourages the use of or, facilitates the supply of banned or illegal substances to athletes shall be subject to termination without notice. An employee, who it is established by evidence, witness or conviction, has stolen VC property or stolen property at a VC event, shall be terminated without notice. An employee who is convicted of criminal offences outside of any VC connection may be subject to a notice of termination. Unsatisfactory work performance shall be cause for termination only if all the appropriate corrective actions and consultative steps, as outlined in 'Performance Review', have been exhausted, and a reasonable time frame for improvement has elapsed. Termination to be effective in accordance with the Provincial Employment Standards Act of the province of Employment, as it is from the date that the notice in writing is received by the employee.

6.10.1 Notice—a) All employees leaving the organization are requested to give the organization appropriate and reasonable notice reflective of their position within the organization. b) Volleyball Canada will provide reasonable and appropriate notice, and reason for dismissal i.e., funding cuts, redundant position, etc., to all employees whose services may no longer be required. At a minimum, the notice required by law will be provided. Every attempt will be made to provide as much advance notice as possible.

6.10.2 Benefits Owing—Volleyball Canada shall pay the employee any cash in lieu of vacation time owing.

6.10.3 Severance—Volleyball Canada shall adhere to appropriate labour legislation with respect to severance payments, i.e., when required, notice in lieu of, amounts, etc.

6.10.4 Exit Interview—Exit interviews may be conducted at the discretion of the Director General, or in the case of the Director General at the discretion of the President.

6.11 Statutory Holidays: Employees are entitled to the following designated holidays: New Year's Day, Good Friday, Easter Monday, Victoria Day, Canada Day, Civic Holiday (where applicable), Labour Day, Thanksgiving Day, Remembrance Day, Christmas Day, Boxing Day

6.11.1 Chrismas Hours—The offices of Volleyball Canada shall close at noon on December 24th, and will re-open the first business day following New Year's Day, unless otherwise designated by the VC Director General.

6.11.2 Religious Observances and Recognition of Non-Christian Faiths—a) It is recognized that not all employees of Volleyball Canada observe the Christian Holiday calendar, reflected above. In recognition of this, and in respect of Volleyball Canada's policy recognizing religious preference, Volleyball Canada provides that employees requiring variance from the established days as noted above will work out a comparable schedule with the Director General, the total days of which will equal 11. b) Identification of other options to respect the religious holidays and observances of employees may be identified and exercised by the Director General i.e., application of overtime when the employee wishes the traditional Christian time off as well.

6.12 Vacation Leaves: All permanent employees are entitled to annual leave. Leave may not be carried forward from one year to the next without the written permission of the Director General. The Director General will require the permission of the President to carry leave forward. Any leave carried forward will be taken at the earliest possible time. All annual leave must be scheduled in advance and cleared with the Director General. In the case of the Director General, leave must be approved by the President. Permanent employees at a Senior Staff level are entitled to the following paid vacation, as earned, following completion of respective years of employment.

- after 1 year, 15 days
- after 5 years, 20 days
- after 15 years, 25 days

Permanent employees at a support staff level are entitled to the following paid vacation, as earned, following completion of respective years of employment.

- after 1 year, 15 days
- after 10 year 20 days

6.13 Educational Leave: Time off from work to take educational courses beyond professional development, i.e., degree credits at a recognized institution is at the discretion of the Director General or in the case of the Director General at the discretion of the President - as to whether time will be granted and whether any time granted must be made up. Factors taken under consideration will include the number of hours of absence each week, length of term of the course, relevancy to their position with Volleyball Canada, time and scheduling demands on the position given the time of year.

6.14 Other Leave With Pay

6.14.1 Sick Leave—a) Permanent full-time employees shall accumulate sick leave credits of .5 days per month. Extended leaves of absence, may be covered by association health insurance regarding short and long-term disability coverage. After the appropriate period of time this health policy coverage will kick in covering employee salary. b) Sick leave may be accumulated up to a maximum of 30 days. Employees may not accumulate sick leave credits during extended periods of absence of 14 or more working days duration. c) Employees will not receive pay for accumulated sick days upon termination of employment or retirement. d) An employee must notify his or her supervisor as soon as possible of any absence. Volleyball Canada reserves the right to request a medical certificate from an employee to establish validity of the claim and/or applicability of related medical insurance coverage regarding STD and/or LTD. e) An employee must complete their probationary period to be eligible for sick leave.

6.14.2 Compassionate/Bereavement Leave—a) Employees shall be granted up to three (3) days off work, with pay, in the event of death or life-threatening illness in the immediate family. The length of such leave may be extended under extenuating circumstances upon request to the Director General with consideration given to travel time involved, and complexity of the individual situation. Immediate family is defined as spouse, common-law spouse, children, brother, sister, or parent. b) Necessary time off may be granted in the event of the death of a grandparent, or inlaw, or to attend the funeral of another person.

6.14.3 Court Appearance or Jury Duty—a) An employee who is summoned for jury duty or who receives a summons or subpoena to appear as a witness in a court proceeding, not occasioned by the employee's private affairs, will receive regular pay. The employee will be required to forward any fees paid by the courts to the association within one pay period after such fees are received by the employee. b) Employees shall be entitled to five (5) days maternity support leave (for an employee who is partner of an expectant mother) at or around the time of birth; five (5) days for the birth of a child; and five (5) days leave for the adoption of a child.

6.15 Other Leave Without Pay: Leaves of absence without pay may be granted, upon approval of the Director General and Executive Committee. Employees on leave without pay shall not accumulate sick days or vacation days. Volleyball Canada shall retain and continue to provide existing benefits, i.e., medical, dental, etc., for the employee on approved leaves of absence. The employee shall pay his or her share of group insurance premiums owing during the leave of absence. The employee shall be entitled to return to the same position or a position of equal responsibility and remuneration upon completion of the leave of absence, should the leave of absence be six months or shorter. Longer leaves of absence must be approved by the Director General and Executive Committee, and the position guarantee is to be negotiated at that time. Leave of absence without pay after five (5) years employment may be granted to an employee upon their written request at the discretion of the Board of Directors with a recommendation from the Director General. Overstaying a leave of absence without notification and without valid reason in the opinion of the Director General, or in the case of the Director General of the President, may result in termination of the employee. Employees may apply for benefits to Employment Immigration Canada for maternity leave, parental leave, and adoption leave provided the employee meets their minimum requirements. Volleyball Canada does not provide for additional remuneration during maternity, parental or adoption leave beyond that provided for by Employment Immigration Canada.

6.15.1 Pregnancy and Parental Leave (As per ESA Regulations)—a) Pregnant employees have the right to take Pregnancy Leave of up to 17 weeks of unpaid time off work. In some cases the leave may be longer. b) Both new parents have the right to take Parental Leave—unpaid time off work. Birth mothers who took pregnancy leave are entitled to up to 35 weeks' leave. Employees who didn't take pregnancy leave are entitled to up to 37 weeks' leave. c)

Parental leave isn't part of pregnancy leave. A birth mother can take both pregnancy and parental leave. d) Both parents can be on leave at the same time. e) Employees are entitled to pregnancy and parental leave regardless of the type of employment relationship they have—full-time or part-time, permanent or contract.

6.15.2 Qualifying for Parental Leave—a) To qualify, an employee who is a new parent must have been hired at least 13 weeks before the leave begins. b) The employee doesn't have to actively work for 13 weeks to be eligible for parental leave. The employee could be on layoff, vacation, sick leave or pregnancy leave for all or part of the 13-week qualifying period and still be entitled to parental leave.

6.15.3 A "Parent" Includes: a) a birth parent; b) an adoptive parent (whether or not the adoption has been legally finalized); or c) a person who is in a relationship of some permanence with a parent of the child and who plans on treating the child as his or her own. This includes same-sex couples.

6.15.4 When a Parental Leave Can Begin—a) A birth mother who takes pregnancy leave must ordinarily begin her parental leave as soon as her pregnancy leave ends. b) However, an employee's baby may not yet have come into her care for the first time when the pregnancy leave ends. For example, perhaps her baby has been hospitalized since birth and is still in the hospital's care when the pregnancy leave ends. c) If this is the case, the employee can choose to return to work and start her parental leave once the baby comes home. However, she doesn't have to wait until the baby comes home to begin her parental leave. d) All other parents must begin their parental leave no later than 52 weeks after: the date their baby is born; OR the date their child first came into their care, custody and control. e) The parental leave doesn't have to be completed within this 52-week period. It just has to be started.

6.15.5 Length of a Parental Leave—a) Birth mothers who take pregnancy leave are entitled to take up to 35 weeks of parental leave. b) All other new parents are entitled to take up to 37 weeks of parental leave. c) Employees may decide to take a shorter leave if they wish. However, once an employee has started parental leave, he or she must take it all at one time. The employee can't use up part of the leave, return to work for the employer and then go back on parental leave for the unused portion.

6.16 Professional Development: VC may support the professional development of its employees, however approval for financial support must be received from the employer prior to registration or enrollment. Support may cover any portion of the costs up to 100% and may include leave with pay, for the purposes of professional development related to the performance of the employee's duties. Volleyball Canada will attempt to set aside each year, finances permitting, a fixed amount of money in the annual budget for the professional development of both its staff and its primary volunteers. The employee will be required to pay for their professional Development opportunity first and then, if money is available, they will be reimbursed. Such funds may be used for the professional development and/or education of individuals as it directly relates to the performance of their duties for Volleyball Canada. Non-job related development is not eligible for consideration. As well, professional development for specific staff may not be possible at certain times of the year due to compressed demands on their time and their required availability previous to, at, or post certain functions, i.e., AGM. Volleyball Canada support for professional development may take the form of:

- covering the cost of tuition fees, conference fees, related travel and meals
- providing time off for the pursuit of professional development.

Reimbursement of agreed upon support will be provided only on proof of completion of the professional development activity and with the provision of proper receipts. Requests for professional development by professional or support staff must be made to the Director General. Requests for professional development for the President must be approved by VC Board in consultation with the Director General. Requests for professional development for the Director General must be made to the President.

Requests for professional development for other critical volunteers must be approved by the President in consultation with the Director General.

7. Review and Approval

7.1 This policy was approved by the Volleyball Board of Directors on the 12th day of January, 2003.

7.2 Date of last review:

7.3 Original policy development lead: Kristine Drakich

Reprinted, by permission, from Volleyball Canada.

References

Adler, P., & Adler, A. (1987). Role conflict and identity salience: College athletics and the academic role. *Social Science Journal, 245,* 443-455.

Amis, J., & Slack, T. (1996). The size-structure relationship in voluntary sport organizations. *Journal of Sport Management, 10,* 76-86.

Amis, J., Slack, T., & Berret, T. (1995). The structural antecedents of conflict in voluntary sport organizations. *Leisure Studies, 14*(1), 1-16.

Argent, E. (2005). *From the locker room to the boardroom: Developing leaders through sport.* In Proceedings of the 12th EASM Sport Management Congress, 197-198.

Auld, C. (1994). Changes in professional and volunteer administrator relationships: Implications for managers in the leisure industry. *Australian Journal of Leisure and Recreation, 4*(2), 14-22.

Auld, C. (1997). Professionalization of Australian sport administration: The effects on organizational decision making. *European Journal for Sport Management, 4*(2), 17-39.

Australian Sports Commission. (2002). *National sporting organizations. Governance: Principles of best practice.* Canberra, Australia.

Balyi, I., & Hamilton, A. (2000). Key to success: Long term athlete development. *Sport coach, 23*(1), 30-32.

Barnard, C. (1938). *The functions of the executive.* Cambridge, MA: Harvard University Press.

Bass, B.M. (1985). *Leadership and performance beyond expectations.* New York: The Free Press.

Bayle, E., & Madella, A. (2002). Development of a taxonomy of performance for national sport organizations. *European Journal of Sport Science, 2*(2), 21.

Beamish, R. (1985). Sport executives and voluntary associations: A review of the literature and introduction to some theoretical issues. *Sociology of Sport Journal, 2,* 218-232.

Beaumont, P.B. (1993). *Human resource management.* London: Sage.

Berger, P., & Luckmann, T. (1967). *The social construction of reality: A treatise on sociology of knowledge.* London: Penguin.

Blanc, X. (1999). *L'activation des bénévoles dans le management de projets sportifs (The activation of the volunteers in the management of sport projects).* Papers of the symposium held in Lausanne, 24th, 25th, 26th November 1999.

Blau, P., & Schoenherr, R.A. (1971). *The structure of organizations.* New York: Basic Books.

Bloom, B. (1985). *Developing talent in young people.* New York: Ballantine.

Borms, J. (1996). Early identification of athletic talent. Keynote address at the Pre-Olympic Congress, Dallas.

Bouchet-Virette M. (1999). *Le programme des volontaires de la Coupe du Monde de football "France 98" (The Programme of the volunteers of the football World Cup "France 98").* Paper presented at the 33rd AGFIS Congress, Osaka, Japan.

Bowen, D.E., & Lawler, E.E. (1992, Spring). The empowerment of service workers: What, why, how, and when. *Sloan Management Review, 33,* 31-39.

Braun, S. (2000). Elite and Elitenbildung (Elite and Elite Construction), Teil II. *Leistungssport,* 30, 4, July 58-62.

Brickson, S. (2000). The impact of identity orientation on individual and organizational outcomes in demographically diverse settings. *Academy of Management Review, 25*(1), 82-101.

Brown, W.A., & Yoshioka, C.F. (2003). Mission attachment and satisfaction as factors in employee retention. *Nonprofit Management & Leadership, 14*(1), 5-18.

Cameron, K.S., & Quinn, R.E. (1999). *Diagnosing and changing organizational culture.* Reading, MA: Addison-Wesley.

Camy, J., Cljisen, L., Madella, A., Pilkington, A. (2004). *Améliorer l'emploi dans le domaine du sport en Europe par la formation professionnelle (Improving employment in the field of sport in Europe through vocational training).* VOCASPORT project, supported by the European Commission (DG Education and Culture, Contract no. 2003-4463/001-001.

Canadian Olympic Association. (1986). *The state of the volunteer-professional relationship in amateur sport in Canada.* Montreal: Canadian Olympic Association.

Canadian Olympic Association, Coaching Association of Canada, Sport Canada. (1999). Canadian Sports Centers, Position Paper. Montreal: Canadian Olympic Association.

Carlson, S. (1979). *Executive behavior: A study of the workload and the working methods of managing directors.* New York: Arno Press. (Original work published in 1951.)

Cases Pallarès, B. (2001). Managing human resources in Barcelona '92: The volunteer project. Communication at the MEMOS module 3, Rome 26, March 2001.

Cenci, M., & Semprini, M. (2001). *The organization of the human resources during the IXth Games of the Small States of Europe, San Marino 2001.* Proceedings of the 9th European Congress of Sport Management, Vitoria-Gasteiz, Spain.

Chantelat, P. (2001). *La professionalisation des organizations sportives.* Paris: L'Harmattan.

Chappelet, J.L. (2000). Volunteer management at a major sports event: The case of the Olympic Games. In M. de Moragas et al. (Eds.), *Volunteers, global society and the Olympic movement.* Lausanne: IOC Editions.

Chappelet, J.L., & Bayle, E. (2004). *Strategic and performance management of Olympic sport organisations.* Champaign, IL: Human Kinetics.

Chelladurai, P. (1987). The design of sport governing bodies: A Parsonian perspective. In T. Slack & C.R. Hinings (Eds.), *The organization and administration of sport.* London, Canada: Sports Dynamics.

Chelladurai, P. (1993). Leadership. In R.N. Singer, M. Murphy & K. Tennant (Eds.), *The handbook on research in sport psychology.* New York: MacMillan.

Chelladurai, P. (1999). *Management of human resources in sport and recreation.* Champaign, IL: Human Kinetics.

Chelladurai, P. (2001). *Athletic teams as models for managing diversity.* Opening Keynote presentation at the 9th Congress of the European Association for Sport Management. Vittoria-Gasteiz, Spain. September 19-23, 2001.

Chelladurai, P. (2001). *Managing organizations for sport & physical activity: A systems perspective.* Scottsdale, AZ: Holcomb Hathaway Publishers.

Chelladurai, P. (2005). *Leadership in the pursuit of excellence in sports.* Presented at 9th Annual Eastern Canada Sport and Exercise Psychology Symposium, University of Windsor, Windsor, Ontario Canada. (March 11-12, 2005).

Chelladurai, P. (2005). *Mananging organizations for sport and physical activity.* (2nd ed.). Scottsdale, AZ: Holcomb Hathaway.

Chelladurai, P. (2006). *Managing human resources in sport and recreation.* (2nd ed.). Champaign, IL: Human Kinetics.

Chelladurai, P., and Haggerty, T.R. (1991). Differentiation in national sport organizations in Canada. *Canadian Journal of Sport Sciences,* 16(2), 117-125.

Chelladurai, P., Szyszlo, M., & Haggerty, T.R. (1987). Systems-based dimensions of effectiveness: The case of national sport organizations. *Canadian Journal of Sport Sciences, 12*(2), 111-119.

Child, J. (1972). Organizational structure, environment and performance: The role of strategic choice. *Sociology, 6,* 1-22.

Chin, R., Benne, K.D. (1961). General strategies for effecting changes in human systems. In W.G. Bennis, K.D. Benne, R. Chin, (Eds.), *The Planning of Change* (4th ed.). (pp. 22-45). Fort Worth, TX: Harcourt Brace Jovanovich, Inc.

Clarkson, M.B.E. (1995). A stakeholder framework for analyzing and evaluating corporate social performance. *Academy of Management Review, 20,* 92-117.

Clegg, S., & Dunkerley, D. (1980). *Organization, class and control.* London: Routledge.

Collins, C.W. (1994). Sport management in New Zealand: From kitchen table to board room. In *Proceedings of the Second Congress on Sport Management,* Florence, 161-199.

Collins, R. (1975). *Conflict sociology: Toward an explanatory science.* New York: The Academic Press.

Connors, T.D. (1988). The board of directors. In T.D. Connors (Ed.), *The nonprofit organization handbook* (2nd ed.). New York: McGraw-Hill.

Cook, S.D., & Yanow, D. (1993). Culture and organizational learning. *Journal of Management Inquiry, 2*(4), December. Reprinted in M. Cohen & L.S. Sproull (Eds.), *Organizational learning* (1995). Thousands Oaks, CA: Sage.

Cox, T. Jr., & Beale, R.L. (1997). *Developing competency to manage diversity: Readings, cases, & activities.* San Francisco: Berrett-Koehler.

Crozier, M., & Friedberg, E. (1977). *L'acteur et le système.* Paris: Seuil.

Cunningham, D., Slack, T., & Hinings, C.R. (1987). Changing design archetypes in amateur sport organizations. In T. Slack & C.R. Hinings (Eds.), *The organization and administration of sport.* London, Canada: Sports Dynamics.

Cuskelly, G., & Boag, A. (1999). Differences in organizational commitment between paid and volunteer administrators in sport. *European Journal for Sport Management,* Special Issue, June, 39-61.

Daft, R.L. (2001). *Organization theory and design.* St. Paul, MN: South Western College Publishing.

Danylchuk, K., & Chelladurai, P. (1999). The nature of managerial work in Canadian intercollegiate athletics. *Journal of Sport Management, 13,* 280-297.

Davidson, J. (1990). Competition is healthy if approached correctly – and unhealthy is it isn't, Management Quarterly, 31, Spring 42-48

De Coster, M. (1978). *L'analogie en sciences humaines (The analogy in human sciences).* Paris: P.U.F.

Delavallée, E. (1999). Changement organisationnel et Gestion des Ressources Humaines. In D. Weiss (Ed.), *Le ressources humaines.* Paris: Editions d'Organisation.

De Martelaer, K., Van Hoecke, J., de Knop, P., van Heddegem, L., & Theboom, M. (2002). Marketing in organised sport: Participation, expectations and experiences. *European Sport Management Quarterly, 2*(2), 113-134.

Denison, D.R. (1990). *Corporate culture and organizational effectiveness.* New York: Wiley.

Digel, H. (2005). Comparison of successful sport systems. *New Studies in Athletics, 20*(2), 7-18.

Di Maggio, P.J., & Powell, W. (1983). The Iron Cage revisited: Institutional isomorphism. *American Sociological Review, 48,* 147-160.

Doherty, A., & Chelladurai, P. (1999). Managing cultural diversity in sport organizations: A theoretical perspective. *Journal of Sport Management, 13,* 280-297.

Donnadieu, G. (1999). Stratégies et politiques de rémunération (Strategies and politics of remuneration). In D. Weiss (Ed.), *Le ressources humaines* (The human resources). Paris: Editions d'Organisation.

Donnelly, P. (1993). Subcultures in sport, resilience and transformations. In A. Ingham & J. Loy (Eds.), *Sport in social development: Traditions, transitions, and transformations.* Champaign, IL: Human Kinetics.

Donovan, F., & Jackson, A.C. (1991). *Managing human service organizations.* Sydney: Prentice Hall.

Drucker, P. (1989). What business can learn from non profits. *Harvard Business Review,* July-August, 88-93.

EOSE (2004). European Observatoire of Sports Employment. Rome, Italy: School of Sport, Italian Olympic Committee (CONI).

Ericsson, K.A. (1996). (Ed.). *The road to excellence: The acquisition of expert performance in the arts, and sciences, sports and games.* Mahwah, NJ: Erlbaum.

Ericsson, K.A., & Charness, N. (1994). Expert performance: Its structure and acquisition. *American Psychologist,* 49(8), 725-747.

Esposito, G., & Madella, A. (2003). Quanto corre l'atletica? La valutazione della performance organizzativa del "sistema atletica" in Italia (The evaluation of the organizational effectiveness of the "athletic system" in Italy). *Atleticastudi,* 3-4, 3-26.

Etzioni, A. (1975). *A comparative analysis of complex organizations.* New York: The Free Press.

Ferrand, A., & Torrigiani, L. (2005). *Marketing of Olympic sport organisations.* Champaign, IL: Human Kinetics.

Fiedler, F.E. (1967). *A theory of leadership effectiveness.* New York: McGraw-Hill.

Filin, V.P. (1978). *La preparazione sportive giovanile.* Roma: CONI-Scuola dello Sport.

Fink, J., & Pastore, D.L. (1997). Gender equity? Differences in athletes perceptions of equity in sport. *Journal of the Legal Aspects of Sport, 7,* 130-144.

Fink, J.S., Pastore, D.L., & Riemer, H.A. (2001). Do differences make a difference? Managing diversity in Division IA intercollegiate athletics. *Journal of Sport Management, 15,* 10-50.

Freeman, R.E. (1984). *Strategic management: A stakeholder approach.* Boston: Pitman.

French, J.R.P., & Raven, B. (1959). The bases of social power. In D. Cartwright (Ed.), *Studies in social power.* Ann Arbor, MI: University of Michigan Press.

Friedman, M., Parent, M., & Mason, D. (2004). Building a framework for issues management in sport through stakeholder theory. *European Sport Management Quarterly, 4,* 170-190.

Gidron, B. (1983). Volunteer work and its rewards. *Volunteer Administration, 11*(3), 18-32.

Goddard, R.W. (1986). The healthy side of conflict, *Management Weekly,* June, 8-10

Goffmann, E. (1961). *Asylums. Essays on the Social Situation of Mental Patients and Other Inmates.* New York: Anchor Books.

Gordon, G.C., & Cummins, W.M. (1979). *Managing management climate.* Lexington, MA: Lexington Books.

Gouldner, A. (1954). *Patterns of industrial bureaucracy.* New York: The Free Press.

Green, C. (2005). Building sport programs to optimize athlete recruitment, retention, and transition: Toward a normative theory of sport development. *Journal of Sport Management, 19,* 233-253.

Green, C., & Chalip, L. (1998). Sport volunteers: Research agenda and application. *Sport Marketing Quarterly, 7*(2), 14-23.

Grossmann, J.B., & Furano, E. (2002). Making the most of volunteers. *Public/Private Ventures Briefs,* July, 1-24.

Haase, H. (1986). Management von Spitzenleistungen (Management of top performance). *Leistungssport, 5,* 32-38.

Haase, H. (1987). Olympiastuetpunkte: Anforderungen an den wissenschaftlichen service (Olympia support centres: Requirements from the scientific services). *Leistungssport, 3,* 5-10.

Hackman, J.R. (1980). Work redesign and motivation. *Professional Psychology, 11 (3),* 445-455.

Hagedorn, G. (1987). Olympiastuetpunkte – eine Zukunftschance? *Leistungssport, 6,* 5-9.

Hager, M.A., & Brudney, J.L. (2004). *Volunteer management practices and retention of volunteers.* Washington: The Urban Institute.

Halba B., & Le Net, M. (1997). *Bénévolat et volontariat (Volunteering),* Edit. La Documentation française, Paris.

Hall, R.H., Haas, J.E., & Johnson, N.J. (1967). Organizational size, complexity and formalization. *American Sociological Review,* December 1967, 903-12.

Harvey, J., Thibault, L., & Rail, G. (1995). Neo-corporatism: The political management system in Canadian amateur sport and fitness. *Journal of Sport and Social Issues, 19*(3), 249-265.

Hedley, R., & Davis Smith, J. (1992). *Volunteering and society.* London: Bedford Square Press.

Heinemann, K. (2004). *Sportorganisationen.* Schorndorf: Karl Hoffmann.

Henry, I., & Theodoraki, E. (2000). Management, organizations and theories of governance. In J. Coakley & E. Dunning (Eds.), *Handbook of sports studies.* London: Sage.

Henry, I.P., Radzi, W., Rich, E.J., Shelton, C., Theodoraki, E. and White, A. (2004). *Women and Leadership in the Olympic Movement.* Lausanne: International Olympic Committee.

Herman, R.D., & Heimovics, R.D. (1991). *Executive leadership in nonprofit organizations.* San Francisco: Jossey Bass.

Herzberg, F. (1966). *Work and the nature of man.* New York: World.

Hinings, C.R., & Slack, T. (1987). The dynamics of quadrennial plan implementation in national sport organizations. In T. Slack & C.R. Hinings (Eds.), *The organization and administration of sport.* London, Canada: Sports Dynamics.

Hinings, C.R., Thibault, L., Slack, T., & Kikulis, L. (1996). Values and organizational structure. *Human Relations, 49*(7), 885-916.

Hoeber, L., & Frisby, W. (2001). Gender equity for athletes: Rewriting the narrative for this organizational value. *European Sport Management Quarterly, 3,* 179-209.

Hofstede, R. (1991). *Cultures and organizations. Software of the mind.* London: McGraw-Hill.

Holbeche, L. (2005). *The high performance organization: Creating dynamic stability and sustainable success.* Amsterdam: Elsevier Butterworth Heinemann

Horch, H.D. (1996). The German sport club and the Japanese firm. *European Journal of Sport Management, 3*(1), 21-34.

Houlihan, B. (1997). *Sport, policy and politics: A comparative analysis.* London: Routledge.

House, R.J. (1971). A path-goal theory of leader effectiveness. *Administrative Science Quarterly, 16,* 321-38.

House, R.J., & Dessler, G. (1974). The path-goal theory of leadership: Some post hoc and a priori tests. In J.G. Hunt & L.L. Larson (Eds.), *Contingency approaches to leadership.* Carbondale, IL: Southern Illinois University Press.

Hovden, J. (2000). Gender and leadership selection processes in Norwegian organizations. *International Review for the Sociology of Sport, 35,* 75-82.

Hoye, R., & Cuskelly, G. (2003). Board power and performance within voluntary organizations. *European Sport Management Quarterly, 3,* 103-119.

Inglis, S. (1997). Roles of board in amateur sport organizations. *Journal of Sport Management, 11,* 160-176.

Kent, A., & Weese, J. (2000). Do effective organizations have better executive leadership and/or organizational cultures? A selected study of sport organizations in Canada. *European Journal of Sport Management,* 7(2), 4-21.

Kikulis, L. (1989). A structural taxonomy of amateur sport organizations. *Journal of Sport Management, 3,* 129-150.

Kikulis, L., Slack, T., & Hinings, C.R. (1992). Institutionally specific design archetypes: A framework for understanding change in national sport organizations. *International Review for the Sociology of Sport, 27,* 343-370.

Knoke, D. (1986). Associations and interest groups. *Annual Review of Sociology, 12,* 1-21.

Knoke, D., & Prensky, D. (1984). What relevance do organization theories have for voluntary associations? *Social Science Quarterly, 65,* 3-20.

Kokolakakis, T. (1997). *The economic impact of sports in UK,* Proceedings of the 5th European Congress of Sports Management, 192-197. Glasgow: EASM

Kolb, D. (1984). *Experiential learning: Experience as a source of learning and development.* Englewood Cliffs, NJ: Prentice Hall.

Kolb, D., & Fry, R. (1972). Toward an applied theory of experiential learning. In C. Cooper (Ed.), *Theories of group process.* London: J. Wiley.

Koski, P., & Heikkala, J. (1998). Professionalization and the organization of mixed rationale: The case of Finnish national sport organizations. *European Journal of Sport Management, 5*(1), 7-30.

Kotter, J.J. (1990, May-June). What leaders really do. *Harvard Business Review, 68*(3), 103-111.

Kotter, J.P., & Schlesinger, L.A. (1979). Choosing strategies for change. *Harvard Business Review,* March-April, 106-114.

Kouri, M.K. (1990). *Volunteerism and older adults.* Santa Barbara, CA: ABC-CLIO, Inc.

Lamprecht, M., & Stamm, H. (1997). *La situation des clubs sportifs en Suisse,* Edit. AOS, Berne.

Lanfranchi, P., & Taylor, M. (2001). *Moving with the ball: The migration of professional footballers.* Oxford: Berg.

Langhorn, K., & Hinings, B. (1987). Integrated planning and organizational conflict. *Canadian Public Administration, 30,* 550-565.

Lawler, E.E. (1984). The strategic design of reward systems. In C. Fombrun, N.M. Tichy, & M.A. Devanna (Eds.), *Strategic human resource management.* New York: J. Wiley.

Lawler, E.E., Mohrman, S.A., & Benson, G. (2001). *Organizing for high performance: Employee involvement, TQM, reengineering, and knowledge management in the Fortune 1000.* San Francisco: Jossey Bass.

Leiter, J. (1986). Reactions to subordination: Attitudes of southern textile workers. *Social Forces, 64,* 948-974.

Lewin, K. (1951). *Field theory in social sciences.* New York: Harper and Row.

Lyle, J. (2004). *"Ships that pass in the night": An examination of the assumed symbiosis between sport-for-all and elite sport.* In Proceedings of the 12th EASM Sport Management Congress, 26-27. Ghent, Flanders/ Belgium. September 22-25, 2004.

McCann, J.E. (1991), Design principles for an innovating company. *Academy of Management Executive,* 5, May, 76-93

MacIntosh, D., & Whitson, D. (1990). *The game planners: Transforming Canada's sport system.* Montreal and Kingston: McGill-Queen's University Press.

MacIntosh, E., & Doherty, A. (2005). Leader intentions and employees perception of organizational culture in a private fitness corporation. *European Sport Management Quarterly, 5*(1), 1-22.

Madella, A. (2001). Les paradoxes de la professionalisation de la fédération italienne d'thletisme. In P. Chantelat (Ed.), *La professionalisation des organisations sportives.* Paris: L'armattan.

Madella, A. (2003). *La qualità delle organizzazioni sportive: cos'è e come si misura (The quality of sport organizations: what is it and how to measure it?). SDS, Rivista di Cultura Sportiva,* 58-59, Lug-dic 2003, 2-8.

Madella, A. (2004). *Performance sportive et son contexte: Recherches menées en Italie (Sport performance and its context: Research carried out in Italy).* Paper presented at the 3èmes Journées Internationales de Sciences du Sport, Paris: INSEP 24 November 2004

March, J.G., & Simon, H. (1958). *Organizations.* New York: J. Wiley.

Martin, J. (1992). *Cultures in organizations. Three perspectives.* Toronto: Oxford University Press.

Matveev, L.P. (1984). *La base de l'entrainement* (The basis of training). Paris: Vigot.

McClelland, D.C., & Burnham, D.H. (1976). Power is the great motivator. *Harvard Business Review, 54,* 100-110.

McIntyre, N., & Pigram, J.J. (1992). Recreation specialization reexamined: The case of vehicle based campers. *Leisure Sciences, 14,* 3-15.

McKay, J. (1997). *Managing gender: Affirmative action and organizational power in Australian, Canadian, and New Zealand sport.* New York: State University of New York.

Mc Pherson, B.D. (1986). Policy-oriented research in youth sport: An analysis of the process and product. In C.R. Rees & A.W. Miracle (Eds.), *Sport and social theory.* Champaign, IL: Human Kinetics.

Merton, R.K. (1936). The unanticipated consequences of purposive social action. *American Sociological Review, 1,* 894-904.

Merton, R.K. (1982). *Social research and practicing professions.* Cambridge, MA: ABT Books.

Meyer, J.W., & Rowan, B. (1977). Institutionalized organizations: Formal structures as myth and ceremony. *American Journal of Sociology, 83,* 340-363.

Meyerson, D.E., & Martin, J. (1987). Cultural change: An integration of three different views. *Journal of Management Studies, 24,* 623-647.

Michels, R. (1962). *Political parties.* New York: The Free Press.

Middleton, M. (1987). Non profit boards of directors: Beyond the governance function. In W.W. Powell (Ed.), *The non profit sector: A research handbook.* London: Yale University Press.

Miles, R.H. (1980). *Macro organizational behavior.* Santa Monica, CA: Goodyear.

Miller, D., & Friesen, P. (1984). *Organizations: A quantum view.* Englewood Cliffs, NJ: Prentice Hall.

Mintzberg, H. (1979). *The structuring of organizations.* Englewood Cliffs, NJ: Prentice Hall.

Mintzberg, H. (1983). *Power in and around organizations.* Englewood Cliffs, NJ: Prentice Hall.

Morgan, G. (1986). *Images of organization.* Thousands Oaks, CA: Sage.

Morrow, P.C., & Goetze, J.F. (1988). Professionalism as a form of work commitment. *Journal of Vocational Behavior, 32,* 92-111.

Mowday, R.T., Porter, L.W., & Steers, R.M. (1982). *Employee-organization linkages: The psychology of commitment, absenteeism and turnover.* New York: Academic Press.

Murray, V., Bradshaw, P., & Wolpin, J. (1992). Power in and around nonprofit boards. A neglected dimension of governance. *Nonprofit management and leadership, 3*(2), 165-182.

Neilsen, E.E. (1972). Understanding and managing intergroup conflict. In J.W. Lorsch & P.R. Lawrence (Eds.), *Managing group and intergroup relations.* Homewood, IL: R.D. Irwin.

Nier, O., & Sheard, K. (1999). Managing change: The "economic", "social" and "symbolic" dimensions of professionalisation in five European elite rugby clubs. *European Journal for Sport Management, 6*(2), 5-33.

Oakley, B., & Green, M. (2001). The production of Olympic champions: International perspectives on elite sport development systems. *European Journal for Sport Management, 8,* Special Issue, 83-105.

Omotho, A.M., Snyder, M., & Martino, S.C. (2000). Volunteerism and the life course: Investigating age-related agendas for action. *Basic and Applied Social Psychology, 22*(3), 181-197.

O'Reilly, C., & Chatman, J. (1986). Organizational commitment and psychological attachment: The effects of compliance, identification, and internalization of prosocial behaviour. *Journal of Applied Psychology, 71,* 492-499.

Osborn, R.N., & Hunt, J.G. (1975). An adaptive-reactive theory of leadership: The role of macrovariables in leadership research. In J.G. Hunt & L.L. Larson (Eds.), *Leadership frontiers.* Kent, OH: Kent State University.

Palisi, B.J., & Jacobson, P.E. (1977). Dominant statuses and involvement in types of instrumental and expressive voluntary associations. *Journal of Voluntary Action Research, 6,* 80-88.

Palm, J. (1991). *Sport for all: Approaches from utopia to reality.* Schorndorf, Germany: Karl Hoffmann.

Papadimitriou, D. (1999). Voluntary boards of directors in Greek sport governing bodies. *European Journal for Sport Management,* Special Issue, 78-103.

Papadimitriou, D. (2001). An exploratory examination of the prime beneficiary approach of organisational effectiveness: The case of elite athletes of Olympic and non-Olympic sports. *European Journal for Sport Management,* Special Issue, 63-82.

Parker, M. (2000). *Organizational culture and identity.* Thousands Oaks, CA: Sage.

Parlier, M. (1999), Stratégies de formation et de développement des compétences dans l'entreprise (Corporate strategies of training and development of competencies). In D. Weiss (ed.), *Le ressources humaines,* pp. 414-462; Paris: Editions d'Organisation.

Parsons, T. (1960). *Structure and process in modern societies.* Glencoe, IL: The Free Press.

Pelled, L.H., Eisenhardt, K.M., & Xin, K.R. (1999). Exploring the black box: An analysis of work group diversity, conflict, and performance. *Administrative Science Quarterly, 44,* 1-28.

Pettigrew, A. (1985). *The awakening giant: Continuity and change in ICI.* Oxford: Blackwell.

Pettigrew, A., & Whipp, R. (1991). *Managing change for competitive success.* Oxford: Blackwell.

Pfeffer, J. (1972). Size and composition of corporate boards of directors: The organization and its environment. *Administrative Science Quarterly, 17,* 218-228.

Pfeffer, J. (1973). Size, composition, and function of hospital boards of directors: A study of organization-environment linkage. *Administrative Science Quarterly, 18,* 349-364.

Pfeffer, J. (1981). *Power in organizations.* Marshfield, MA: Pitman.

Piore, M., & Sabel, B. (1984). *The second industrial divide.* New York: Basic Books.

Price, J.G. (1963). The impact of governing bodies on organizational effectiveness and morale. *Administrative Science Quarterly, 8,* 361-377.

Provan, K.G. (1980). Board power and organizational effectiveness among human services agencies. *Academy of Management Journal, 23,* 221-236.

Pugh, D.S., & Hickson, D.J. (1976). *Organizational structure in the context: The Aston programme.* Lexington, MA: Lexington Books

Pugh, D.S., Hickson, D.J., Hinings, C.R., & Turner, C. (1969). The context of organization structures. *Administrative Science Quarterly,* March, 91-114.

Quinn, J. (1980). *Strategies for change: Logical incrementalism.* Homewood, IL: Irwin.

Richardson, D., Gilbourne, D., & Littlewood, M. (2004). Developing support mechanisms for elite young players in a professional soccer academy: Creative reflections in action research. *European Sport Management Quarterly, 4,* 195-214.

Robbins, S.P. (1990). *Organization theory: Structure, design and applications.* Upper Saddle River, NJ: Prentice Hall.

Robbins, S.P., & Barnwell, N. (1998). *Organisation theory: Concepts and cases.* Sydney: Prentice Hall.

Robinson, G., & Dechant, K. (1997). Building a business case for diversity. *Academy of Management Executive, 11*(3), 21-31.

Rodriguez, N. (2003). *Women and management in international Olympic federations.* Unpublished Masters Project, Executive Masters in Sports Organization Management (MEMOS), Claude Bernard University, Lyon, France.

Salamon, L.M., Sokolowski, S.W., & List, R. (2003). Global civil society: An overview. Center for Civil Society Studies, Institute for Policy Studies, The Johns Hopkins University.

Salmela, J. (1997). Detections des talents (Talent detection). *Education Physique et Sport, 267,* 27-29.

Sargent, L.D., & Sue-Chan, C. (2001). Does diversity affect group efficacy? The intervening role of cohesion and task interdependence. *Small Group Research, 32*(4), 426-450.

Schein, E.H. (1969). *Process consultation.* Reading, MA: Addison-Wesley Pub. Co.

Schein, E.H. (1985). *Organizational culture and leadership.* San Francisco: Jossey Bass.

Schein, E.H. (1991). What is culture? In P.J. Frost, L.F. Moore, M.R. Louis, C.C. Lundberg, & J. Martin (Eds.), *Reframing organizational culture.* Beverly Hills, CA: Sage.

Schnitzer, M. (2004). *Managing volunteers at the Winter Universiade Innsbruck/Seefeld 205.* Unpublished Masters Project, Executive Masters in Sports Organization Management (MEMOS), Claude Bernard University, Lyon, France.

Schon, D.A. (1983). *The reflective practitioner.* New York: Basic Books.

Scott, W.R. (1995). *Institutions and organizations.* Thousands Oaks, CA: Sage.

Sheremata, W.A. (2000). Centrifugal and centripetal forces in radical new product development under time pressure. *Academy of Management Review, 25,* 389-408.

Shibli, S. (1999). The characteristics of volunteers in UK sport clubs. *European Journal for Sport Management,* Special Issue, June, 10-27.

Sills, D.L. (1972). Voluntary associations: Sociological aspects. In *International encyclopedia of the social sciences (vol. 16).* New York: Cromwell, Collier and MacMillan.

Slack, T. (1997). *Understanding sport organizations.* Champaign, IL: Human Kinetics.

Slack, T., Berrett, T., & Mistry, K. (1994). Rational planning systems as a source of organizational conflict. *International Review for the Sociology of Sport, 29*(3), 317-327.

Smart, D.L., & Wolfe, R.A. (2000). Examining sustainable competitive advantage in intercollegiate athletics: A resource-based view. *Journal for Sport Management, 14,* 133-153.

Smart, D.L., & Wolfe, R.A. (2003). The contribution of leadership to organizational success. *European Sport Management Quarterly, 3,* 165-188.

Smircich, L. (1983). Concepts of culture and organisational analysis. *Administrative Science Quarterly, 28,* 339-58.

Smith, D.H. (1981). Altruism, volunteers, and volunteerism. *Journal of Voluntary Action Research, 10,* 21-36.

Smith, D.H. (1993). Public benefit and member benefit nonprofit, voluntary groups. *Nonprofit and Voluntary Sector Quarterly, 22,* 53-68.

Soucie, D. (1994). The emergence of sport management as a professional occupation: A North American perspective. *European Journal for Sport Management, 1*(2), September, 13-30.

Spitz, L., & Ziegler, J. (2005). Analyse der Olympischen Spiel Athen (Analysis of Athens Olympic Games), 2004. *Leistungssport,* 35(1), 5-20.

Sport and Recreation Victoria (2006). Volunteer Management Plan workbook. Retrieved February 12, 2006 from (http://www.sport.vic.gov.au/web9/srvimages.nsf/Images/VMPWorkbook/$File/VMPWorkbook.doc).

Sport England. (2002). *Volunteering in England.* London: Sport England.

Spreitzer, G.M. (1995). Psychological empowerment in the workplace: Dimensions, measurement, and validation. *Academy of Management Journal, 38,* 1442-1465.

Theodoraki, E.I., & Henry, I.P. (1994). Organisational structures and contexts, British national governing bodies of sport. *International Review for Sociology of Sport,* 29(3), 243-267.

Thibault, L., & Babiak, K. (2005). Organizational changes in Canada's sport system: Toward an athlete-centred approach. *European Sport Management Quarterly,* 5(2), 105-132.

Thibault, L., Slack, T., & Hinings, B. (1991). Professionalism, structures and systems: The impact of professional staff on voluntary organizations. *International Review for the Sociology of Sport, 26*(2), 83-97.

Thomas, R.R. (1996). *Redefining diversity.* New York: AMACOM.

Thompson, J.D. (1967). *Organizations in action.* New York: McGraw-Hill.

Unger, L.S. (1991). Altruism as motivation to volunteer. *Journal of Economic Psychology, 12,* 71-100.

Vaillancourt, F., & Payette, M. (1986). The supply of volunteer work: The case of Canada. *Journal of Voluntary Action Research, 15*(4), 45-56.

Van de Ven, A.H., Delbecq, A.L., & Koenig, R. (1976). Determinants of coordination modes of organizations. *American Sociological Review, 41,* 322-338.

Verhoeven, M., Laporte, W., De Knop, P., Bollaert, L., Taks, M., & Vincke, J. (1999). In search of macro-, meso-, and microsociological antecedents of conflict in voluntary sports federations and clubs with the Flemish situation as a case study. *European Journal for Sport Management,* Special Issue, June, 62-77.

Weber, M. (1922). *Wirtschaft und gesellschaft (Econmoy and society).* Tubingen, Germany: Mohr.

Weber, R., Del Campo, F. Pelucchi, M. (2002). Dentro lo sport. Primo Rapporto sullo sport in Italia, Il Sole 24 Ore Libri, € 34,00.

Weese, J. (1995). Leadership and organizational culture: An investigation of Big Ten and Mid-American conference campus recreation administrations. *Journal of Sport Management, 9,* 110-134.

Weick, K.L., & Westley, F. (1996). Organizational learning: Affirming an oxymoron. In S. Clegg, C. Hardy, & W.R. Nord (Eds.), *Handbook of organization studies.* London: Sage.

Weiner, N. (1997). *Making cultural diversity work.* Scarborough, ON, Canada: Carswell (Thompson Professional Publishing).

Werber, J.D., & Gilliland, S.W. (1999). Person-environment fit in the selection process. *Research in Personnel and Human Resources Management, 17,* 209-243.

Westerbeek, H. (1999). A research classification model and some (marketing oriented) reasons for studying the culture of sport organisations. *European Journal for Sport Management, 6*(2), 69-85.

Williams, A.M., & Reilly, T. (2000). Talent identification and development in soccer. *Journal of Sport Sciences, 18,* 657-667.

Wolfe, R.A., Hoeber, L., & Babiak, K. (2002). Perceptions of the effectiveness of sport organisations. *European Sport Management Quarterly, 2*(2), 135-156.

Young, D.R. (1998). Non profit management studies in the United States: The state of the art. *European Journal for Sport Management, 5*(2), 30-43.

Young, E. (1989). On the naming of the rose: Interests and multiple meanings as elements of organizational culture. *Organization Studies, 10,* 187-206.

Yukl, G., & Van Fleet, D.D. (1992). Theory and research on leadership in organizations. In M.D. Dunnette & L.M. Hough (Eds.), *Handbook of industrial and organizational psychology.* Palo Alto, CA: Consulting Psychologists Press.

Ziemainz, H., & Gulbin, J. (2002). Talent selection: Identification and development exemplified in the Australian Talent Search Programme. *New Studies in Athletics, 17,* 27-32.

MEMOS

Master Exécutif en Management des Organisations Sportives

Executive Masters in Sports Organisation Management

Avec le soutien de la Solidarité Olympique, Comité International Olympique

With support from Olympic Solidarity, International Olympic Committee

Directeur du MEMOS / *MEMOS Director:* Prof. Jean-Loup Chappelet
IDHEAP Institut de hautes études en administration publique
Swiss Graduate School of Public Administration
associé à l'Université de Lausanne et à l'Ecole polytechnique fédérale de Lausanne,
membre de l'Académie internationale des sciences et technique du sport (AiSTS)
21, route de la Maladière / CH-1022 Chavannes-Lausanne (Suisse/*Switzerland*)
Tél. +41(0)21 557 40 00 / Fax +41(0)21 557 40 09 / jean-loup.chappelet@idheap.unil.ch
www.unil.ch/idheap/MEMOS.htm

Expand your MEMOS series collection with these books from Human Kinetics!

Improve the management and performance of sport organisations

This book covers the first of three courses in the MEMOS programme and emphasizes the importance of the history and development of the Olympic movement. It highlights new issues at stake as the Olympic movement evolves, and it helps readers to grasp the specific management framework of Olympic sport organisations and other sport federations. Packed with case studies and examples of strategic plans used in Olympic sport organisations, readers will learn to:

- Identify and formulate a mission
- Assess external threats and opportunities as well as internal strengths and weaknesses
- Define organizational goals and steps to reach them
- Evaluate the results of actions for future planning

Strategic and Performance Management of Olympic Sport Organisations
Jean-Loup Chappelet, PhD, and Emmanuel Bayle, PhD
©2005 • Paperback • 144 pp • ISBN 0-7360-5829-X

Successful marketing strategies for sport organisations

Marketing of Olympic Sport Organisations offers valuable insight into the purposes of Olympic sport organisations and addresses in detail the combination of social and economic issues within the Olympic movement that create unique challenges and influence the effectiveness of marketing, sponsorship, and sales programs for sport organisations. Each chapter in *Marketing of Olympic Sport Organisations* contains a case study from a different European country that shows how different sport organisations have marketed themselves and improved their standing. Readers will learn how to do the following:

- Improve brand equity management by assessing and managing its assets and liabilities
- Analyze stakeholders' expectations and decision-making processes in order to deliver the right service
- Market strategically by gaining strong positioning in the marketplace
- Manage strategic sponsorships by specifying the persuasive impact and developing a model to work out strategic choices

Marketing of Olympic Sport Organisations
Alain Ferrand, PhD, and Luiggino Torrigiani
©2005 • Paperback • 144 pp • ISBN 0-7360-5930-X

HUMAN KINETICS
The Information Leader in Physical Activity
P.O. Box 5076 • Champaign, IL 61825-5076 USA

For a complete description or to order
Call (800) 747-4457 US • (800) 465-7301 CDN
44 (0) 113-255-5665 UK • (08) 8277-1555 AUS
(09) 448-1207 NZ • (217) 351-5076 International
or visit www.HumanKinetics.com!

LEARNING RESOURCES CENTRE